Determinants of Health Status in India

Keya Sengupta

Determinants of Health Status in India

Springer

Keya Sengupta
Indian Institute of Management
Nongthymmai, Shillong, India

ISBN 978-81-322-2534-8 ISBN 978-81-322-2535-5 (eBook)
DOI 10.1007/978-81-322-2535-5

Library of Congress Control Number: 2015950910

Springer New Delhi Heidelberg New York Dordrecht London

Printed on acid-free paper

Springer (India) Pvt. Ltd. is part of Springer Science+Business Media (www.springer.com)

Dedicated to my loving parents

Preface

Studying the health sector of a nation is, on one hand, a very simple and also a very complex task. It is simple because health affects each and every person in a country, and at the micro level, every person seems to be able to be equipped to a large extent to take care of his/her health. It is complex, particularly at the macro level, because no single factor can determine good health, and health issues operate in a complex dynamic socioeconomic set-up. Health status, therefore, has being the subject of intense research by economists, sociologists, policy makers as well as the medical sciences.

Health status of the population of a nation has therefore emerged unanimously as a crucial determinant of economic development throughout the world. Unfortunately, however, health is an area which has received the least importance in the development plans of most emerging nations including India. Investment in the health sector in India is one of the lowest in the world. India for instance, which has experienced almost 9 p.c. growth rate consistently for the last decade, has emerged as one of the nations in the world with high growth potential and has been the centre of attention by investors all over the world. However, records of health statistics in the country are lower than even some of the less developing countries of the world. In terms of the various health statistics also, India ranks much lower than the medium human development nations, whose growth rate is much lower than India.

Understanding the gravity of the problem of the health sector is incomplete without the knowledge of health economics. The work, therefore, touches upon the basic issues of health economics so that the reader is able to understand the tools and techniques that can be utilised to understand the real life problems of the health sector.

The rapid growth of the private health sector makes accessibility and affordability more difficult for the rural poor, who still dominate the demographic structure of India. Though India has a very strong network of public health system, spread throughout the entire country, health care delivery suffers due to rampant corruption in the health sector at the service delivery point, which has a depressing effect on the health status in the country. All this is the result of inadequate application of management skills and non-professional attitude in the public health system. The result is that in spite of some of the most innovative policies in the health sector in India, the desired and requisite health outcomes have not been achieved. Therefore in spite of slowly but gradually rising investment in the health sector and announcement of new policies in the health sector, India not only is burdened with poor health indicators, but also has been increasingly facing the dual problems of emerging infectious diseases as well as chronic degenerative diseases. The former is the result of poor implementation of public health programmes, and the latter is due to demographic transition with increase in life expectancy. The work has therefore touched upon the discussion of the various issues related to management, which becomes highly relevant for the successful functioning of the health sector and deriving the desired health outcomes.

It is evident that if India desires to be among the progressive nations of the world, there is no alternative but to have a serious relook into the functioning of the health sector and its associated problems. It is also imperative to understand the behavioural pattern of the health outcomes both in the urban and rural sectors of the country. Due to wide diversity of the socioeconomic and environmental factors prevalent in the urban and rural areas in India, all determinant factors of the health outcomes cannot be expected to behave in a similar manner to provide the policy and decision makers in the health sector with a holistic picture of the health status and their determinants. The present work therefore has been undertaken with the objective of identifying the relevant and crucial factors which determine each and every outcome of the health sector, along with their relevant weightage. This has been done separately for the urban and the rural sector so that no uniform health policy is applied at all times and at all places, with the wrong notion that health outcomes too will be uniform at all times and all places. The present work therefore attempts to take each individual determinant of the various indicators of health status and study their importance in influencing each individual health indicator. It is hoped that policy makers will be able to appreciate the relative weight of the various determinants of health in India from the findings of the study and formulate policies on health accordingly.

Shillong, India Keya Sengupta

Acknowledgement

My interest in the health sector developed during the course of my several visits to the Indian Institute of Advanced Study, Shimla, as an associate for 3 years. This interest in health economics was further strengthened after I read the various works on the subject by Amartya Sen and after many years of my work on human development. My work on human development made me ponder on the multi-dimensional reasons for the low level of health and education performance in India, due to which India continues to be so low in the Human Development Index among the countries of the world. The present work is the result of several years of research in the area of health sector. I am thankful to different scholars and experts in the area, my discussion and interaction with whom has benefitted me immensely for undertaking the work.

I am also thankful to all those who helped me during the course on my visit to Indian Institute of Advanced Studies, Shimla; Fondation Maison des Sciences de l'Hommes, Paris; and Pantheon-Sorbonne University, Paris.

I am immensely thankful to my students from whom I have benefitted immensely through my discussion with them and also for providing me technical assistance.

Last but most importantly, I am thankful to my parents who have been constantly prodding and encouraging me for the completion of the work, without which I would have taken much more time to complete the work.

March, 2015 Keya Sengupta

Contents

List of Diagrams

List of Figures

About the Author

Keya Sengupta is a Professor of Economics, Dean, Academics at the Indian Institute of Management, Shillong, India. She has been teaching economics to the postgraduate and PhD students for about 30 years. Her research of over 35 years was focused on price theory. She later shifted to the study of various aspects of the social sector such as human development, education and health. She has published many papers in this field and has also authored three books on issues of human development, marketed surplus and price theory. Prof. Sengupta was selected for the Indo-French Social Scientist Exchange Programme to visit Fondation Maison des Sciences l'Hommes, Paris, France, to study the health sector of the country. She has also visited many other countries in connection with various academic assignments. She was also an associate for 3 years at the Indian Institute of Advanced Studies, Shimla, India. Prof. Sengupta was honoured with the Dewang Mehta Award for the best teacher in Economics in Business Schools for the year 2011 and the National Educational Leadership Award by Economics Times NOW in 2013.

Chapter 1
Significance of the Study of Health Economics

1.1 Introduction

Development of a nation is crucially connected with the condition of health of its people, and health is now been accepted as an important determinant of economic development of a nation. It is only a nation with a healthy labour force who has the ability and the capability to undertake the task of expediting the growth and development of the economy. According to Development Economists, health condition of the people is also one of the important ends of all developmental efforts. Impressive achievement in the health sector has paved the way for excellent record not only in the level of economic development as revealed by the experience of most nations, but in human development as well. This has been the experience of the South East Asian nations as well as the Nordic nations. Inadequate and unplanned investment in the health sector results in frequent break out of epidemics and deaths, which can seriously retard the current and the future growth potentiality of those nations. Such has been the unfortunate experience of some of the African nations.

It is therefore at great peril that policy makers can ignore the vital relationship between health status of nations and their economic development. The relationship has been proved repeatedly by numerous empirical evidences. A workforce which is healthy can help to raise the overall productivity in the economy. Higher level of output can result only in an economy characterised by a strong and hardworking labour force since it results in lower level of absenteeism due to ill health and sickness. Scarce resources in a less developed economy need not be diverted for financing health expenditure of an unproductive nature or tackling the problems of frequent epidemics if adequate and timely attention is given to the health needs of the population. Opportunity cost of such scarce capital in poor countries is very high because these resources could have been used for the purpose of economic development. It is also true that there is no evidence of any direct relationship between economic growth and good health. Evidences have revealed that nations with the same level of GDP have recorded a wide disparity with respect to performance in

K. Sengupta, *Determinants of Health Status in India*,
DOI 10.1007/978-81-322-2535-5_1

the health sector. Economic growth is a necessary but not a sufficient condition either for removing poverty or for improving the health condition of the population. Economic growth may enhance income, but inaccessibility to social goods such as health may persist. Due to these reasons, the World Health Organisation has set up the Commission on Macroeconomics and Health (CMH) in 2000. This was done in an attempt at assessing the place of health in global economic development.

It is essentially for this purpose that social investment at the macro level and household expenditure on health at the micro level assumes importance. Thus the evolution "what constitutes health" brought to the foreground the interconnectivity between economic growth, poverty and social goods namely health, adding new dimensions to the understanding of development economics" (IHR 2005). Poverty of the nation as well as the individual households restricts accessibility to health facilities like any other facilities. It is a common experience throughout the world that poor people are the victims of higher level of morbidity and mortality. Poor health diverts a higher proportion of expenditure at the micro level for meeting health expenses. This is often at the cost of rising debt volumes, mostly at very high interest rates. In the Indian condition, a significant proportion or rural debt is for meeting medical expenses. This section of the population are consequently caught up in a vicious circle of low income, poor health, low productivity, lower earning capacity and therefore higher debt. Such problems assume serious proportion in countries such as India characterised by high degree of poverty. Good health is therefore not only a means of economic development but also an end by itself. The interlink between good health, workers' productivity, income earning capacity and economic growth has been a well-accepted fact (Savedoff and Schultz 2000; Schultz 1999a, b, 2002; Schultz and Tansel 1992; Strauss and Thomas 1998). There is a circular relationship between good health and higher income. This is only natural because when a person has adequately good income, he/she is in a position to look after his own health and that of his family members. He can afford better and good education which helps to increase the awareness about the importance of good health. Such people understand the significance of hygiene and good health will ensure and can also afford clean in life style. As a result such people are less likely to be the victims of water-borne diseases and various illnesses due to the absence of sanitation or the inability to maintain a healthy life style. This in turn improves their working ability as they can work much harder and for longer hours in comparison to those who fall ill and are victims of infant and child mortality and shorter life expectancy, due to inadequate awareness, education and income. The former group is naturally able to have higher income earning capacity and are able to contribute more productively to the economic growth of their respective nations. It is therefore evident that good health status is not only a determinant and imperative for economic growth, but also the result of economic growth, because only when the economy expands and grows, more employment can be generated thereby increasing the income earning capacity of the health consumers. Such an economy is also in a position to spend more by way of public health spending, especially for those who are unable to afford spending on health care needs on their own. This in turn can improve the overall health status of the nation. Relationship of this nature is further supported by a good number of empirical work. Significant among them is the work of Weil (2005), who postulates that adult heights and survival rates move together, and maintains that there is a stable relationship between the height and health of the population and adult survival. He then goes on to examine the relationship between adult survival rates as a proxy for good health and labour productivity across countries. According to his findings, 1 p.c. increase in adult survival rates results in 1.68 p.c. rise in labour productivity, implying that a worker with good health status and with low mortality rate will be 70 p.c. more productive in comparison to a worker with low mortality. According to his study, it means that health differential account for 17 p.c. of the differential in output per worker. Therefore it implies that health is as important as physical capital for the purpose of economic development.

Similar kind of study by Bloom and Canning (2000), maintains increase by 1 p.c. in adult survival rates, result in increase in labour productivity by about 2.8 p.c.

It is therefore evident that study of health status of the people of a nation is an integral part of the study of economic growth. Any programme of economic growth that ignores the health of its people faces a bleak future which may jeopardise the very process of economic growth. Gunner Myrdal had rightly focussed attention to the vital role of health in economic development (Myrdal 1968). According to him, health should not be viewed in isolation from the development process. Health is determined not only by the socioeconomic factors like education and the level of income, but health in turn also determines the ability and the capability for better earning opportunities and better education. Just as labour productivity depends on health conditions for an adult, similarly the ability to go to school and acquire good education also depends on good health. Myrdal therefore opines that planning for better health should be an integral part of general planning for economic growth. He further maintains that the sole emphasis on physical infrastructure for development, at the cost of social infrastructure such as health is totally fallacious. The western paradigm of economic growth based totally on the capital output ratio can be dangerous if accepted for less developing nations with poor health record. Only one part of economic development can be explained by physical investment, but the crucial part with long-term implications can be explained by investment in health and education (Bryant 1969). Health like education therefore occupies the centre stage of human capability which in turn is the core of the broader development issues. Health conditions can therefore be considered as inputs to aggregate production function. It is therefore no wonder that labour productivity in developed nations, which experiences better health records, is many times more than their less developed counterparts. One of the important reasons is that mortality rates, especially child mortality rates in developing countries are ten times higher than the rich countries. It is estimated that the lives of more than ten million children can be saved in the developing nations, if child mortality rates in such countries were equal to that of the developed ones. Even those who survive are the victims of different types of chronic and infectious diseases (Todaro and Smith 2003). It is therefore evident that good health status in a nation increases both the quality as well as the quantity in terms of both the number of work force as well as the number of hours of work put in by the labourers. Improved health status necessitates spending less for healthcare and to that extent enables the citizens of a poor nation to spend more on other necessities of life. Thus better health not only improves the general well-being, but improves the standard of living. It is therefore pertinent to mention here the definition of health as accepted by WHO (1947) as "state of complete physical and social wellbeing and not merely the absence of disease or infirmity". It is therefore too evident that health is a holistic concept, implying both physical and social health.

From the above discussion, it is only too apparent that public health policy which aims at better health condition of the general population of a nation plays a crucial role for economic growth. Instances and evidences of the benefit of health needs are so great and economic benefits so visible that there is no challenging the wisdom of the health programme and policies of public health (Bryant 1969). Further, successful health programmes tend to improve general attitudes, such as the recognition, that change is possible and encourage innovative thinking that cannot be expected of a nation characterised by unhealthy people.

Support of all health programmes necessitates expenditure on improving health status, irrespective of the level of development of the country concerned. The crucial question is who incurs the expenditure on health. Health infrastructure has undoubtedly to be provided by the state or made through private investment. Programmes for eradication of diseases and illness and arresting outbreak of epidemics is more acute and urgent in poor nations, since such nations are more prone to these problems. In poor countries, since individuals are often unable to meet such expenditure or have to incur huge debt for meeting medical expenditure, the state has step in and bear a major part of the burden of health expenditure. Investment in health therefore forms a significant component of overall investment for economic development, which no modern nation, be it developed or underdeveloped can ignore only at great perils to its future growth prospects. According to a study by E.F. Dennison (Dennison), it is maintained that population in US would have been less by 13 million, since 1990, if death rates had not declined. The contribution of this 13 million amounts to an additional amount of $ 60 billion to national income, when valued at 1960 prices, which is mainly the result of improvement in health status of its population.

It is therefore too clear that one of the crucial concerns of health economics is the cost benefit analysis of health expenditure. Benefit is measured in terms of reduction of death rates, morbidity prevented or the economic loss that is prevented. Cost is the total amount of expenditure incurred by the government to improve these health indicators.

The study of the importance of health economics is relevant in three related ways. Firstly, it reveals the contribution of the health sector to the overall economy. Secondly, the national policy concerns which results from the importance many people attach to the economic problems they face in pursuing and maintaining their health; and thirdly, the many health issues that have a substantial economic element (Folland et al. 2009).

1.2 Role of State and the Health Sector in Developing Economies

If the health sector is left entirely to the market forces, the sole responsibility for the provision of health services would rest on the individual, whatever may be his level of income. The consequence will be the emergence of acute form of social inequity and wide divergence in health indicators between the ones who can afford private health care and the ones who cannot. Such has been the experience of those nations which have adopted the neo classical model of growth. Strategies of growth based on such models would automatically exclude such vital issues with their disastrous consequences for long-term sustainable development. Developmental economics therefore necessitates assigning these responsibilities to the state so that the requisite health standard can be assured even to the deprived and the poverty stricken people.

Economic growth has to be combined with the distribution of income by providing minimum health care facilities in a manner that is politically and socially acceptable. Economic growth if properly managed through policy measures can be made effective through the trickle down process. This can be achieved by transferring resources from the rich to the poor by allocating resources for the health sector. All these efforts would directly contribute in raising human development. Though initial returns from such involvements may be negative and hence may be against the basic tenets of neo classical economy, yet developmental economists maintain that such investments can make the growth process more effective and meaningful in the long run.

In poor and less developing nations, the poor tend to incur more health expenditure than their counterparts in the rich and developed nations. In poor nations, incidences of diseases and epidemics are much higher than in the rich nations, whereas availability of doctors, nurses, hospitals and other medical infrastructure is much less. The result is per capita availability of medical assistance in such nations is lower and often unaffordable. There are numerous instances of poor people in India who have sold out their entire assets, got steeped in permanent indebtedness just to meet the medical expenses of some of their close relatives' illnesses. This compels the poor people to refrain from medical help, which in turn increases the morbidity and mortality rates. It is therefore only too evident that the state in such nations needs to step in to provide universal health care to its citizens. Inspite of the growing role of the market forces during the recent decades, the role of the state in the health sector particularly in those nations which are overpopulated and mostly rural dominated cannot be overemphasised. This is mainly because the poor cannot afford health care that is often extremely exorbitant. Health care provided by the state under such circumstances can not only alleviate poverty but may also increase productivity and reduce curative health expenses, which may often constitute significant proportion of a nation's GDP. Some health-promoting actions are public goods that create large positive externalities which cannot be expected to be produced by the private sector. Public welfare may thus be raised by state intervention especially in areas of health insurance and health care activities. WDR (2000) postulates that the role of the state in providing health care services should consist of formulating a sound health policy with a definite vision and direction. Setting the minimum standard for health services and their delivery mechanism, framing laws and enforcing them, evaluation of the impact of health policies on the health indicators as well as ensuring universal access for the purpose of equity and quality can be undertaken only by the state. Such activities fall outside the purview of the market forces. In poor countries, it is therefore imperative that the state should extend its areas of operation to immunization, family planning, services to ensure pregnancy related care and other infectious diseases. The state has also to make the necessary institutional arrangements so that health services may be provided to the poor and the needy. It is aptly stated by Dr Brundtland, Director General of WHO that, "The challenge facing governments in low income countries is to reduce the regressive burden of out-of-pocket payment for health by expanding pre-payment schemes, which spread financial risk and reduce the spectre of health care expenditures".

In addition to the direct intervention in health care activities and expenditure, the role of the state in providing health care also extends to provision of safe drinking water, sanitation, health education and health awareness campaigns. These provision of universal system of health care has become one of the core functions of the government because health is an important determinant of human development, which is being now accepted by good number of nations as the new paradigm of evaluating the trickle-down effect of economic growth.

The role of the state in providing health services particularly during the period when market forces have assumed a growing role has been a matter of intense debate. It is maintained by some that the role of the state in health sector has resulted in wastage of precious resources particularly in poor nations in maintaining a huge administrative setup. Such a set-up has resulted more in corruption rather than in providing the necessary health services to the needy. While this view cannot be totally ruled out, at the same time as mentioned, there are certain areas of health care system which if left outside their purview will only result in growing misery among the poor. One of the most important reasons for the controversy over the role of the state is the inadequate understanding about the role of the state in either changing the economic scenario or the health scenario. As a result, there have always been inadequate resources for the health sector. Added to this is also the rising problem of equally inadequate monitoring system and absence of accountability. Consequently what should be one of the most important social investments has lost its relevance and appears to be wastage of resources in a good number of nations.

The other associated problem has been a lack of priority regarding allocation of resources. The result has been gross misallocation of resources. Lack of prioritization has also resulted in "financial and human resources being spread too thinly for impact". Studies have revealed that states in India which have experienced equity in terms of service coverage and in delivery of basic preventive services to poor and disadvantaged groups have consistently better health outcomes. This reveals the importance of equitable access to health services by poor and disadvantaged groups which can be ensured only by the state (IHR 2005). Apart from these functions, areas of health education and public awareness, planning, management and monitoring of services sensitivity to local community needs can best be ensured by the state machinery. Therefore role of the state even during period of growing role of the private sector can at best be restructured but cannot be done away with.

The issues that need to be addressed are development of models to identify ways and means to optimise the performance of the state in various spheres of health related activities. Development of such models is a holistic approach which has to extend to the overall issues of good governance supported by a strong health management system, discussed in the subsequent chapters of the present study, which extends to both political as well as administrative reforms. Inadequate attention to this holistic approach to health care planning with only emphasis on the provision of merely medical care has resulted in greater number of people left to avail of private health care services in most poor countries, including India. This inspite of the fact that the average cost of treatment in the private sector for the rural inpatients was 2.1 times higher, and for urban inpatients 2.4 times higher than in the public sector during 1995–1996 according to NSS data in India. This is mainly because advances in technology have made the average cost of health care services more expensive rather than cheaper all over the world.

1.3 Allocation of Resources in the Health Sector

It is therefore imperative that attention needs to be diverted to various means of generating sufficient resources for the health sector and their optimum allocation among the various areas of the health sector. Resources also need to be optimally allocated between rural and urban areas between medical research and technology.

Allocation of resources in the health sector has always been a debatable issue though it is seen as a crucial determinant affecting the health sector of a nation. One of the reasons for the problem as maintained by some studies is that (Eike 2007), when resources are construed as social goods, allocation may proceed either in terms of competition between individuals on the basis of the relative strengths of their competition rights or on aggregate basis by evaluating which distribution would produce the greatest amount of good for the greatest number of people. One therefore needs to be very clear about the three distinct level of decision making for allocation of resources.

- Firstly, it is the allocation of resources to health care vis-a-vis other social needs
- Secondly, is the issue of allocation within the health care sector itself.
- Thirdly, allocation among individual patients.

Most of these issues of allocation have become highly debatable, because not only resources are limited but demand and the costs of the health care sector have become very expensive. As is the case with allocation of resources in other sectors, in health care sector too, the issue is resolved depending on the nature of resources themselves. The consideration of the greatest amount of benefit for the greatest number of people may be the sole consideration if resources are taken as social goods. In contrast, if resources are taken merely as physical and material resources, the idea of economic considerations assumes supremacy. Ability to pay at the micro level assumes dominance and at the macro level the main consideration is 'whether the economic structure that governs the cost/price relationship for commodities is sufficiently robust to allow for the survival of the economic enterprise that is associated with the production and sale of the goods in question' (Eike 2007).

The resource constraint in health sector like any other sector has given rise to the concept of 'healthcare rationing', which has assumed importance in recent times. The newly emerged concept refers to the conscious decision to exclude certain people from health service or treatment that they need. Rationing may take place when the government decodes who is eligible for free medical treatment or medicine, which sectors are eligible for medical insurance. For allocation of resources in the health care sector, it is essential to realise that financial, physical and manpower resources are equally important to realise the objectives of health. The places, the instruments and the personnel who are able to deliver health care need special investment and not everywhere and everyone, without any equipment can deliver health care services. There is always a mismatch between demand and supply due to which the use of econometric models based on health economics is essential to assess the exact nature and type of the health care sector concerned. Such models can also indicate the relative importance of various types of investment for raising the health status, so that the respective intersectoral health resource allocation may be done.

1.4 Economics and Its Relevance for Health Sector

It is here that the role of economics for the health sector assumes importance. The awareness of the crucial role of economics in the health sector has brought to the forefront the branch of study known as 'health economics' for the first time by the Nobel Laureate, Kenneth Arrow (1963). Arrow highlighted the role of 'uncertainty' an important element in the study of demand and supply in health economics. The concept of health economics has however become much broader at present and is extended to the services to promote health and to prevent and treat diseases and illnesses. Health services more of which will be discussed in the subsequent chapters includes medical care, public health services and environment. World Health Organisation (WHO) also, as mentioned in the earlier section, defines health as state of complete physical, mental and social well-being and not merely the absence of disease or infirmity. Cost of health services also incorporates the cost of education and training of medical personnel and medical research. The health sector in all countries employs a significant percentage of its population serving as an important source of employment. It is estimated that in the US economy, in 2003, almost 10 p.c. of US population was engaged in the health sector. Greater resource allocation to the health sector also means higher opportunities for employment in the sector.

Like other sectors which are affected by rising price, inflation in the health sector also results in a rise in health expenditure, which affects the common man, due to which the poor in less developing countries have to be deprived of adequate medical care. This makes them the victims of diseases and illness, which could perhaps be avoided if health sector was not the victim of often exorbitant rise in prices. Besides this, the production, costs and insurance of health are not the only areas of study which come under the purview of health economics. The exercise of 'choice' by the health care user, among the various alternative forms of health service delivery and the most affordable way of treatment, directly encompasses the study of health within the framework of economics. The use of 'choice' arises in health economics because resources are scarce both to the individual as well as to the public authorities. As a result, the scarce resources have to be spent most judiciously and are therefore allocated only in those areas where their return is expected to be the highest. The exercise of choice proceeds on the assumption that the stakeholder who incurs the expenditure is a 'rational entity' because she/he wants that return from the scarce resource should be the highest. This is an important characteristic feature of someone who spends the scarce resource. For making 'rational choice', resource is spent by measuring the additional cost and the resultant additional benefit derived, which is mentally measured for every dose of additional expenditure. This brings the consumer directly under the purview of marginal analysis of study, which is an important tool of analysis in economics. Finally, to understand the behavioural aspect of any variable in the health sector and to make predictions about the future behaviour, econometric models' are used to study the health sector. The use of economics come directly into the picture when medical practitioners charge different prices for the same services rendered by them from a rich patient, charging a higher fee and a lower fee from a poor patient, implying the use of 'price discrimination' in a monopolistic competitive market.

It is thus the use of economic tools and techniques and the powerful analytical method of the subject that can provide adequate guidance to the policy makers as how best to utilise the scarce resources for obtaining the optimum health outcomes. The goal of improving the various health outcomes analysed within the purview of economic framework gives a new and different insight of looking into the problems confronting the health sector. It is in this connection that the issues relevant for health management arises and the knowledge from the study of health economics can be utilised for the purpose of health management. Economics basically work with the idea of unlimited demands, because there is no limit to the wants of mankind. In the health sector too, there are unlimited demands that require urgent attention. However, the basic problem in economics is limited resources to satisfy these unlimited claims and demands. It is here that models and tools of analysis in economics are used to study health economics, and the analytical tools of overcoming these problems are been used to study the health related issues in an organised manner. The framework developed based on economic models is then used to predict health-related economic behaviour. The many conflicting demands of the health sector can thus be attempted to be optimally satisfied by the use of these tools.

It is therefore the need of using the economic tools of analysis for identifying and studying health-related problems that has given rise to a new branch of economics known as 'Health Economics'. The new discipline of health economics had started emerging when economists began to work with these problems confronting the health sector. Health economics is a relatively new branch of economics which emerged during the sixties. Some of the pioneering academic work which deserves mention in this connection are the works of Kenneth Arrow (1963), C. M. Lindsay (1969), S. J. Muskin (1962a, b) and M. S. Feldstein (1967). Economists dealing with health-related problems study issues ranging from supply of health services such as health personnel and specialists, health infrastructure and the demand and the market demand for health care services. Their costs, revenues and evaluation also come under the purview of health economics. Study of the alternative ways of addressing health related problems, the opportunity costs of investments in health, cost–benefit analysis of health investment, all of which are included in the micro-economic framework of health economics, play a pivotal role in decision making for the policy makers in the health sector. On the other hand, study related to health which addresses issues for the society or the country as a whole, such as the performance, accessibility, affordability, effectiveness of the health system, or the determinants of the health status of a nation, or the comparisons of the health standards among different nations are the subject matter of the study of macroeconomic framework of health economics.

It is a growing and serious concern in all nations and more particularly in the developing ones that the objectives of attaining the optimum goal in the health sector has been more and more elusive, rising health expenditure notwithstanding. Among the factors responsible for such anomalies is the absence of the technical knowledge about health economics. The absence of scientific guidelines for identifying the right choices for making allocation of resources for the health sector and the optimum distribution of the health services among those sectors where their optimum utilisation lies has been one of the causes for not attaining the targets of the health sector. Absence of such guidelines when inadequate attention is paid to health economics can have disastrous long tern consequences for the economy.

When the desired health outcome is not forthcoming, it may indicate that investments are made in the wrong kinds of health services or in those health technologies which are expensive and have low health outcome. Knowledge of health economics enables the policy makers to take decision on how to acquire resources for the health sector, and how best to use the scarce resources for the production of health services. It also helps the policy makers to guide for which section of the population, these limited health services are to be used. Health economists also evaluate the health situation in an objective manner and identify the factors responsible for the problems in the health sector, which may range from the uses of resources, various health outcomes, health expenditure, infrastructure or even the health delivery mechanism from the perspective of economics. Depending on the economic evaluative studies, alternative methods are suggested which are expected to have better outcomes or save resources for the economy.

Decisions relating to the health sector on the demand for health services, the supply of health services and the equilibrium market price may either be left to the market forces or may be planned. In the former case, it is the private sector which dominates the health sector and in the latter case it is the state which decides where, how, when and for whom decisions relating to the health sector are to be taken. Activities in the health sector when they proceed in a planned manner revolve around the crucial question of 'what is the best way'. Accordingly different strategies and approaches are worked out for the best allocation of resources. Economic tools and techniques are evolved to obtain the desired results in the best possible manner. Another important issue that often emerges in health economics is the question of equity and efficiency. While market forces depend on the price mechanism for the allocation of resources is guided by the principle of *efficiency*, health planning by the state is guided more by the principle of *equity*. A trade-off between equity and efficiency in the health sector is an issue that has being long debated. While equity meaning easy accessibility to health services is of utmost importance in a poor nation, sacrificing efficiency for a long period may also make health services unsustainable.

Knowledge of health economics is essential not only from the point of view of the provider of health services but also from the view point of the users of health services. For instance, the users need to be familiar with the idea of maximising their utility of health services by the use of their limited resources. Within the constraints, the consumers of health services have to exercise their preferences. The individual consumers' tastes and preferences on health services, prices of such services and the income are important in guiding them in taking decisions on the type and nature of health services that they prefer to avail. In taking all such decisions, knowledge of health economics is imperative. Concepts of price elasticity of demand and income elasticity of demand which examine the responsiveness of demand for health services to changes in price and income is a crucial economic tool which enables the provider of health services to know the exact amount by which such services are to be increased whenever there is a change either in price or income. Such studies assume crucial importance for policy purposes in the health sector on whether taxes are to be imposed in certain areas of health items or whether subsidies are to be given for others.

The structure of the market which is an important branch of the study in economics has a pivotal role to play in determining the price and delivery of health services provided. The market may consist of a single provider of health services which is termed as a monopolist. A monopolist in the health delivery and health care system may charge any price that he likes. Under such conditions, unregulated monopoly may imply depriving the poor and the needy from such services. In other forms of market structures, there may be only a few providers of health services termed as oligopolistic markets. Still in others, many providers may characterise the health care services. Depending on the type of market for health delivery mechanisms, the appropriate policy decisions need to be taken. It is therefore evident that the knowledge of health economics is essential both for the provider, user as well as the policy makers.

1.5 Health System

Study and understanding of health status without a mention of the health system would be meaningless and sterile, as one would fail to grasp the responsibility of the providers of health services which is determined by the health system of a nation. However, health systems by itself do not determine the health status of a nation. It is the relationship between the users, payers, providers and regulators which constitutes the health system of a nation and it is the health system of a nation which in turn determines the health status of a nation. These relationships among the providers of health services take place within the market system. The bargaining power of the sellers as determined by the market structure or the buyers as determined by the users of health services determines the health system, though they are often not as explicit as in the case of markets for other products.

One of the major debates of a health system is the alternative ways of health funding and financing. Unlike the 'need' that is mentioned in pure economics and which is always insatiable, health care needs are all expected to be met. This is defined not in terms of the needs of the individual but the possibility of intervention to meet the health need. This is mainly because health care need is much more complicated than all other types of need. It is defined not in terms of the size of the absolute nature of health problems but in terms of the feasibility of intervention to remove or reduce the problems (Mathew 1971). Intervention is necessary because unlike as in pure rational behaviour in economics, where the benefit of the need has to always exceed the cost, in health economics all needs are not evaluated merely by cost benefit analysis. When individuals meet their own health needs, they take the help of price mechanism to ensure that that their resources are allocated in terms of their demand in the most rational manner. This is undertaken by the use of the marginal analysis and resources are diverted away from those sectors where the return is the lowest to those areas where the return is the highest.

Though spending in the health sector broadly follows the principal of marginal analysis, yet spending resources for health needs are viewed from a social perspective also. Just as the individual demand curve slopes downwards, in a similar manner, the social demand curve which is derived by summation of all the individuals demand curve represents the idea of social marginal valuations, which is also based on diminishing marginal return. However, priorities will be quite different for individuals and social demand curves. For instance, health expenditure for prevention of any epidemic will be extremely low for lower income groups, since the best allocation of their limited resources would necessitate spending on basic necessities of life. In contrast, since this section of the population is more vulnerable to diseases and illnesses and when there is an outbreak of epidemics, social demand function requires spending the most for this section of the population, since they are unable to spend on health preventive measures on their own. For the well-off section of the community on the other hand, due to greater degree of awareness and better education, health spending for preventive purposes is relatively higher and social spending on this group is therefore relatively lower.

Health policies determine the alternative ways of organising health financing. This in turn has wide implications for ownership of health providing and health financing institutions, the organisational and the hierarchical structure of the health system. All these factors determine the flow of resources within and between institutions.

In no nation, the state directly has a role to play in the health system, though the degree and extent of its role varies from nation to nation. In most cases, health system is managed by the state. There is some form of either subsidy or tax for the users of health services in all nations. There is also some form of monitoring and regulation by the state for the minimum qualification of doctors and other medical staff, hospitals and all other health infrastructure, even if they fall under the private domain of health system. However, in most other cases, it is the tax revenue which finances building of medical infrastructure, employment of medical staff who works within the health system and the supply of all drugs and other inputs. The question of funding health needs therefore assumes crucial significance in this connection.

One of the important features of any health system is *health insurance,* where users pay regularly for the maintenance of health system. On the other hand, they are assured of regular health care which they otherwise could not have normally afforded due to high costs. Public health systems are also a form of insurance, with the relevant share of tax which is more or less equivalent to health insurance premium. Even the type of health insurance varies from one country to another. It is therefore clear that health systems in all countries are a blending of different degrees of state regulation and payments where one of the features may dominate while in the others some other features might play the leading role. In some countries, health system is totally financed publicly and centrally, and all medical services are provided free of charges to the users. Private sector had a very limited role to play and all medical staff were appointed by the state. Such was the type of health system prevalent in the former Communist nations of Central and Eastern Europe. The other type of health system though largely provided and financed publicly also includes user charges. It may also have a private insurance sector outside the public system. Such is the health system prevalent in UK and adopted in a good number of other countries of Africa and Asia in a slightly modified form.

A major challenge confronting the public health system is inadequate and poor management of resources. The result has often been the inability to deliver the desired results and outcome. The result has been that the private sector has filled in the gap.

Most of the industrialised nations are characterised by the *social insurance* system. Under this system, major chunk of the population are insured compulsorily and a small proportion is insured voluntarily and the others are insured privately. The proportion of private and public providers varies from time to time and from places to place. Both the private and public operate on contract to the statutory sickness funds and there are minor co-payments made by the users at the time of use. Such systems prevail in Germany and in Brazil. There are also nations where the three important subsystems such as public, social insurance and private operate simultaneously. Such is the health system prevalent in most of the Latin American countries.

Another type of system is dominated totally by the private sector, and the state steps in only for those who do not come under the purview of the private sector. Such a system is prevalent in US where employers provide insurance coverage to the employees and their dependents, and the rest provides insurance for themselves. State provides insurance coverage only for the elderly and the poor (McPake et al. 2002.

1.6 Health Management and Health Economics

There is an integral connection between health economics and health management. The limited resources available for the health sector for their optimum use and maximum health benefits to the users can be given proper direction and channelized into desired objectives only through the right management techniques. The optimum use of limited resources can thus be attained only through various management tools. Health management uses various managerial tools and techniques in an attempt to undertake the challenges of limited resources, inadequate health infrastructure both physical and human as well as spatial problems of health delivery and other critical issues of delivering health services to the needy. Decision about such managerial tools and techniques is determined by the type of health problems confronting the people and the nation. It is also decided by the national income of the country, the per capita income of the people and their health expenditure, the population composition of the nation as well as the literacy of the population, all of which come under the purview of health economics. Identification of these factors and their relative weightage on health status needs to be examined before deciding upon the managerial techniques to achieve the health objectives. It is thus evident that a holistic study of health economics is incomplete without a study of issues of health management.

It also needs to be noted that the choice of health management tools are determined by the challenges posed by the type of diseases, mortality and morbidity rates, infant and maternal mortality rates. The priority given in solving each of these problems and the formulation of health goals and objectives, which come under the purview of health policies, are in reality addressed by health management. Development of programs, costestimation, alternative and cheaper programs and strategies for attaining the health objectives can all be achieved with the help of knowledge of health management. Study to evaluate the effectiveness of different health programmes, their modifications, expansion or even replacement or innovation is undertaken only with the help of management tools. The primary role of management is the same everywhere, be it in the service sector, production and manufacturing sector or sale of goods and commodities. Basic objective are the same with a difference of only the complexities of the respective enterprises. The complexities of the health sector have been only increasing in recent times. As an organisation tries to handle these complex issues, managerial competence from top to bottom faces greater and greater challenges. Managerial experience of not only the health officials but even the health providers assumes crucial significance. Successful and professional functioning of the health sector requires managers who can control and make the health sector function effectively so the health delivery system can successfully meet its goal and objectives.

With the expanding health sector, investment in the sector too has been rising at an increasing rate. Efficient management of financial resources necessitates knowledge of financial management, which will not only reduce wastage but will also ensure optimum utilisation of scare resources, which is one of the goals of the study of microeconomics. It is also essential that proper health administration demands efficient personnel management and human resource management. Teamwork effort in the health sector and other types of soft skills is the key to the success of the health sector. All these efforts both at the organisational level and at the national level require a vision and a mission, which can only be effectively devised and handled by managerial techniques.

Health management therefore deals extensively with the evaluation of health programmes and cost accounting, cost benefit and cost effectiveness of health expenditure. As a result, health economics plays a pivotal role in the study of hospitals, medical curricula with the purpose of making health management standardised and effective. Hence the study and integration of Health Economics and Health Management is of crucial importance which neither any economist nor any health manager can afford to ignore, the detailed study of which will be discussed in Chapter six.

1.7 Objectives of the Present Study

The present study with its emphasis on Health Economics will examine the health problems within a macroeconomic framework. The focus of the study will be on Health Status and their determinants in the Indian context. Health status in India leaves a lot to be desired inspite of India being one of the fastest growing emerging economies in the world. Life expectancy in India according to Human Development Report (HDR 2011) is only 65.4 years as against 80.0 years for the highly developed nations and 73.1 years for the Arab countries. Even the medium category nations of human development to which India belongs has a higher life expectancy of 69.7 years. Even the figures for maternal mortality i.e. the death of women per 1,00,000 live births in India is one of the highest in the world. The figure stands at 230 as against 15 and 51 for very high and high human development nations and 133 for medium human development nation, the group of countries to which India belongs. Similar is the extremely disturbing figure for mortality rate under 5 years, which was as high as 66 in 2009. This is much higher than the mortality rates of 6 and 19 for very high and high human development nations and 44 for the medium human development nations. These figures only go to reveal the extremely appalling health condition in India. It also raises the natural curiosity as to why inspite of such satisfactory figures for economic indicators health status in the country still continues to be so poor. It also raises the question as to whether economic growth could have been expedited even further with a healthy lot of population with better health record. Such doubts are raised when it is revealed (HDR 2011) that the loss due to inequality in life expectancy in India is as high as 27.1 p.c. though the figure for the medium category human development nations is only 19.2 p.c. The figure is indeed alarming because the figures for very high and high human development nations are 5.2 p.c. and 12.4 p.c., respectively. It also needs to be mentioned here that public expenditure on health as a percentage of GDP in India is 1.1 p.c., which is the lowest among all categories of nations in the world.

Health status can not only be defined in terms of quality, but can also be quantified. Therefore no single factor can measure the health status of a country. A number of factors are needed to determine the health status of a nation in a holistic manner. Health status represents the overall quality of life and therefore no single health indicator taken alone can represent the overall quality of life. In the Indian context, it is urgently required to identify the factors responsible for the appalling overall health condition of the country inspite of its expanding and growing economy. The objective of the present study will therefore be to identify the determinants of the various parameters of health status in the country, as studying the overall health status without segregating it into its various components will not convey any meaningful analysis of the study of health status and its determinant factors.

The indicators of health status that will be selected for the purpose of the study will be

- Infant mortality rates
- Maternal mortality rates
- Death rates
- Life expectancy
- Children with stunted growth (Diagram 1.1)

Identification of the pivotal determinates of the parameters of health status will enable the policy makers to determine the allocation of resources for health sector in terms of their relative importance instead of wasting valuable resources and allocating them in areas which deserve perhaps not so much of importance for the purpose of resource allocation. Another new dimension of the work will be to highlight the fact that health status and their determinants is not the same in the rural and urban areas in any nation, and more so in a vast country like India with so much of diversity in almost every aspect of life. Therefore uniform health policies in terms of their goals and resource allocation for the two sectors may not deliver the desired health outcomes. Consequently, the work will attempt to identify the determinants of health status for the urban and rural sector separately. The components of the health status selected for our purpose is represented in a diagrammatic form.

Since health is a multi-dimensional complex issue, there are numerous determinants of is status. Some of these play a direct role and others an indirect role. Some factors are tangible others are intangible ones. Some factors have an immediate and direct impact on health status; some others may have long term and indirect impact. Out of these many determinants, some are determined by the provider of health

Diagram 1.1 Indicators of health status

services, whereas others are determined by the income, socio economic status, religious beliefs, psychological factors and sentiments of the users of the health care services. It is therefore an impossible task to incorporate all these determinant factors to study and examine their impact on health status. The study has therefore confined itself to only some of the most crucial factors and studied their relative importance. The determinant factors for health, selected for the purpose of the present study, are therefore divided into two broad groups, the primary and the secondary determinants.

Primary Determinants

1. Financial allocation for this sector
2. Level of general education judged by the literacy rate
3. Female education as indicated by the female literacy rate
4. Immunisation rates
5. Clean drinking water
6. Sanitation facilities

The parameters thus selected are represented below diagrammatically (Diagram 1.2).

The primary factors mentioned above determine the health status directly and hence policy makers assign greater importance to such factors.

As mentioned above, there are also certain factors which are normally not considered to have any significance for the purpose of determining health status, but they play an extremely crucial role particularly in a country like India, which is not only a vast country, but characterised by huge population, majority of whom are in the rural areas. Major proportion of the population do not have any education and

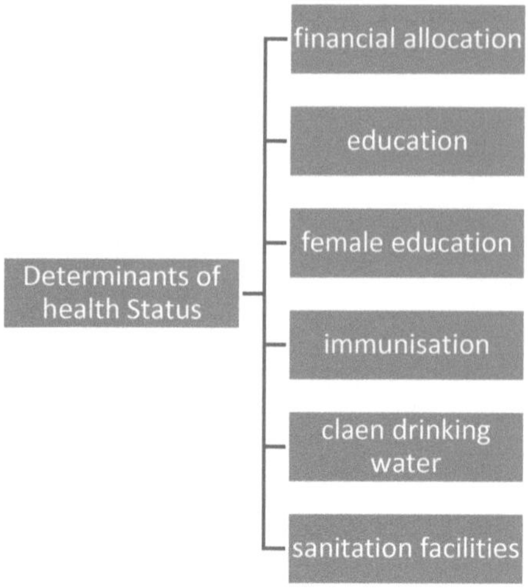

Diagram 1.2 Primary determinants of health status

lack awareness about good health and are also are under the burden of high incidence of poverty. In a developed country, factors which do not appear to be of any consideration may assume even a greater importance than the primary factors for a less developing country like India. For instance, there may be higher incidence of infant, child and maternal mortality simply because the health centres are located too far away for the patients to be transported to them. Therefore distance of the nearest primary health centres can assume to be of high importance in such places, where patients may have to be transported in carts and rickshaws. Then the very awareness of basic hygiene, health benefits of sanitation facilities and clean drinking water can go a long way in improving health condition. Use of open defecation is a normal practice, the impact of sanitation for good health needs to be actually explained to a majority of rural people. These are some of the issues which do not have much significance for health status for an already developed nation with high level of literacy. For policy consideration on health status, such factors are not assigned the due importance they deserve in comparison to the primary factors mentioned above in any country, whether developed or developing. However, in less developing countries with a high degree of illiteracy, such factors can be ignored only at great peril to the health of its general public, particularly in the rural sector. The result is health status will continue to record poor performance inspite of sufficient and adequate resource allocation. We term such factors as secondary determinants of health status some of which are mentioned below:

Secondary Determinants

7. Availability of manpower such as doctors, nurses, lab technicians and others
8. Physical infrastructure such as hospitals, number of beds in the hospitals, public health centres, sub-centres, etc.
9. Existence of health, sanitation and hygiene committees (in the rural areas)
10. Distance from the nearest health centre

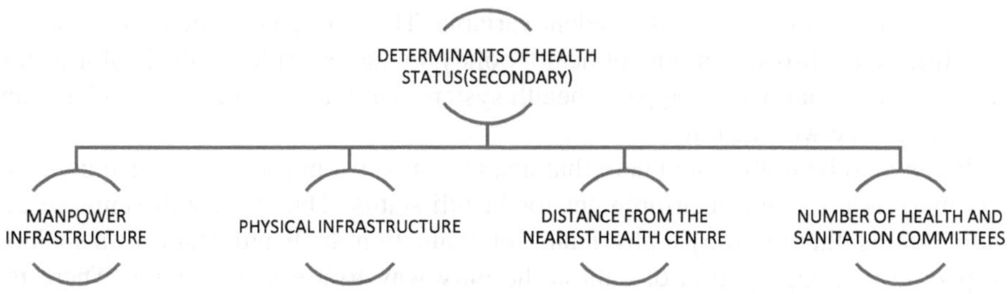

Diagram 1.3 Secondary determinants of health status

The factors having a secondary impact on health status is represented below in the form of a Chart Diagram (Diagram 1.3).

After the identification of the relative importance of various determinants of health status, the allocation of resources on such lines will be examined. In view of the pivotal role of health financing in a macro economic framework, the proper allocation of scarce resources plays an equally pivotal role. Consequently, investment in the health sector will also be examined. All these issues will then be examined within the context of health management since it is the appropriate management strategies and techniques which will in the ultimate analysis enable the economy to attain its desired objectives.

Data used for the purpose of the study is cross-sectional secondary data from across all the states and union territories of India. The sources from which data has been collected are the various issues on Health Bulletins, Health Statistics of India, Census Reports and World Health Organisation Reports. Raw data collected have been converted into percentages for the sake of uniformity and used in the econometric models outlined in the respective chapters.

1.8 Methodology of the Study

The study will first highlight the role and significance of economics for the study of the health sector of a nation. This will be done in a purely analytical manner by drawing liberally from studies of similar nature that has already been undertaken in the past. To strengthen the analysis, examination of the tools and techniques of economics which needs to be used for the purpose of productive and allocative efficiency will also be highlighted in the study. However, the main focus of the work will be to identify the crucial economic and socioeconomic factors that determine the health status of a nation. With the help of econometric tools of analysis, we will make an attempt to also identify the relative weigtage of these factors at the national level. For this purpose, the study will use multiple regression models with the various parameters of health status as the dependent variable and the determinant factors as the explanatory independent variable. This will enable the policy makers to delineate the broad contours of health policy so that priorities in the health sector can be worked out and the type of health system that the nation needs to adopt can accordingly be worked out.

It needs to be highlighted here that health status is a multi-dimensional concept and there is no single measurement for health status. Though health status of an individual is diagnosed by a physician, for evaluation the health status of a society or population, aggregation of data is the only way to assess the status. There is, however, no comprehensive or absolute measure for the health status of a population. Normally, average life span, prevention of preventable diseases or deaths, availability of health services at the macro level, are accepted as indicators of health status. There is however no ideal situation of perfect health status.

For policy purposes and also for sectoral allocation of funds for the health sector, it is extremely crucial that the determinants of health status are identified. As all determinants do not affect all the health indicators of health status in an identical manner, it is important to understand the variation in the relative weightage of these determinants for different indicators. In fact, the manner in which certain determinants affect a certain health indicator in rural area may not be the same as it affects the same indicator in the urban sector. This is more true for a vast country like India with such disparity between urban and rural areas in terms of health status and their determinants. As a result, the analysis of the entire study through the use of econometric models will be done separately for the rural and urban sectors as far as feasible. Such a methodology can give us the exact spatial spectrum of health status and disaggregative data can convey a clearer idea which may facilitate the policy makers.

References

Arrow KJ (1963) Uncertainty and the welfare economics of medical care. Am Econ Rev 53:941–973

Barro R (1996) Health and economic growth. Mimeo, Harvard University, Cambridge

Bloom D, Canning D (2000) The health wealth of nations. Science 287:1207–1208

Bloom DE, Canning D, Sevilla J (2001) The effect of health on economic growth: theory and evidence. Working paper. National Bureau of Economic Research. http://www.nber.org/paper/w8587

Bryant J (1969) Health and the developing world. Cornell University Press, Ithaca

Commission on Macroeconomics and Health (2010) Macroeconomics and health: investing in health for economic development. WHO, Geneva

Denison EF (1967) Why growth rates differ: post war experience in nine western countries. Brookings Institutions, Washington, DC

Eike HWK (2007) Resource allocation in healthcare. Med Gen Med 9(1):57

Feldstein MS (1967) Economic analysis for health service efficiency: econometric studies of the British national health service. North Holland, Amsterdam

Folland S, Goodman AC, Stano M (2009) The economics of health and health care. Pearson, Prentice Hall

Human Development Report (2011) UNDP. New York, Palgrave Macmillan

International Health Regulations (2005) Strengthening health security by implementing the international health regulations. WHO, Lyon
Lindsay Cotton M (1969) Medical care and the economics of sharing. Economica 36(144): 351–362
Mathew GK (1971) Measuring need and enhancing services. In: McLachlan G (ed) Portfolios for wealth: the role and programme of the DHSS in health services research, sixth service. Oxford University Press for Nuffield Provincial Hospital Trust, London
McPake B, Kumaranayake L, Normand C (2002) Health economics-an international perspective. London, New York
Muskin SJ (1962a) Health as an investment. Part-2 Investments in human being. J Polit Econ 70(5):129–157
Muskin SJ (1962b) Health as an investment. J Polit Econ 70:129–157
Myrdal G (1968) Asian drama "an enquiry into the poverty of nations". Pantheon, New York
Narayan S (2010) Investigating the relationship between health and economic growth, empirical evidence from a panel of 5 Asian countries. J Asian Econ 21:404–411
Sala-I-Martin X (1997a) I just ran four million regressions, Working paper, no 6252. NBER, Cambridge, MA
Sala-I-Martin X (1997b) I just ran two million regressions. Am Econ Rev Pap Proc 87(2):178–183
Savedoff WP, Schultz TP (2000) Wealth from health. Inter-American Development Bank, Washington, DC
Schultz P (1999a) Health and schooling investments in Africa. J Econ Perspect 13930:67–88
Schultz P (1999b) Productive benefits of improved health: evidence from low income countries. Yale University, Hartford
Schultz P (2002) Formation of human capital and the economic development of Africa "Returns to health and schooling investments". Working paper series 171, African Development Bank
Schultz P, Tansel A (1992) "Measurement of returns to adult health". Morbidity effects of wage rate in Cate d'Ivoire and Ghana, Discussion paper no 663. Yale University, Economic Growth Centre, New Haven
Sen A (1998) Mortality as an indicator of success and failure. Econ J 108:1–25
Sen A (2001) Economic progress and health. In: Leon D, Watt G (eds) Poverty, inequality and health: an international perspective. Oxford University Press, Oxford
Sengupta K (2009) Genesis of human development in North East India. Concept, New Delhi
Sengupta K (ed) (2010) Multi-dimensional approach to human development. Concept, New Delhi
Shastry GK, Neil DN (2003) How much of cross country income variation is explained by health? J Eur Econ Assoc 192(3):387–396
Sorkin AL (1977) Health economics in developing countries. "An Economic Perspective". Lexington Books, Lexington
Strauss J, Thomas D (1998) Health, nutrition and economic development. J Econ Lit 36:766–817
Todaro MP, Smith SC (2003) Economic development. Pearson, Delhi, India
Weil DN (2005) Accounting for the effect of health on economic growth. Q J Econ 122(3):1265–1306,08
WHO (1947) World Health Organisation Act, 1947, First Schedule

Chapter 2
Economic Tools Used for the Analysis of Health Sector

2.1 Introduction

Though the study of health problems do not appear to be included within the realm of Economics, but is considered to be the concern of only the scientists and medical practitioners; yet in modern times no work on health sector is complete without the application of the knowledge of economics. This is not only because the complexity of the health sector has increased manifold with the complexities of the society, but also because over the last 50 years or so, most nations of the world have experienced rapid increase in health care spending. This has resulted in the emergence of health economics as an independent area of study.

Some of the problems that characterise the health sector, such as the acute pressure of demand for different types of health services, the inadequacy of supply of health services and health infrastructure and the determinants of demand and supply of these health services are precisely the areas of study of economics. These problems in the health sector arises because resources for the use in the health are always scarce, whereas due to rise in population and health related problems, demand for health services is forever rising. The various ways in which the limited resources can be used in the health sector and how these limited resources are to be used for the different subsectors of health in a manner that yields the highest returns can be determined only by the principals of economics. The economic models that are developed to study the health sector can predict in quantitative terms the relative weightage of the determinants of the different parameters of the health sector. In a similar manner, economic models developed for the health sector for examining the relative importance of the different subsectors of demand side can predict the future trend of demand in the health sector.

On the basis of such study, health economists can either examine or study how choices and decisions are made in the health sector. On the other hand, on the basis of such studies, health economists can judge a situation and examine whether such choices or events are good for the nation or the society and the best possible ways

K. Sengupta, *Determinants of Health Status in India*,
DOI 10.1007/978-81-322-2535-5_2

in which they are to be made. The former type of studies is called *positive studies* and the latter type the *normative studies*. Based on such studies, future course of action and policies in the health sector are decided upon. However, for making such studies which may be extremely complex and may involve collection of huge mass of data related to the health sector, can be undertaken only with the economic tools of analysis. Therefore study of health economics without the knowledge of the economic tools of analysis will be incomplete and sterile.

Accessibility to health services has at all times and at all places being unequal. Non-affordability to health services especially for expensive ones is being ascribed as the main factor behind inequality and inaccessibility. The ones who are able to pay can afford to avail of better health facilities and have therefore a better health status. The ones who are unable to meet the price of health services have poor health indicators and are therefore characterised by poor health status. However, state which is the custodian of thc welfare of all section of the population cannot allow the section of the people to suffer from ill health disease and deaths. As a result state spends for those who are unable to pay for medical services. However, government spending on health expenditure for the poor may have long-term economic effect, expenditure on health do not have any immediate short-run benefits. Money spent without any return is termed as bad investment in economics; because as per the principals of economics, limited resources have to be spent where return is the highest, and that is when efficiency in resource allocation is brought about. Efficiency criteria go against the criteria of equity according to which state has to reduce the gap between the rich and the poor. The question therefore that arises is whether such spending which are against the principal of efficiency but promotes equity should be incurred by the state. From here arises the question of trade-off between the principals of equity and efficiency, issues which are extremely important for health economics.

The status of health in any society is determined by the operation of the health institutions for which the understanding of the concept of medical price mechanism, return on investment of health technology, medical equipment and facilities, the cost benefit and effectiveness of medical programmes is essential. All these areas necessitate the knowledge of the application of economics to the health sector. Such knowledge is also crucial for the production of medical industry such as medical equipment, drugs, pharmaceutical industry and health corporate sectors. Allocation of scarce resources for the production and services of the health sector would be incomplete without the knowledge of the science of economics. Knowledge of the best allocation of scarce resources also play a pivotal role for addressing the long-term health objectives of a nation such as providing a healthy environment, water and sanitation, a comprehensive system of preventive treatment and care and rehabilitation services. Managed in a proper manner all these measures can contribute to a healthy life which can reduce morbidity and increase life expectancy. However, mismanagement of scarce financial resources without the adequate application of the knowledge of economics may prevent the country from attaining the requisite health standard.

2.2 Role of Demand in Health Economics

Some of the crucial tools of economics without which no study in health economics is complete will be focussed attention in this section. For instance, demand for goods and services and their supply are the two pivotal pillars around which the entire subject of economics evolves. Unless and until there is generation of demand, supply will not be forthcoming. Why, how and when demand is generated, the nature and extent of demand and the changes therein and the factors responsible for such changes constitute the wide spectrum of the study of demand. Though health needs are slightly different from the needs for other goods and commodities, yet it is the demand for health care which is the basis of survival of the health sector. In fact, greater and greater demand for health care services has been a matter of great concern because such huge demand often goes unsatisfied due to inadequate resources and the inability of supply to meet the health demands.

Like demand, supply is the parallel force in economics, and the interaction of the two crucial forces of demand and supply determines the prices of medical services, drugs and medicines. Supply of health-related products and services, the investment on which is decided by the extent of demand, is decided by the training and production of adequate numbers of doctors, specialists, paramedical personnel, nurses, establishments of health centres, clinics, production of medicines and medical equipment, all of which are needed to satisfy the health demands of a nation. The demand for medical and health services in turn is determined not only by the income level of the health service/care users but also by the socio economic and cultural background of such users. It is also determined by the educational level in general and female education in particular, all of which will be addressed at greater length in the latter section.

2.3 Determinants of Demand in Health Economics

We will therefore begin by examining the various aspects of the concept of demand in economics and their relevance for the study of health economics. Demand for health care and medical services like the demand for all other goods and commodities is firstly determined by the price of the health care and its services. This relationship between demand for a product and its corresponding demand is termed as *Law of Demand in Economics*, which represents an inverse relationship between price and demand. Higher the price of the product lower is the demand for the product and vice versa. It is true that demand for health care which is an urgent necessity of life may not always be determined only by its price, because when it is a matter of life and death, as in the case of health service requirement/demand, resorting to borrowing and replenishing one's own savings is not uncommon. Nevertheless, one cannot ignore the broad contour of relationship between price and quantity. It is a fact that when certain types of medical care are too expensive, consumers switch over to its substitute, if its price is lower and more affordable, so that the demand for the original product declines. Therefore apart from price which is the most crucial determinant of demand, *the price and availability of its substitute* also constitute other important determinants of demand. For instance, if allopathic treatment is too expensive and similar treatment can be done by homeopathy, the price of which is much lower, some consumers may prefer to go in for the lower priced product.

Due to normally inverse relationship between the demand for medical care and the price of medical care, the demand curve for medical care like the demand for any other product takes the shape of a downward sloping curve, as represented in the diagram below. Figure 2.1 below shows that when the price of medical care items or services is high the demand is low. As the price begins to fall, the affordability rises and therefore the demand too begins to increase. The slope of the curve however is determined by the rate at which the price falls and the corresponding responsiveness of demand, which will be discussed in the subsequent section on the elasticity of demand. Any movement on the demand curve *D*, for health care services, therefore implies the quantum of medical care services at a certain price. Such a phenomenon enables the policy makers to assess the demand or affordability of medical care at a certain price. Pharmaceutical or even the health sector can also assess the demand for their products according to which they can decide upon the prices for their products.

However, it also needs to be mentioned that unlike other regular products of consumption, use of medical services may be a matter of life and death, due to which there may be exceptions to such accepted laws of demand revealing inverse relationship between price and demand. Under such situations, health consumers are willing to pay high price and still demand more of the health care services, if the demand is of an urgent nature. The exceptions will, however, be studied on a case to case basis by the health sector.

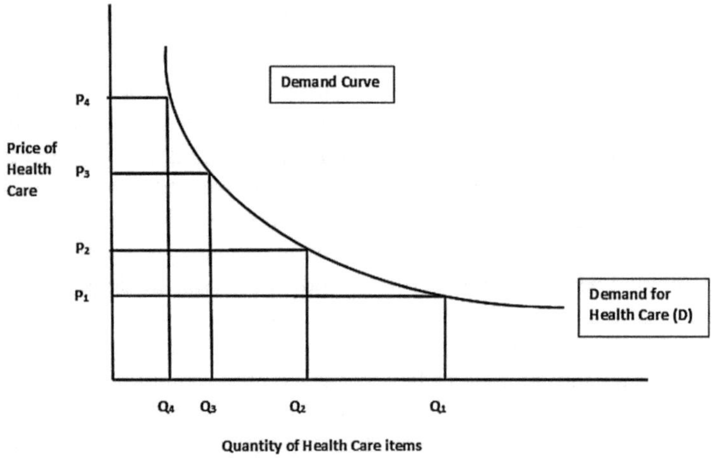

Fig. 2.1 Demand curve for health care/services

Income of the consumers constitutes the other determinant of demand. Consumers belonging to the higher income group can afford to pay a higher price for any product including medical care. Marginal utility of money of the rich people is lower and therefore they do not mind paying exorbitant prices for medical care. The health gyms, for example, are used only by the very rich, because, though maintenance of good health is important, yet is not as urgent as spending on basic live saving drugs which consumers with lower income are unable to afford. Therefore in a nation or in a society with a lower level of income, private medical spending is much lower than in a society with affluent and well off consumers. Under such circumstances of the former type, the state might have to step in to maintain a minimum level of health status of its people. Per capita medical expenditure and per capita government spending on health are thus important determinants of health status of a nation. Therefore the income level and the spending capacity of the public in general assume importance for government's health policy.

The demand for a particular health service may rise, even if there is no change in its price, provided there is a rise in the *price of its substitute*. When the price of allopathic medicine rises, those who were consuming allopathic medicines might switch over to the purchase of homeopathic medicines due to its lower price. As a result, the demand for homeopathic medicines will rise without any corresponding fall in its price. Similar may be the case with the *price of complementary goods.* For instance, for the purpose of injecting medicines, syringes and the liquid medicine is required together. If the price of liquid medicines rises, its demand will fall, but the demand for syringes will also fall, though there is no fall in its price.

Another determinant of demand, though it may not play an important role in case of health economics, is the *expectations of future movements in price.* When consumers expect prices to fall further in the future they postpone the purchase of the commodity, even if prices reveal a declining trend, in the hope of buying more when prices touch the minimum level in the future. Under such a situation, demand may fall inspite of the fact that prices are also falling. Therefore instead of inverse relationship, demand and price may reveal direct relationship. The opposite may be the case when prices reveal an upward trend. In the expectation that prices may rise even further in the future consumers may buy in greater quantity inspite of the fact that prices are rising. In other words, higher the price higher also is the demand. Law of demand is not followed under such situations. However, it needs to be mentioned that in case of medical expenditure such a possibility occurs very rarely. This is because demand for health care facilities is a *derived demand.* Such demand arises not directly for their own sake, but the demand for such services or products is derived from illness, disease and other medical problems. Therefore, it may not be possible to put off the purchases of medical services or items even if there is an expectation of future fall of prices, because such needs are often immediate and very urgent. In a similar manner, for the fear of prices rising in the future normally, consumer do not stock medicines or medical care for the future when prices are low. However, inspite of the difference in the nature of demand for medical services from other normal goods and commodities, one cannot totally rule out such reverse tendency in case of less urgent and immediate medical requirements. Therefore, when there is an increase in demand for health products/services due to the above-mentioned reasons without a corresponding fall in its price, the effect can be traced not through the movement on the same demand curve as depicted in Fig. 2.1, but in this case, the demand curve itself shifts its position to the right. On the other hand, when the demand falls without any rise in the price of medical services there is a movement of the demand curve to the left. The various movements of the demand curve, either to the right or left, without any corresponding change in the price, are represented in Fig. 2.2.

In the above diagram for instance, when price of the medical service is P_4 the quantity of the health services demanded and consumed was Q_4 when the consumers are at the demand curve D_1. However, at the same price of P_4, when consumers demand an increased quantum of medical services of Q_5 they move to a demand curve to the right which is now D_2 instead of being on the original demand curve D_1 as the quantity of Q_5 and price P_4 cannot be accommodated on the demand curve D_1 but can be accommodated only on a demand curve to the right at D_2. Therefore, any increase in the demand for medical product or service at the same price results in the movement to the right of the demand curve itself. Such a situation can occur in an economy when there is a rise in the population or there is an epidemic or incidence of sudden rise in diseases and illnesses necessitating the provision of higher medical services. The health sector must therefore be ready with medical services and items of certain nature whose demand is likely to increase without a corresponding fall in their price. The health sector industry thereby has to be equally prepared to have increased supply of certain items of medicines and health services irrespective of their prices. The normal law of demand may not work under such circumstances.

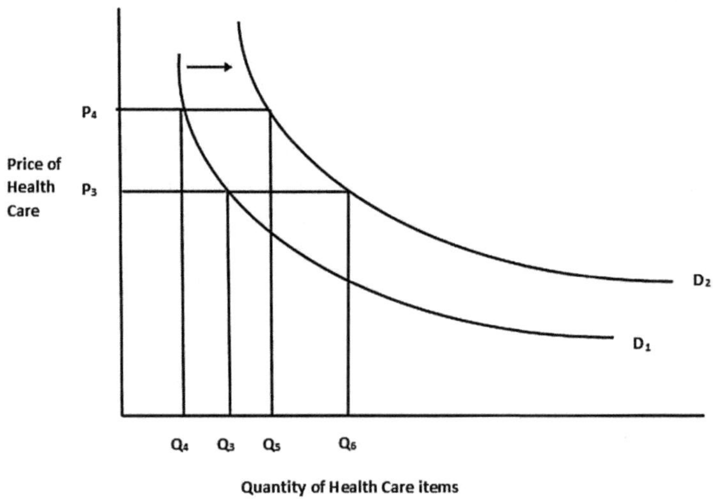

Fig. 2.2 Shift in demand for health care/services with no change in price

Opposite may be the case when the demand for certain medical services may fall without any corresponding rise in their prices. This may be the case when a country records an improvement in the health status. A decline in the incidence of malaria, TB, polio or other such illness in India for instance, has resulted in a decline in the consumption and demand of those medicines and related health care services. The result of this will be a shift of the demand curve to the left from D_2 to D_1 when the demand decreases from Q_6 to Q_3 at the same price of P_3. Under such circumstances, the government department, health sector as well as the health industry has to gear itself up accordingly. Being guided only by the price of health service under such a situation will bring about distortion in the sector, which would result in a misallocation of scarce resources in the health sector.

These features associated with principals of demand side of health economics can be used to understand the demand for health care and health services in general in the health sector. This is important both for the public health sector and more importantly for understanding the health market economy of the health industry. There are many occasions when the public health sector is not guided strictly by the market forces of demand and supply, since public welfare is the guiding principle of public health policy. However the private sector whose dominant guiding principle is maximisation of revenue and generation of profit, market forces of health economy in terms of the demand and supply can hardly be over looked. For this, it is also crucial that we understand the nature of demand for health and health services. Firstly, demand for health is a *derived demand* as mentioned earlier and therefore is determined by many factors and is not a direct demand for other commodities like food or clothing. Good health depends not only on the type and quality of medical care and services but also on the quality of clean drinking water, sanitation facilities, clean living condition, good food, vaccinations and immunisation, medical expenditure as well as awareness about health and general education. Therefore demand for health is a complicated affair and needs greater attention and a thorough study as it is embedded in a complex web of numerous factors.

Demand for medical services arises from the ones who are affected by illness and diseases. It is such demand which compels the users to spend on medical needs such as payments of medical fees for treatment and consultation, hospitalisation expenses, drugs and medicine expenses.

2.4 The Uniqueness of Health Care and Its Demand

Though demand for medical care is extremely crucial, the behavioural pattern of demand in the sector is different from the general demand for other commodities. It has a multi-dimensional demand and is also of an extremely complex nature. It therefore necessitates a different understanding, as well as viewing the nature of demand for health in a manner which is different from the demand for other goods and commodities, though within the same framework of demand and supply. Choices for medical services may not be subject to the same rational behaviour in case of choice of other goods and commodities since some choices on expenses on medical care may be matter of life and death and consumers are even ready and often do sell their assets to meet such expenses or go into heavy debts for meeting medical expenditure.

Medical expenses are also extremely uncertain as most consumers do not know when they will fall ill with the exception of expenses such as regular health check-ups which is characterised by demand of a steady nature. This kind of uncertain medical expenses is totally different from other normal expenditure. It is also a fact, that under normal choices the law of demand behaves in a predictable manner, when consumers purchase less with a rise in the price. However for medical expenses the choice is extremely limited as consumers may have to make the purchases under extreme compulsion and therefore have to buy even if prices and services are exorbitant. Similarly, unlike the normal goods medical items cannot be stored when prices are falling as no one knows with certainty the type of medicines a person may require in the future. It is due to all these reasons that some medical services are provided free of costs particularly for consumers who are not able to afford the expenses. This is unlike most other expenses where very quantum of free services is provided to the consumers. This is because medical expenses are a matter of life and death. At the same time some other type of demand for health such as leading a healthier life style eating healthier food, better housing, clean drinking water proper sanitation, regular check-ups may rise with arise in income and may fall with a fall in come. However it may also be mentioned that such medical expenses have a long term effect on health condition and may not affect direct health condition when consumers fall ill and need immediate medical treatment.

It is therefore pertinent to mention with regards to health care, that the demand for health care is uncertain, and therefore the firms providing the health care services are also not certain about their customer's demand. Uncertainty also exists from the side of the products. Consumers do not know the outcomes of the treatments, and has to depend totally on the physician's advice. In exactly the same manner, physicians too cannot predict with certainty the effect of their treatments. Asymmetric information is to a large extent attributed to be the cause of some degree of uncertainty. Insufficient information, particularly with regards to the exact time of use of the services or whether they will ever demand the products/services, necessitates changes in the behavioural aspect of the health service provider. Firms cannot proceed as in pure economic models with the assumption that there is perfect knowledge on the part of the customers.

However inspite of some different characteristics of demand for medical care, it is extremely essential that the planning of medical care requires some assessment of demand for health. Study of demand of the health sector also enables the pricing of health products and services. The government sector after making an assessment of health demand also plans the type and nature of free medical services that needs to be provided to the type of consumers with varying level of income. Consequently the same principle that is applied for studying demand in economics is equally applied to the health sector.

2.5 Elasticity of Demand and Its Significance for Health Care Sector

A very important aspect associated with demand for health services/products is the responsiveness of demand for health to changes in its important determinants such as price, income and the price of its substitute or related commodities. The extent of responsiveness or changes in such demand to the extent of change in these variables is termed as *elasticity of demand.* Elasticity of demand for any service or good including that of health services determines the direction that policy issues and formulation should take. In order to have an idea about the extent of increase or decrease in demand for health care services that is desired, policy makers may like to know the percentage of change in price or other factors that needs to be initiated.

The measurement of the proportionate change in demand due to a proportionate change in price is termed as *price elasticity of demand.* In a similar fashion, demand also responds to changes in income of the person, because it is a common perception that when income rises there is generally an increase in demand for the product or the service concerned. In a similar fashion, a decrease in income results in a decline in demand, irrespective of the changes in price. Such responsiveness of demand and its measurement to changes in income is termed as *income elasticity of demand.* It is therefore seen that with an increase in income users of health care services can afford better health facilities. People belonging to the lower income group are for exactly the opposite reason unable to afford the bare minimum health facilities. This is evident from the fact that instances of illness, diseases, epidemics and deaths are more common among the poor income group rather than the upper income group. Health care consumers of the upper income group can therefore afford luxurious health services.

When policy makers want that the use of certain lifesaving drugs should increase and the poor are unable to use the same due to its high price, the price is reduced in an attempt to raise its demand and use. However, the extent to which prices should to be reduced and the extent of responsiveness of demand can be known only with the help of price elasticity of demand. When the state desires to restrict or stop the consumption of any harmful drugs, the best answer is to raise its prices. The question that arises is the extent to which prices should be raised so that consumers are discouraged from purchasing such drugs. Policy makers also need to know that there are also certain medicines or minimum health care services which must be used when medical needs are acute, irrespective of the level of their prices. In such cases even if prices are raised, demand may not go down. Such services or commodities are said to have *inelastic demand.* Inelastic demand implies that there is no responsiveness of demand to a change in price.

Elastic demand, on the other hand, implies demand which is highly responsive to a small change in demand. For instance if a 15 % fall in price results in 2 % rise in demand, it is said to have inelastic demand, whereas if a similar fall in demand results in 25 % rise in demand, demand is said to be highly elastic or responsive.

However, if a similar decline in the price level results in absolutely no change in demand, demand is said to be *totally or perfectly inelastic*. Whether demand will be highly elastic, inelastic or absolutely inelastic is determined by the nature of the health product or service whose elasticity is being determined. Health care services which are extremely essential for life and without which survival is impossible or extremely difficult are said to have inelastic demand, as the service has to be availed for survival whatever may be the price. Another unique feature of health care services is that a major category of services under health care falls under this category. In contrast, expensive health care goods and services which are consumed mostly for their status symbol or for the sake of pleasure and are not included under the basic necessities of life are said to have elastic demand. It is possible to survive or continue life even without the consumption of these commodities. Therefore if their prices rise there may be a fall in the demand for such services.

The methodology for measuring this kind of responsiveness in demand to price is to divide the proportionate change in the quantity by the proportionate change in price. The change in demand for goods and commodities can be measured directly in terms of the change in quantity demanded, whereas change in the demand for services is measured in terms of the amount spent on the service. For the purpose of measurement of price elasticity of demand, the following methodology is used

$$E_d = \%\Delta Q_d / \%\Delta P$$

where ΔQ_d and ΔP are the changes in the quantity and price of the health care services respectively.

The figure below depicts three types of price elasticity of demand, namely, highly or very elastic demand, unitary elastic demand and low elastic or very inelastic demand depending on the extent of responsiveness of demand for health care services to its price change. The price of the medical care service is represented in the vertical axis and the quantity demanded on the horizontal axis. E_d denotes the elasticity of demand, and $\% \Delta Q_d/\%\Delta P$ represents the change in quantity of medical care services demanded due to a change in its price. The curve representing elasticity of demand depicts three types of elasticity for any product including health products/services. The upper range shows demand which is highly elastic, where the responsive of demand is more than the change in price. In contrast, the lower part of the diagram represents highly inelastic demand, where change in demand is less than the change in price. The middle portion shows unitary elastic demand, meaning that the change in the quantity and the price demanded is similar (Fig. 2.3).

On the basis of the above method, once the percentage change in both price and quantity are known, the price elasticity of demand is estimated. Price elasticity is always in terms of a certain number and is also always a negative term. It needs to be noted further, that for estimating large changes, it is essential to estimate the proportionate change both in price and demand.

Responsiveness of demand to changes in price often differs from one price range to another. For instance, for a small percentage change in price the demand may still continue to be inelastic because the consumers might have to spend an extra amount

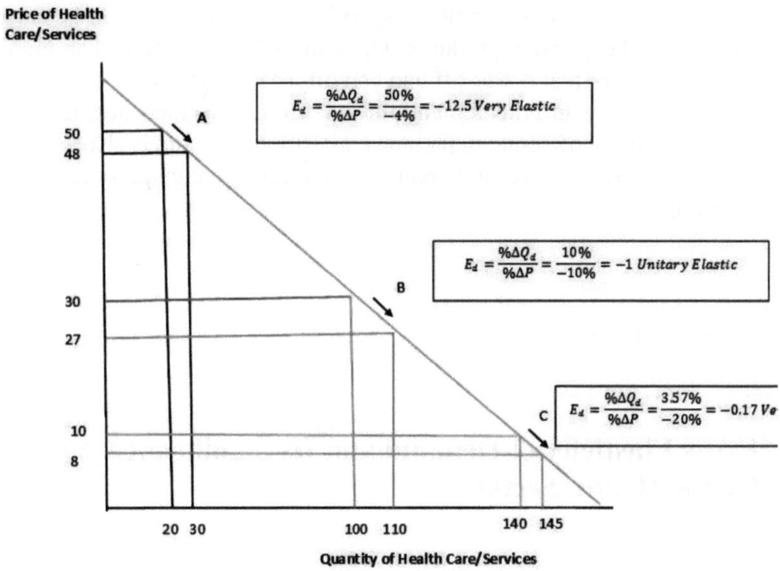

Fig. 2.3 Elasticity of demand for health care services

which may constitute a small percentage of the income. The usefulness of the product may be too high even to reduce small percentage of its consumption. As a result the consumption of the commodity is not reduced. However, for the same commodity when price rise is of a significant proportion the consumer might be compelled to reduce the consumption of the commodity and the demand may be elastic at that range of price. Policy makers therefore need to realise for the purpose of policy formulation that the same product may display different variety of elasticity at different price ranges.

2.6 Income Elasticity of Demand for Health Sector

Just as price elasticity of demand assumes importance, in a similar manner income elasticity of demand too is crucial for policy makers and thereby for health status. Though it is normally assumed that consumption rises with a rise in income, this may not always be true for all categories of products, especially health products. Certain medicines and drugs cannot be consumed in higher proportion even if income rises. When the consumption of a product rises along with a rise in income, the product is said to have positive income elasticity. Such products are called normal products, because that is what is normally expected. However, there are also certain products whose demand actually declines with a rise in income. Such products are said to have negative income elasticity of demand. Products, goods or services which are "inferior" have negative elasticity of demand. Such products are particularly used by consumers belonging to lower strata of income because they are unable to afford expensive products. Therefore whenever there is an increase in income the consumers feel better off and can afford to switch over to more expensive substitutes. As a result, the demand for the original products decline.

Like price elasticity of demand, income elasticity of demand is also estimated by examining the relative change in demand and the relative change in income in the following manner

$$E_d = \% \Delta Q_d / \% \Delta Y$$

where ΔY is the change in income

2.7 Cross Elasticity of Demand and Its Significance for the Health Sector

Another important term associated with elasticity is the cross elasticity of demand which relates to the elasticity of demand for a product in terms of its relationship with the price of its related or complementary product. Complementary product implies when two products have to used simultaneously to satisfy one consumption need. For instance, syringes and needles are used together for the injecting injection. The demand for needles will be affected due to a change in the price or demand for syringes even if there might be no change in the price or direct demand for needles. Therefore the demand for needles is determined by its complementary goods. Such demands are called cross elasticity of demand.

2.8 Elasticity of Demand and the Heath Sector

In health sector too, nature of demand for health care and health services ranges from absolute necessities to luxurious items of consumption. It is therefore crucial that policy makers in the health sector firstly identify the nature of the demand for the health services. Accordingly, they may take the decision regarding the extent of price changes that needs to be initiated in order to attain the desired objectives in the health sector. Accordingly, it is then decided whether to subsidise health care, if so, to what extent or whether to provide health care totally free of cost. These objectives and policies in turn are some of the important determinants of health status of a nation. It is therefore evident that without the knowledge of health economics the task of the policy makers on health would be incomplete and hazardous. It is very important for the policy makers as well as the ones who work in the health sector to have thorough knowledge about such tools of measurement in economics.

It is therefore essential for policy makers in the health sector to be able to identify the consumers of the particular health product or service. Do they belong to the poorer section of the society or are they the well-off section of the society? Are the health products or services the essentials or luxurious items of consumption? What effect the rises in price have on the total market demand? What in turn will be the impact of such change be on the industry or the firm engaged in health product? Answer to all these issues necessitates a thorough examination and study of the economics of the health sector.

Whenever there is an increase in the cost of health infrastructure and production of health services, medicines and drugs, the policy makers needs to examine whether the rise in cost can be passed on to the consumers. If the demand is inelastic because they are the essential health services and there are no substitutes which are available, the rise in cost can be passed on to the consumers and the consumers are bound to spend more. If they are not so essential demand will be elastic and there will be decline in revenue because the increased cost cannot be passed on to the consumers. Study therefore needs to be conducted on the effect on welfare of the consumers, due to price rise or due to a reduction in consumption or due to having to spend more because of price rise. The overall impact of all these on the health status of a nation is extremely crucial for any study related to the health sector.

It is in this connection that the desirability of imposition of taxes on health products needs to be viewed. Taxes may be imposed on those harmful items the consumption of which may be harmful for health status. The impact of tax imposition on health products, the percentage of taxes and the rates of different health products and the targeted group who has to bear the impact of tax imposition are areas which come under the purview of health economics. Information on all these aspects of health sector plays a pivotal role for the study of health status of a nation. Just as imposition of taxes can influence the consumption and thereby the welfare of the health consumers, in a similar manner providing subsidy to health consumer, especially on those health products consumed by the poor can raise the welfare of the poor section of the consumers. The responsiveness of demand to provision of subsidy are also crucial areas in health economics which all policy makers in the health sector needs to be highly familiar with.

Study on health status therefore is associated with the knowledge of taxes and subsidies in an attempt to have knowledge about the nature and types of taxes and subsidies that are to be proposed by the policy makers. Such policies can influence the consumption in the health care sector which in a broader sense can influence the health status in general.

This is the reason for free medical centres in the rural areas under rural health centres as also the different health-related schemes which are meant particularly for the poor. This in turn also helps the policy makers to decide the amount of investment that needs to be made in the health sector.

Income elasticity of demand too helps the policy makers to understand and take decisions accordingly, relating to rise in the standard of living and income of the poor and its effect on the demand for health products. Provision of subsidy which is similar to a rise in income may also impact the demand for the particular health product depending upon the nature of the health product, whether it is an inferior product or a normal product. Income elasticity of demand can thus be examined in case of those health products and policy decisions are then taken to decide whether subsidy can be provided in case of those products and if so the extent to which subsidy can be provided. In a similar manner, imposition of a tax on harmful items of consumption not only provides revenue to the government but more importantly the objectives are to improve health status by discouraging the consumption of such items through stiff rates of taxation. The knowledge of health economics is essential here as the objectives of the policy for reduction in consumption may be a complete failure if the burden of taxes is not shifted on to the consumers by way of high prices. In case it is shifted to the consumers to what extent, is it the full amount of the tax or a small proportion which may make no difference to the amount consumed if the demand for the product happens to be of an inelastic nature. In such a case the policy objectives cannot be achieved. It is therefore necessary to examine the *impact, shifting and incidence* of the imposition of taxes, the areas on public economics which again become important for health sector. In this connection, it needs to be mentioned that if taxes are imposed on medical care items of emergency nature, which may be matter of life and death like costs of life saving drugs or surgeries of an emergent nature, the burden would fall only on the actual users since the use of such goods and services is highly inelastic and can hardly be reduced. Therefore all policy makers need to be extremely cautious before imposing taxes, about the nature of the health item/service or the socio economic status of the health consumers.

2.9 Production Cost of Health Care Services

No study of Health Economics is complete without a discussion of the cost incurred on either producing health products or delivering health services to the health care users. The items on which these costs are incurred are called production inputs. Various types of skills are required for delivering health care services ranging from highly technical to soft skills, sophisticated equipment, expensive drugs and various types of health infrastructure which are all indispensable for the purpose of delivering health care services to the users of health services. The costs incurred on these inputs for production of health services need to be worked out for the purpose of determining the prices of health care services to be provided as well as the extent of taxes or subsidies that may need to be provided for the use of health care.

The knowledge of cost and production techniques studied in economics is therefore extremely crucial for the purpose of studying health economics. Scarcity of financial resources as well as other scarce inputs necessitate that highest level of efficiency with the help of economic tools of analysis is acquired. This will not only provide productive efficiency but also achieve allocative efficiency. Study of economics reveals the ways in which the scare health resources may be used in the best possible manner or the ways of acquiring the inputs at the lowest price. All such decisions become extremely significant when the health providers have to operate within strict competitive environment.

In every production process, there are three distinct areas like inputs, the production process and the final output, all of which are interrelated. Inputs are the various resources such as manpower resources, physical inputs and capital that are necessary for the productive process. Productive process defines the transformation or productive technique which changes inputs into desired outputs, which are the end result of production. In economics, all these relationships are explored within the framework of the production function. Production functions therefore are the ways of representing both qualitatively and quantitatively the relationship that exists between such types of inputs and outputs. The various ways the quantities of labour (L) and capital (K) are combined by a certain process (T), which assumes a fixed technology or a particular production process shows the efficiency of the system.

As far as health sector is concerned, clear cut relationship between input and output through production process is very difficult to establish. This is due to the complexities of the health sector which is not like any production unit, because of the dynamic nature of the sector which uses different inputs in a multiplicity of ways. They use different types of inputs simultaneously. The way these inputs are reduced is not understood and it is difficult to relate to any particular output to any one intervention or activity. Different inputs are used in the health sector unlike only capital and labour in pure production process with the result that they are not only difficult to measure and value these inputs but they are even more difficult to identify. It is even more difficult to define the output of the health sector, which are multi-dimensional and complex and then measure and value them taking their costs for the final valuation of the output. However, all these difficulties notwithstanding techniques are now being developed to measure the outcomes of health services for the purpose of health planning and evaluation.

Production of any health related product or services require the combination of various inputs, chief among them being capital and labour inputs. Such inputs are always scarce in supply and therefore have to be utilised in the best possible way so that the highest level of health outcome can be obtained. There are various ways in which the inputs can be combined for the production of the final health outcome which are denoted by different types of production function. A production function in general represents the relationship between inputs and outputs which are highly mathematical in nature. A simple production function assumes the following nature:

$$Q = A(L,K)$$

where Q represents total output and L the labour inputs and K the capital inputs respectively and A the technical relationship between input and output.

The knowledge of economic tools of analysis can be used as a guide to attain the minimum cost that need to be incurred for acquiring and also combining L and K in a manner using different technology A, so that Q or the health outcome is the maximum.

It is with the above objective that certain terms and concepts in economics, relating to the production function, becomes relevant for the purpose of examining cost and production of health services. For instance, when we mention about efficient use of resources it is implied that there are no better use of the resources for the production of that particular health service. The inputs could also have been combined for the production of some other health services but had to be sacrificed for the production of the present health service under consideration. The production of the health outcome, that has been sacrificed but could have been produced with the concerned inputs, is termed as *the opportunity cost.* When the opportunity cost of any combination of the factor inputs is high, it implies that the present combination for the production of the present health outcome is certainly not the best one. Under such circumstances, production of the particular health service with the combination of the inputs is certainly less than the efficient. It is therefore essential that the producer have familiarity with the various combinations of the factor inputs so that he is able to select the best out of the available ones. This however may not always be possible, particularly in the health sector, when consideration of equity dominates over efficiency, especially in the public health sector, where subsidisation of health services is the norm rather than the exception. However in the private sector and in the health industry such issues become the only guiding principle of production of health services. The subject of economics, however, proceeds entirely on the basis of such assumptions. However, what it actually tries to convey is the idea of choosing the best combination of the inputs so that there is always an effort to strive for the highest level of efficiency, which is so essential in an economy characterised by acute shortage of valuable resources (Fig. 2.4).

The various combinations of the factor inputs in different forms for the purpose of the requisite output or health outcome are represented in the figure above. The figure reveals that the various combinations of factor inputs which produces the same quantum of output is represented by a convex curve known as *production*

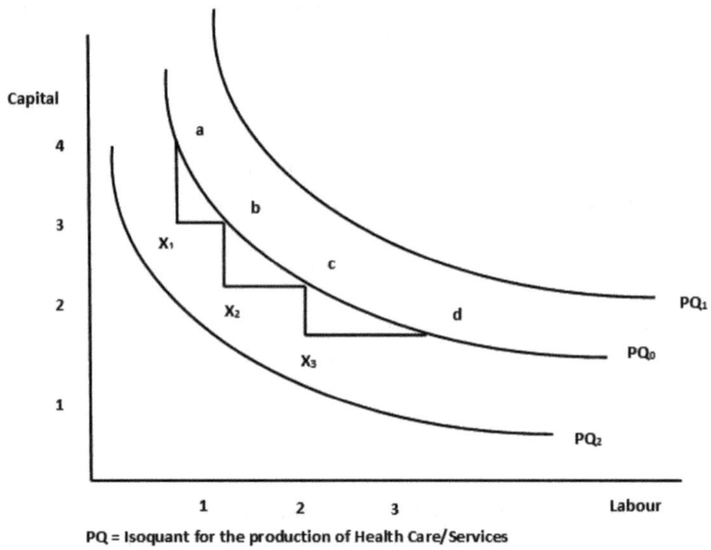

Fig. 2.4 Production isoquants of the health sector

isoquants. If the two axis represents labour (L) and capital (K), different points on the convex curve means the increasing use of one input at the cost of decreasing the use other input. The slope of the production isoquant therefore shows the rate at which one input can be substituted by the other. This technique is termed as *marginal rate of technical substitution (MRTS)*, which is practised by all production sectors. For instance, for the production of an X-ray machine, there might be a combination of either four units of capital and two units of labour or two units of capital and three units of labour. The producer whether in the general production or in the health care sector has to decide which will be the best combination of the factor inputs that needs to decide so that the production cost can be kept at the lowest. If the factor inputs are perfect substitutes, the slope of the isoquant will be a downward sloping straight line. Whereas if the factor inputs are perfect complements which is most often the case with respect to health care delivery services and has to be used in fixed proportions to derive a certain output, isoquants are L shaped.

It is also necessary in this connection to understand about the marginal productivity of a factor of production so that decision regarding the choice of the quantum of factor inputs may be made. When more and more of any particular factor of production is used, keeping the amount the other factor as constant, the productivity of the additional units of that particular factor will go on diminishing. This is termed as *diminishing marginal productivity* of a factor input. For example, if a doctor can examine 20 patients in a day for which he requires two nurses and certain number of medical equipment. Suppose the number of doctor is increased to two without increasing the number of nurses or the other subsidiaries. The total number of patients that will be examined will not be doubled to forty but less than that. This is mainly because one single doctor by himself cannot treat twenty patients. He needs the assistance of nurses and other equipment, but since their number is not increased the services of the existing nurses and equipment has to be over utilised and only some additional patients over and above the normal number can be treated. The overall effect will be that the productivity of the second doctor will be less than that of the first. This is termed as *diminishing marginal productivity* of a factor input, because the doctor here is considered as an input for delivering health services, but it is more important to understand the right combination of the number of doctors, nurses and other health equipment, so that health outcome can be the highest. Therefore, the knowledge of economics is extremely crucial for health services because it reveals the best possible way of delivering health care services to the actual users.

It also needs to be highlighted that the production of goods (output) as in an industry and delivery of health care services which is synomnous as output are not identical, and certain adjustments need to be made with respect to health care services. Output in health sector can be defined as number of children immunised, cases of diseases prevented, death prevention and longevity gained. As a result, suppose, emergency medical units which always needs to be ready for any kind of medical service at any time, even if they are not in use such units cannot be termed as underutilised and therefore inefficient. This is due to the nature or the goals of medical services which have different characteristics then pure productive economic activity. The problem arises in terms of differences in definitional aspect where the exact definition of output is very difficult in health services. If the target is immunisation of a certain number of children, which is much easier than treating a certain number of patients in the hospital where the fixed number of patients (output) is known in advance.

Some of the other terms with respect to costs and production that are important to health economists are variable inputs and fixed inputs and the costs incurred for them as the variable costs and fixed costs. Those costs which vary in proportion to the variation in output such as labour costs and costs of raw materials are termed as *variable cost*. An increase in the use of such inputs results in an increase in output, just as a decrease in such inputs results in a decrease in output. In the health sector, expenditure on syringes, medicines and lifesaving drugs are all instances of variable costs, because they vary with a variation in the level of activity or services rendered which is equivalent to the level of output in terms of production activity. On the other hand, those inputs such as expensive machines of costly infrastructure remain more or less constant whatever be the level of output. Such inputs are therefore termed as fixed inputs and costs incurred on them as *fixed costs*. Medical infrastructure, such as hospitals, and expensive medical equipment are included under fixed costs and expenditure on them do not vary with a variation in the level of output.

2.10 Economic Efficiency and Economic Evaluation of the Health Sector

Utility of the study of health economics lies mainly in the best use of the limited resources. Economic efficiency therefore implies transforming inputs into outputs with minimum of expenses, minimum of wastes and getting the highest returns. Highest return in health sector means best value for indicators of health status, such as infant mortality, maternal mortality, lower level of morbidity and disease, longer life span, better nutrition, etc.

For such a purpose, two crucial criteria such as effectiveness and efficiency are to be used simultaneously. The former identifies the technical possibilities for transforming inputs into outputs, whereas efficiency means ranking these alternatives by comparing the costs of inputs with the value of outputs. Firstly, it has to decided how much of resources are to be invested in the health sector in contrast to other social sectors. Efficiency in health sector requires that resources are to be allocated to productive activities in the best possible manner. Health and health services are not the only things that are valued by the society, and society may prefer health over more urgent needs. Policy makers need to assess and compare the value of health and their costs with the value and costs of other services in the society and select accordingly how much of health services/care to produce. In practical situation such a comparison though extremely useful is also very difficult. A number of techniques have been developed that attempts to make this procedure simple. Some of these techniques are cost effectiveness analysis, cost benefit analysis and cost utility analysis. These techniques differ in their degree of sophistication, and the particular technique selected is determined by the degree of specificity that is required.

The core of the study of economics lies in the best use of scarce resources, the decisions relating to which is taken by those who are entrusted with such responsibilities. In health sector too, there are crucial decisions which has to be taken by the health and hospital administrators. In a hospital, decision has to be taken for instance on the amount of capital investment that needs to be made and where they can be best utilised. Policy makers in the health sector must decide how much of subsidy needs to be provided in the health sector and who should be the beneficiaries of such subsidy. These are crucial economic decisions which are taken on the basis of evaluation of cost and benefits of the total amount of expenditure incurred in the concerned sector. Such decisions are taken by the application of economic tools of analysis, since they all attempt to find out ways and means of improving the use of resources so that the health delivery services can be improved either to the patients at the individual, group or at the level of the society.

Decision making with respect to investment and spending on health sector affects vitally the quality of life, the health statistics and the health indicators of a nation. It is therefore extremely vital that such decisions be taken in an extremely systematic and professional manner. This calls for an economic evaluation of the decision taken in terms of the costs and benefits of the various alternative course of action so that the best out of these may be selected. A medical treatment option is not considered in isolation from all other treatment options that are alternatives to treating a well-defined medical condition. Evaluation is made on the basis of the costs and consequences of these alternative options. Economic efficiency in the health sector therefore studies the best possible use of scarce resources so that maximum health benefits can be provided to the users of health care. However, best possible use of scarce resource differs from private health expenditure to public health expenditure where choice of health expenses in the former case may not always be guided by rational economic behaviour and optimum levels of efficiency. For public health expenses, it is extremely essential to meet the criteria of effectiveness and efficiency, keeping in view the broad characteristics of the health sector. Effectiveness measures the methods of transforming resources into health outcomes and efficiency evaluates the various ways of comparing costs of the resources with the value of the health outcomes in terms of their ranks.

Economic evaluations are therefore the specific measurements to evaluate the viability of health services. Health outcomes are studied with the help of economic tools and econometric models to examine the viability of investments in different sectors of health and make a comparative analysis.

The four types of economic evaluations which are predominantly used in economics as well as in Health Economics are firstly represented in a diagrammatic form followed by a brief discussion on their conceptual framework (Diagram 2.1).

Diagram 2.1 Techniques of cost benefit evaluation

- *Cost Accounting* (CA) which means the set of procedures for determining the cost of a product or the various activities involved in its manufacture and sales and for planning and measuring performances is the cost accounting. This method determines and analysis costs for the purpose of evaluating the operating efficiency of each division, deals with the accumulation and utilisation of cost data for purposes of controlling costs. As a management tool the method helps to estimate the cost of production of every unit, work order and processes and thereby indicate various forms of waste in terms of material and labour.
- *Cost Effective Analysis* (CEA) is the methodology in which comparison is made in achieving one particular objective in various ways. The CEA uses the monetary method of measurement and attempts to concentrate on one major desired outcome such as health improvement with respect to one disease or reduction of incidence of any particular disease. However, when different options for measurement are used, the method assumes that cost or effectiveness is constant for the various alternative options. It attempts to examine which one of the equally costly alternative policy actions is likely to be most effective or which one of equally effective policy action is expected to be least expensive.
- *Cost Utility Analysis* (CUA) is a measure to find out the various ways of bringing down the cost of medical care. This technique is used extensively in health sector for which knowledge of economics is extremely crucial. In the health sector, CUA estimates the ratio between the costs of health related intervention and the benefit it produces in terms of the number of years lived in full health by the beneficiaries. Cost is here measured in terms of monetary costs, whereas benefits are in terms of quality adjusted life years (QALYs). This common unit of measurement in terms of money/QALY gains enables health policy makers, comparisons across different health programmes and policies providing a holistic analysis of total health benefits. However, measuring QALYs according to economists is very subjective and therefore extremely difficult.

- *Cost Benefit Analysis* (CBA) is a method mostly used to justify the adoption or implementation of a certain health programme. It is a method in which comparison is made between the costs of providing service with the gain accruing from the service. Attempts are made to measure all socially relevant health outcome in terms of money, though monetary evaluation of health benefits are extremely difficult. This method is useful for all those health programmes which have a major impact on economic development.

The tests are used mostly to examine the economic feasibility, acceptability, or viability in deciding to implement specific health programmes whether in the public or private sectors. The health services and programmes implemented by the public health sector are adopted for the purchase of the needed medical supplies, equipment and facilities, vaccines for communicable and non-communicable diseases, immunisation programmes, use of contraceptives, etc. Since all these programmes involves huge amount of public resources, judicious planning for allocation of these resources in the various sectors of health is of utmost importance so that maximum return in terms of benefits is assured to the beneficiaries. It also needs to be mentioned here that that most of the benefits of health programmes may not be always measurable in terms of monetary benefits, because assigning monetary benefits to human health benefits is not really a satisfactory procedure. The reasons for the inability to measure the health benefits arise due to the fact that the general socio-economic condition often affects the health condition of the people. Besides, the impact of health services is also determined by the utilisation and maintenance as well as the cooperation by the beneficiaries. Extent of public cooperation in turn is determined by the educational level of the public particularly female education. It is also determined by the income level of the beneficiaries, all of which have been accepted for the present study as determinants of health status. However, till now there is no index of population health status in any country for the measurement of direct benefits. Added to this is also the problem that different medical specialists value a given health impairment differently (Satpathy and Bansal 1982). It is because of all the above reasons that it is only in very rare instances that highly specific cases of estimation of health services on the reduction of health risks and problems have been possible.

2.11 Measurement of Costs of Health Delivery

Monetary costs incurred for health delivery system is determined by some of the crucial decisions that needs to be taken in the health sector. Some of these decisions are taken both at the micro level as well as at the macro level. Individual patients must decide where to go for treatment, whom to go to and how much to incur for medical treatment. He/she takes the decision on the basis of the best alternative choices available to the patient, which again is a matter of economic choice. At the macro level, decision needs to be taken by the policy makers on the investment to be made in the health sector. Sectoral allocation of resources for the health sector and the alternative choices in health policies also come under the purview of health economics.

Given the limited resources both individuals as well as policy makers aim to maximise the return from health investment both to the individual as well as to the society by minimising the costs. It is here that model building in economics is undertaken which helps particularly the policy makers in understanding, explaining, and predicting decision making and costs which plays a pivotal role in health economics.

Costs incurred for health care and services, which can be measured quite easily in case of an individual, cannot be measured in the same manner for the society. Though opportunity costs are crucial indicators of costs foregone, yet costs as far as the health sector is concerned is a much broader concept. Cost of illness to the individual and the society are extremely important information for the policy makers and health economists. Cost of disease, illness, and epidemics to the nation which are both explicit as well as implicit are also very important. Long run as well as short run costs to the society is also very crucial for policy makers. In an interesting study made by Druss et al. (2001) for the US economy, it was revealed that in 1996 that total cost for the treatment of mood disorders diabetes, heart disease, asthma, and hypertension was $62.3 billion. Out of this heart disease and hypertension constituting almost half the total expenditure. The cost of treating coexisting medical condition totalled $207.7 billion. In addition to that, it was also estimated that an additional amount of $36.2 billion was lost due to lost man days due to these five diseases. Therefore the total cost to the society was $306 billion. All these are indirect but extremely important components of health costs. Such costs are the costs to the society by reducing the productive capacity of the people of the economy due to ill health and disease, loss of earning power of the individual, and the other additional costs which are related to ill health and sickness though they are not strictly speaking medical costs. This highlights the difference between *Direct and Indirect Costs* in the health sector. The former category includes the costs of prevention, detection, treatment, rehabilitation, research and training as well as long-term capital investments because of diseases and illnesses. They can be further subdivided into two types: direct medical costs and direct nonmedical costs. The former type of costs are the costs associated with the use of medical resources such as the costs of hospitalisation, medical procedures, laboratory testing, pharmaceutical drugs, costs of medical care, etc. Direct nonmedical costs are the expenses incurred by the patients themselves such as transportation costs, loss of income, and other expenses to help the patients. Indirect costs are costs to the economy and society due to poor health condition of the people such as high degree of morbidity, illness, disability, and deaths. They also include the loss to the economy due to low productivity, loss of manpower due to sick leave, morbidity, and deaths.

Health costs therefore include the expenses incurred by both the producers of health services, use of medical staff of all categories, buildings, materials and medical supplies as well as the costs incurred by the users of medical/health services. All these costs can be divided into (1) *Capital Costs* and (2) *Recurring or Current* Costs. Normally capital expenditure spreads over a longer period, whereas current costs are incurred for meeting the immediate needs. Under the former category are included costs of building, purchase of equipment, and training of medical practitioners. In the latter category are included the costs incurred on medicines and drugs, and all other day-to-day expenses for rendering health care services to the population.

Intangible costs also constitute an important aspect of costs in the health sector. Such costs include pain and suffering, grief and anxiety, which cannot be quantified but has large costs to the society.

Depreciation costs like any other investment is also an important part of health costs. Expensive equipment and building depreciates in value over time due to their continuous use.

2.12 Economic Models

With the help of the economic theories, tools of analysis, and the various concepts of economics, economic models are constructed in the health sector to examine in a simplified manner the relationship between the key variables in an attempt to analyse their relationships. As a word of caution, it needs to be mentioned here that models are never realistic, but convey the general picture of the relationships among variables in real life situation. Economic models do not include all variables. Only important variables which have significant influence in the area of study are considered and non-important variables are either taken as constant or considered to be zero. Consequently, emphasis is laid upon only those relationships that are under study and examine the interrelationships between them. Models are used for the purpose of future decisions based on the interactions of the accepted variables enunciated by theoretical relationships of the variables.

For the purpose of the present study, various economic models in the health sector will be developed based on the theoretical underpinnings of health economics. Based on the results obtained, analysis will be made and conclusions derived relating to the health sector, which may help the policy makers working in the sector to reshape policy decisions.

References

Bhargava A, Jamison DT, Lawrence JL, Murray CJL (2001) Modelling the effects of health on economic growth. J Health Econ 20:423–440

Folland S, Goodman A, Stano M (2009) The economics of health and health care. Pearson Prentice hall

Grossman M (1972) On the concept of health capital and the demand for health. J Polit Econ 80:223–225

Henderson J (2005) Health economics and policy. South-Western, Cengage Learning, India

McPake B, Kumaranayake L, Normand C (2002) Health economics – an international perspective. Routledge, London/New York

Satpathy SK, Bansal RD (1982) Health and population. Perspectives 5(1):23–33

Torrance GW (1997) Preferences for health outcomes and cost utility analysis. Am J Manag Care 3:S8–S20

Vitaliano DF (1987) On the estimation of hospital cost functions. J Health Econ 6:305–318

Wedig GJ (1988) Health status and the demand for health: results on price elasticities. J Health Econ 7:151–163

Weinstein MC, Manning WG Jr (1997) Theoretical issues in cost effectiveness analysis. J Health Econ 16:121–128

Williams A, Cookson R (2000) Equity in health. In: Culyer AJ, Newhouse JP (eds) Handbook of health economics, Vol 1b, Elsevier, Amsterdam

Zuckerman S, Hadley J, Iezzoni L (1994) Measuring hospital efficiency with frontier cost functions. J Health Econ 13:255–280

Chapter 3
Health Economics: A Review

A good number of studies on health economics has been conducted, mostly during the last 50 years. In the Indian context however, a lot more studies in this sector needs to be undertaken, in view of the dearth of adequate research work in this area. Most of the literature surveyed for the purpose of the present work relates to the workdone by health economists of the west. All the work reviewed has been divided broadly into four categories as represented in the diagram below (Diagram 3.1):

3.1 Studies on Theoretical Issues of Health Economics

Rendering health care services to the users of health care resulted in the emergence of the concept of "Health Consumers", a concept which has been the subject of many debates in the late 1960s and 1970s. One school of thought maintains that in modern times recipients of health care services behave in a manner typical of consumers in a market economy. The other school of thought opines that due to practical, ideological and structural differences between the public and private sector, recipients of health care can never behave like the typical consumers of a market economy. However, Rob Irene in the work on "Fabricating 'health consumers' in Health Care Politics" maintains that to fix "the consumer" merely in terms of a set of behavioural traits against which actual behaviour can be assessed, reduces this important and complex term to a one dimensional aspect. He considers consumers as historical product of social and political discourses.

According to Irvine, the emergence of the concept of "health consumers" is the result of creation of the force of resistance, which questions the privileged status of health care providers. It has, according to the author, opened up some creative possibilities for the reform of the patient relationships with the self and strengthens the hand of patients in their transaction with the medical profession and the state. The result of this has paved the way for restructuring the medical sector once again taking into account the concepts of health economics of whether the sector is

K. Sengupta, *Determinants of Health Status in India*,
DOI 10.1007/978-81-322-2535-5_3

Diagram 3.1 Diagrammatic representation of review of literature on health economics

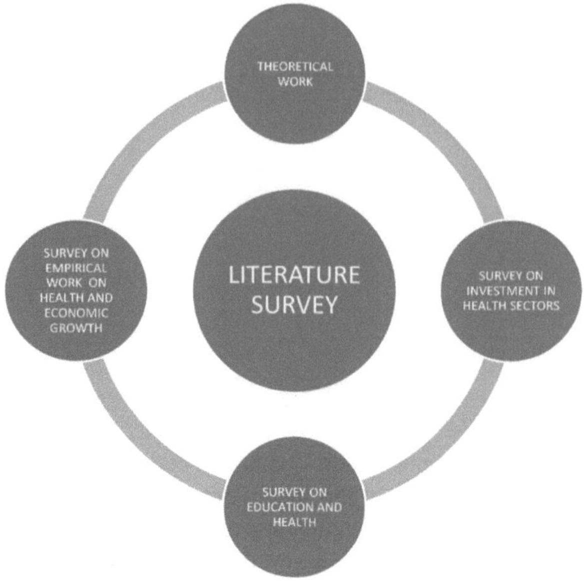

characterised by a seller's market or a buyer's market. However, this has not brought about democratisation of health care organisations in most countries. This new concept of "health consumerism" has only loosened the rules and expectations which constitute the traditional patient role and sets limits and reimpose hierarchical relations in the health care systems. He further opines that with resource constraint particularly for the social sector, health consumerism has been used as a means to redefine the position of the state with respect to the relation to the health profession.

Health Consumers have been found to be playing a crucial role in the health care delivery system in UK. Their characteristics have been found to be similar as the other social groups in the study conducted by Allosop and others in their work on "Health Consumers Groups and the National Policy Process". According to the study such groups help the members with information treatment and services and provide opportunities for social interactions they hold knowledge and expertise and the members communicate with each other and the leadership through various forms of media. Health Consumer Groups in UK are now being involved in a greater way for policy making in the health sector. They also have parliamentary presence and have also effected legislation and policy action. Government finds the experimental knowledge, expertise and networks of such groups highly useful for policy making. This according to the author, however, does not mean that the dominance of the medical profession has in any way lessened.

It needs to be mentioned here that however much important the role of the health consumer groups may play in policy formulations in the health sector, their functions are limited to developed countries where health consumers are educated and are conscious of good health. The problem however is for the health care users of developing countries who lack basic education and health awareness, due to which the health status of such people are also extremely poor. Formation of health Consumers Groups under such circumstances is extremely crucial, but at the same time very difficult. It is for this reason that education has been taken as a proxy for awareness of health consumers as a determinant of health status in our study.

Reliance on the government sector totally for provision of health services is often wrought with difficulties due to the uncertain nature of the demand for such services. At the same time, dependence on the private sector for the provision of such services particularly in less developed countries with high level of poverty may deprive the masses from health care facilities.

In view of the difficulties for the provision of health services, particularly when consumers are poor and lack awareness, the idea of the welfare aspect of health is emphasised by a good number of authors. Kenneth J. Arrow being the prominent among them highlights the different nature of medical services and emphasises the normative nature of health care services. Health care, apart from only medical care, is a very complex issue. Under its purview, according to the author includes income, nutrition, shelter, clothing, sanitation and the services which include physicians, hospitals, and public health. For satisfying the demand for health services by all sections, the author opines that a transfer of assets among individuals will in general change the final supplies of goods and services and the prices paid for them. Thus according to him, a transfer of purchasing power from the well-to-do to ill-to-do, will increase the demand for medical services by the ones who are otherwise unable to afford. This will in the short run result in an increase in the price of medical services and in the long run, an increase in the amount of medical products/services supplied. The redistribution of purchasing power may take the form of taxes and subsidies. If the distributions are not satisfactory, steps can be taken to correct it by subsequent transfers. Thus "by successive approximations, a most preferred social state can be achieved, with resource allocation being handled by the market and public policy confined to the redistribution of money income".

The study by Lindsay (1969) on equality relating to medical care focuses attention to the fact that medical need and not economic status should be the priority for medical care. Provision of health services is to be determined not by the economic status or wealth of the consumer. The idea becomes more relevant in the context of less developing nations where consumer's awareness is less and income low as mentioned above. According to Lindsay, government intervention for the provision of medical services is called for the purpose of greater consumption equality. This in turn promotes greater equality in the share of funds for medical resources. The author names several alternatives which a wealthy individual might employ to promote the desired extension of equality in consumption of medical services. The four alternatives according him are: (1) the burnt offering method, (2) the gift method, (3) the abstention method and (4) the subsidy method. The wealthy person would act rationally and would seek to promote equality to the point where his or her marginal evaluation of a unit of equality was equal to the marginal subjective cost of that unit. He would of course strive to employ the least cost method.

Inequality in the share of the health services may be removed through the market distribution system. According to the author, subsidies through the provision of taxes may be provided to the poor to promote an extension of their consumption increasing the degree of equality "from below". Added to this is also the same restraint on the level of medical consumption which may to be adopted through rationing, extending equality from the top. However, for practical purposes, the cost of administrative overheads involved in the two systems must be taken into account and the assumption of equal "medical need" must be relaxed. Lindsay's work though highly theoretical provides the basic idea upon which the health system should be based. In fact, for a nation characterised by poverty and high population, the idea is ideal though implementation in such countries is equally difficult.

There is therefore a consensus that delivery of health services is different from the delivery of other goods and services. Ensuring the use of such services by the deprived necessitates transfer of wealth and income from the well off to the ones who are not able to afford such services.

This call for examining the nature of the medical care market since the characteristics of such market is also different from that of other markets due to which delivery mechanisms of such services also differ. Kenneth Arrow (1963) draws a distinction between the characteristics of such services and other commodities used regularly by consumers. The demand for medical services is not steady unlike that of the other basic necessitates of life though this is also the most essential item of consumption and provides satisfaction only occasionally as in the case of illness. Inability to spend on health care services involves risk of death, disability and loss of earning power. Arrow also highlights the fact that the providers of health care services have characteristics and nature different from that of the other sellers. There is an element of trust in the services rendered and therefore an ethical consideration dominates the service provider. The author further opines that medical care does not involve competition and thus advertisement, services rendered is completely devoid from self-interest and treatment is dictated by need and not financial considerations. It is pertinent to mention here that with the corporatisation of the medical sector most of these features of health services have indeed disappeared. The author also maintains that the incidence of recovery is unpredictable and thus uncertainty regarding the quality of the product is more intense. Moreover, the entry of the service provider into this sector is limited by licensing and some kind of professional skills. The study also maintains that both the quality and the quantity of the supply of medical care services are being influenced by social non market forces.

3.2 Studies on Investment in the Health Sector

A good number of studies have been conducted on the expenditure incurred for health purposes, which is termed as health investment. Most of these works relate to the expenditure on health which according to them not wasteful expenditure is as is alleged by many, but can have long-term returns. Muskin (1962) in his work on

"Health as an Investment" emphasises the changes in the quality of people through investment in health and the consequent impact on economic growth. According to him, health outlays improve labour productivity and yields a return over a period of time. The labour product created by this care according to him and the savings in health expenditure in the future, if any, as a consequence of reduction in disease is the yield. Like physical capital, human capital formation through expenditure on health may also be counted through cost analysis, which are costs of environmental and curative health services embodied in the life spans in the present labour force according to the author. This cost, Muskin postulates, may be set at the cost of acquisition of the health services in the years they were acquired, they may be determined on a basis of replacement cost basis or constant price prevailing in a base year. Human labor gained according to him is the resource gained as a result of prevention or treatment of diseases. For the purpose of measuring the gains in monetary terms, it is necessary to estimate the addition to total output, both in the past as well as in the future. Death i.e. loss of workers, disability which is defined as the loss of working time and debility defined as loss of productive capacity while at work are the three ways in which to evaluate the effect of sickness on labour force. The yield in output can be measured at two stages, by estimating the gain in productive work time and by assigning monetary value to the output that this added work time represents.

Fuchs (1966) in his work on health economics maintains that in terms of economics, the contribution of an industry is measured in terms of its output. Since resources are scare, the study of health economics assumes importance, because if they were not scarce, all health needs could be met and the study of health economics and health management would not be necessary. Output of health industry is identified by the author by distinguishing between three different kinds of output that flow from health services. The most important is the contribution of health services to health. Economists assume that consumers know what they want and know how to satisfy those wants. According to the author, unlike the health sector, there are very few industries where the consumer is so dependent upon the producer for information for the quality of the product, and in many cases, the consumer is even subject to the producer's recommendation concerning the quantity to be purchased. Consumer's problem with respect to the choice of health services cannot be put in the same category as other goods and commodities. This is mainly because of the inherent uncertainty of the effect of the service on any individual and he is often not in a position to make a cool and rational judgement at the time of purchase when he is ill or a close family member is ill.

On a similar note, Culyer (1971) argues that there are some conceptual difficulties in defining the nature of optimal allocation for health care services when discussing the optimal allocation of health care services for a nation. He puts forth three arguments for consumer's rationality behaviour with respect to health care services. Firstly, "many consumers, though sick, do not hesitate treatment and may even be ignorant of their sickness". Secondly, the mentally sick fit oddly into consumer's sovereignty model" and thirdly patients requiring emergency treatment are often not in a position to reveal their preferences. It is due to all these factors that the demand, cost and the uncertainties relating to the demand for health cannot be worked out exactly in the same way as for other commodities in the market. Culyer maintains four points due to uncertainty of health care which normally prevents attainment of optimal condition. For instance, patients are not able to calculate the exact cost of medical expenses before actually incurring it. It may often happen that they spend more than what they would have actually wanted to pay or may have regrets for not being able to incur more expenditure to save their near and dear ones. It is also maintained that users do not have the choice to explore the possibilities of going in for various alternative forms of medical care as they normally have in case of other commodities. The medical practitioner too have better idea about the treatment to be given rather than the receiver of health care as a result of which most societies have evolved the "doctor-patient" relationship.

Culyer in his work further emphasises the problems of externalities which in turn has great implications for the form of organisation suitable for producing and distributing the services related to health care. Some of these externalities are the benefits of not being immunised when the others are immunised and prevents contacting communicable diseases. Ensuring utilisation of optimum capacity also may not work out exactly in the same way as in case of other manufactured products, since the existence of optimum capacity is always essential as it is unknown when a person will fall ill. He further maintains that if an individual fails to immunise the diseconomy that is being caused to the society in the form of the probability that they will contact the disease needs to be internalised. He also questions as who should bear the expenses for the public benefit when a suboptimal situation is rectified. Economists are generally of the opinion according to him that such activities should be subsidised by the government and financed out of taxation. The burning debate relating to user cost of capital in such cases can be reduced to zero, which in turn enables the public authority to take the decision and encourage the use of such health subsidy. The author further opines that healthcare expenses be considered as "merit good" especially for that category of the population who are either not aware of health problems or not able to afford spending on healthcare services.

3.3 Studies on Education and Health

Numerous studies have been undertaken to highlight the impact of literacy and education on health status. An important work by Bloom et al. (2001) uses production function models of economic growth to incorporate two crucial variables that micro economists have identified as fundamental components of human capital, i.e. work experience and health. Their work reveal that good health has positive, sizeable and statistically significant effect on aggregate output without any substantial variation across countries in average work experience. Work experience reveals that 1 year improvement in a population's life expectancy contributes to an increase of 4 p.c. in output. According to the authors, this is a relatively large effect indicating that increased experience on improving health might be justified on the grounds of their impact on labour productivity. They further opine that improvements in health may increase output. According to their findings, education creates no discernible externalities since the effects of average schooling on national output are consistent with microeconomic estimates of the effects of individual schooling on future earnings.

Another study by Higgins et al. (2008) for Ireland reveals a strong link between education and health. The author opines that education leads to greater chances of finding a secured and well paid employment which is the results of health benefits. Education also leads to more opportunities for social developments and enhances social skills with positive impacts both for the individual and the wider community and subsequently for general health. Education further leads to improved attitudes and behaviour conducive to good health. The authors recommend strategic investment in education in view of the strong links between education and health, since it is revealed by the study that increased health inequalities perpetuates cycles of intergenerational and socioeconomic disadvantage. The authors further opine that educational benefits of health do not accrue equally to all sectors of the population in Ireland. Young people from socioeconomically disadvantaged backgrounds and some ethnic groups are less likely to gain health benefits from education. Most of these advantages are confined to the more advantaged groups.

In another empirical study relating to the effect of education on health outcomes, Brunello et al. (2011) for a study of three European countries comes up with the findings that three additional years of schooling reduces self-reported poor health by 7.1 % for females and 3.1 % for males. Health behaviour, according to the study, is measured by smoking, drinking, exercising and the body mass index. The mediating effect of behaviour, according to the study, account for at most 25–40 % of the entire effect on education on health depending on gender. Most of these health benefits are individual consumption decisions, like abstaining from smoking or drinking. Such changes in health behaviour, according to the study, are also to be distinguished from changes resulting from free benefits of education such as lower stress and better decision making, which in turn leads to political decisions relating to the extent to which subsidisation in education is necessary.

3.4 Empirical Studies of the Impact of Health on Economic Growth

In one of the initial empirical work in the health sector using economic tools was undertaken by Friedman and Kuznets (1945). In their study on the shortage of physicians in the 1930s in US, the study highlighted the fact that although physicians earned 32 p.c. more than the dentists per year, their costs of training was however, 17 p.c. higher. The higher return on investments to the medical profession was explained by the barriers to entry in the medical profession due to the high cost of their training as is revealed in the case of market structure and competition in economics. According to the authors, the value of producing one more physician was higher than the cost of producing one more dentist.

A good number of studies has also been done to examine the relationship of health with economic development. Some of the significant ones are on "Health Economics in Developing Countries" by Sorkin (1997). In this work, the author highlights an important fact through his empirical work that improved status of health in developing countries have a greater impact on economic growth compared to developed countries, where the impact is much less. Reduced mortality rates had an important impact on economic growth during the earlier twentieth century. Therefore health programmes, according to the author, are important for developing countries in improving various indicators of health status, which in turn can positively impact the development of the nation. In a similar way, Jack (1999) in his in his empirical work on "Principals of Health Economics for Developing Countries" shows how labour productivity can be enhanced by investment in human capital and improvement in labour organisation and management. He further highlights how improved health status raises labour productivity through labour organisation and better management. He also focuses in his work that labour productivity is adversely affected by having to spend working hours, having to care for poor health of family members or cut down on schooling years when parents are ill and suffer from poor health.

In another study Grossman (1972) in his work on "The Concept of Health Capital and the Demand for Health "develops a model incorporating health capital formation which is considered as a capital good, the ability to work and earn and in the process produce domestic goods. The time that is lost due to sickness and other health problems can be compensated by increase in health capital. The initial endowment of health capital with which people are born can improve with investment in health. This enhanced productive nature of health can improve performance in education and job, which in turn can lead to economic growth. There are a good number of literature in this regard showing the relationship between health status and economic growth, such as Gellego (2000), who maintains that due to lack of interaction between the contributions of health economics and economic growth theory no solid theoretical structure could be developed. Strauss and Duncan (1998) have worked on the empirical relationship between health and productivity and established correlations between physical productivity and some health indicators. Further the endogenous causality between health and income was studied by Luft (1978) highlighting that many people are poor simply due to their poor health condition and due to poverty many people are not healthy as otherwise they would have been. In the Life Cycle Model, Smith (1999) links up health condition with future income, consumption and welfare. Work on similar lines were conducted by Bloom and Canning (2000), Hammond and Sachs (1999) and others. However, most of these works use life expectancy as an indicator of health status. In reality, however, health status includes a wide range of indicators such as morbidity, infant mortality, mortality rates, maternal mortality, morbidity and children with stunted growth and underweight children. It is due to this reason that most of these studies give only a partial view of the impact on health status and investment. In the present work, we make an attempt to overcome these shortcomings by incorporating most of these health indicators, though we have not included health indicators like depression or psychological cases.

References

Arrow KJ (1963) Uncertainty and the welfare economics of medical care. Am Econ Rev 53:941–973

Bloom DE, Canning D (2000) The health and wealth of nations. Science 287(5456):1207–1209

Bloom DE, Canning D, Sevilla J (2001) The effect of health on economic growth: theory and evidence, Working paper. NBER, Cambridge

Brunello G, Fort M, Schneeweis N, Ebmer R (2011) The casual effect of education on health: what is the role of health behaviour, Working paper. Institute for the Study of Labour, Austria

Culyer AJ (1971) Nature of the commodity "health care" and its efficient allocation. Oxf Econ Pap 23:189–211

Friedman M, Kuznets S (1945) Income from independent professional practice. National Bureau of Economic Research, New York

Fuch VR (1966) The output of the health industry. In: Cooper MH, Culyer T (eds) Health economics. Penguin, London

Gellego R (2000) Introducing purchaser/provider separation in the Catalon health administration: a budget analysis. Public Adm 78:423–442

Grossman M (1972) On the concept of health capital and the demand for health. J Polit Econ 80(2):223–255

Higgins C, Lavin T, Metcalfe O (2008) Health impacts of education. Institute of Public Health, Ireland

Jack W (1999) Principles of health economics for developing countries. World Bank Institute of Development Studies, Washington, DC

Lindsay CM (1969) Medical care and the economics of sharing. Economica 36(144):351–362

Luft H (1978) Poverty and health: economic causes and consequences of health problems. Ballinger Publishing Company, Cambridge, MA

Muskin SJ (1962) Health as an investment. J Polit Econ 70, 129 pp

Smith J (1999) Healthy bodies and Thich wallets: the dual relation between health and economic status. J Econ Perspect 13(2):145–166

Sorkin AL (1997) Health economics in developing countries. Lexington Books, Lexington

Strauss J, Duncan J (1998) Health, nutrition and economic development. J Econ Lit 36(2): 766–817

Chapter 4
Significance of Health Financing and Investment for Health Economics

4.1 Health Expenditure and Health Finance

In view of the crucial role played by cost in determination of health status as examined in Chap. 2, health expenditure and investment in health sector assume significance for the present work. Expenditure on health is viewed more as a long-term investment, which benefits accrue more to the individual in the short run, but it is the society and the nation who ultimately reap the benefit of such expenditure in the long run. Expenditure on health, therefore, like expenditure on any other socioeconomic aspect, can be viewed as investment for enhancing the quality of life of the people. The expenditure incurred for bringing up children and providing them with good health contributes not only for his own self but for providing healthy labour force for the future development of the nation. The GDP of such nations will eventually be much higher and better in comparison to those nations burdened with malnourished children with high morbidity and mortality rates. Resources required for meeting the challenges of health-related problems of such nature has high opportunity costs. Such resources spent in less developed nations could otherwise have been spent more profitably for the purpose of development of the nation had they not been spent for meeting the challenges of poor health of the population. It is not only by way of monetary investment alone, but a nation characterised by high morbidity and mortality rates also loses much of its human resources from whose productive contribution the nation is deprived. Health expenditure is therefore considered as an investment because the benefits are directly in terms of number of lives saved, extent of disability prevented and the amount of monetary loss that can be reduced.

Links between poverty and ill health is now a well-established fact. Ill and malnourished people are not only unable to contribute productively to the development, but their children too are not able to attend schools and receive the best education. This leads to further levels of poverty and thereby lower level of economic development even more. Therefore investment in health for the right people and at the right

K. Sengupta, *Determinants of Health Status in India*,
DOI 10.1007/978-81-322-2535-5_4

time not only ensures a healthy and productive workforce but also ensures the future economic growth for the nation. Higher economic growth, in turn, enables a nation to invest more in the health sector so that people in a rich and developed nation are naturally much healthier and more productive, since most of their basic health needs are taken care of by through public health spending of their respective countries. There is thus a circular relationship between good health and higher economic growth. Good health of the population of a country makes economic growth sustainable. Good health is now accepted as a fundamental determinant of economic growth and therefore investment in the health sector of a nation has assumed to be an important policy matter under the purview of economic growth.

The Report on the Commission on Macroeconomics and Health draws attention to the fact that developing countries should mobilise extra domestic resources for health and make cost-effective use of these resources. According to the Report, public health expenditure therefore should be directed towards the poor and support the health needs of the community and the health programmes. This kind of health expenditure can protect households against disastrous private health expenditure, since in some poor countries, private health expenditure can be as high as 40 %, though in India the percentage is even more. The Report therefore argues for the extension of health interventions beyond national borders through R&D in health, since those areas of health are often underfunded by resource-starved poor countries. Health investment through public health spending is therefore urgently called for in global public goods.

Availability of requisite finance therefore plays a pivotal role in determining the status of health in a society. It is inadequate finance which is mostly responsible for poor health status among the less developing and poor nations. Small percentage of financial allocation on the health sector results in failure to provide adequate health infrastructure such as hospitals, doctors, paramedical staff and all types of technological upgradation related to provision of health-care services. This results in poor quality and insufficient amount of health services while demand continues to surge ahead, creating a wide gap between demand for and supply of health services. The wide gap between the demand and supply of health services, in turn, results in poor health status in the country. As a result, status of health condition deteriorates even further. Insufficient financial allocation for the health sector also compels the individual health-care seekers to spend on health needs from their own income which is termed as 'out of pocket' expenses. For instance, in India, 'out of pocket' expenses on health are one of the highest in the world, which is as high as 85 % of the total health expenditure. This is a major perpetuator of poverty in India. Debt for medical purposes, particularly among the poor in the country, has been rising at an alarming rate. Health insurance, which is one of the most important means to ensure health security to all, is grossly inadequate in most poor nations, India being a glaring example.

Status of health is better in developed nations for the reason that such nations can afford to invest and spend more on the various requirements of the health sector. The people of such countries are therefore much healthier and more productive, which in turn leads to higher level of income, both for themselves and for the nation as a whole. Therefore poverty in any country can be tackled directly by tackling health issues. Health is considered as a 'normal good' on which people spend more with a rise in income. However, initially with a rise in income, private health spending does not rise immediately as rising income is initially spent on basic necessities of life such as food and shelter. However increased expenditure on food is not spent for increasing nutritional level, because the increased expenditure on food is spent to increase food variety rather than on increasing nutrition on increasing the consumption of calories. The market cannot solve these problems automatically and it is here that the role of health policies related to public health expenditure formulated by the government assumes crucial significance.

4.2 Human Capital Approach

Economists use the term *human capital* to denote the investments made in the health sector, raise human capacities and raise labour productivity for the purpose of increasing the wealth of the nation. Health capital plays a crucial role for the development of every nation because it can improve the return to investments in other economic sectors also. Even the return to education is dependent on investments on health. School attendance in the formal sector is dependent on the health condition of the children which in turn is again determined by investments in the health sector. Higher expenditure on health, especially public expenditure, is associated with better health outcomes and higher productivity, evidence of which is more common in poor nations than in the rich ones. Health sector, particularly in poor countries, therefore, demands far more priority than is assigned at present. This in turn implies the need for higher allocation of GDP for the health sector.

Studies have also revealed that the return to investments in health is higher in developing countries than in the developed ones. The reasons attributed to higher return, and therefore the relevance of investments in the health sector in the less developed countries, are due to the fact that such nations are more often affected adversely by much greater burden of disease. The extent of infant and child mortality is much higher in poor nations, where poverty is the real factor behind poor health. A marginal increase in investment per child in preventing infectious diseases such as malaria, diarrhoea and other water-borne diseases or even better nutritious food can drastically reduce the burden of disease and mortality rates. It is revealed that malaria itself results in one million deaths every year in the world and the African nations top the list in this regard. It is also estimated by WHO that 15 % of the children who survive malaria are left with severe neurological problems and learning disabilities. The estimated direct cost of the disease in Africa alone was more than three billion dollars annually in 2000.

Experience in development studies have revealed that return to investment in man, particularly health and education, has compelled social investment (investment in health) to precede physical investment. This is evident from the fact because a number of developed countries have witnessed growth rate of their economy which has been much higher than the growth rate of physical capital investments and rise in labour force. The future returns to investment in health in developed countries in comparison to less developed countries, where due to poverty and resource constraint, health investment which is often inadequate, has focussed attention to the importance of human capital for economic development. All these issues have given rise to the 'theory of human capital'. Though investment in education has received more attention and has been the subject of greater research in areas of human capital theory in comparison to investment in health, the two types of investments are highly interrelated. Return to investments in health is to a large extent determined by investment in education. Labour productivity is not only the outcome of investment in physical capital but more importantly in health and education.

Health expenditure therefore has the component of both investment expenditure and consumption expenditure. When an individual has a better health status, which is a form of consumption good, he also becomes a better producer. However, as far as financing health expenditures is concerned, it is irrelevant which is the source of health financing, because in most countries such finances come partly from private sector and partly from public sources. The combination varies from one country to another depending upon different factors (Muskin 1962).

Investment in health is thus the same as the investment in the enhancing the quality of the people, because, as mentioned earlier, changes in the quality of people means changing the contribution to economic growth. The central concern is the measurement of the addition to labour productivity and contribution to annual output and economic growth due to the additional investments in health care. Benefits can also be measured in terms of the gain in future work by the beneficiaries of health programmes. The present value of the future earning of these people who would not have otherwise survived with the earlier mortality rates is considered as capital asset of health investments, the addition to national income by this group of people. Benefits of investment in man and thereby investment in health are measured in terms of the economic loss avoided, number of lives saved and the extent of disability prevented. It is therefore pertinent for health planners to estimate the cost-benefit ratios of allocation of scarce resources for different health programmes, which is a subject matter under health economics. However health economists are of the opinion that in the absence of any definite methodology for estimating the cost-benefit ratio for health programmes, the problems of measuring the benefits of health investment particularly for the less developed countries become very difficult, mainly because of inadequate health data in these countries.

4.3 Investment in Health

It is now a well-accepted reality that health status of a nation is an important goal as well as outcome of all developmental policies. However, equally crucial is the importance of investment in health, the nature as well as the extent of investment in various sectors of the health economy, all of which can play a pivotal role for economic development of a nation. It is here that the significance of health economics assumes a crucial role, as it focuses attention to the ways and means of allocation of scarce resources and its optimum utilisation in terms of which health investment is generally made. Study of health management, on the other hand, studies about the strategy and the use of such strategies for health investment for the purpose of attaining the optimum return. Health system in this context is an important determinant of the political and administrative commitment to development of health outcome, because it determines the health budget and the amount of public investment on health. Again health management deals with issues of governance of health delivery system, effective supervision and meaningful administration and accountability. It is therefore evident that ensuring the best of health status in a nation is a combination of the understanding of health economics along with health management and good governance.

Since scarce resources compete to be allocated to various sectors in countries which are perennially constrained by inadequate resources, the health sector often suffers from resource constraint. This is more often the case in the poor countries as highlighted earlier, characterised by inadequate resources for developmental purposes. Resources for health sector are based on the economic structures and the national income of the respective countries, tax collection capacity and internal and external debts. Poor countries according to the report on 'Macroeconomics and Health: Investing in Health for Economic Development' (2010) are shockingly poor in health spending. Even if such countries had allocated more of their domestic resources for health, such measures would still not resolve the basic health problems, because they lack the required financial resources for the basic health needs of their population according to the study. The report further reveals that at $30 and $40 per capita for essential interventions, these costs would represent more than 10 % of GNP of the least developed countries, much more than what can be mobilised out of domestic resources.

4.4 Public Health Spending

Public health expenditure consists of recurrent and capital health spending from government (central and state) budgets, external borrowings and grants, including donations from international agencies and non-governmental organisations and social compulsory insurance funds. Total health expenditure is the sum of public and private health expenditure. It covers the provision of health services, preventive and curative, family planning activities, nutrition activities and emerging aid designated for health but does not include water and sanitation.

Public health expenditure is normally incurred on *public health* which is a social and political concept and aims at improving health, prolonging life and improving the quality of life through health promotion programmes, disease prevention and other forms of health intervention. The *new public health* implies spending in various forms of lifestyles and living conditions all of which determine health status and the necessity to mobilise resources and make sound investments in policies, programmes and services which create, maintain and protect healthy lifestyles.

Health expenditure is considered as a merit good, because large positive externalities are associated with health expenditure. In poor and very rich nations, health expenditure is incurred mostly by the individuals themselves. In the case of poor nations, the reason is resource constraint on the part of the state and in case of the rich nations; the state already had invested the optimum level in the health sector. Hence the state is not required to incur any further expenditure, but leaves the expenses to be incurred on the health sector to the private individuals, who incur the expenditure as per their health needs and requirements. The health outcome is however different in the two cases. In the former case, it implies that a greater degree of reliance has to be placed on private delivery of health infrastructure and health services. It also means that there is inadequate access to health services by the poor since public health investment is not adequate. Public Investment in health especially in poor countries are crucial because the inability to do so means that the poor have to spend more from their pockets. Since they cannot afford to spend too much on health, they suffer from disease, malnutrition, ill health and other related problems. For rich nations on the other hand, health service consumers incur health expenses according to their income and requirements and are not dependent on the state for the provision of health care delivery, because the state had already made investments in health infrastructure.

Though direct correlationship between public health expenditure and health outcomes cannot be established, yet, the different indicators of health status such as life expectancy, infant mortality and maternal mortality are unfavourable in those countries where public health expenditure is inadequate in comparison to those nations where health expenditure is on the higher side.

4.5 Theoretical Underpinnings of Public Expenditure on Health

The two most important characteristics of health care and its expenditure are the presence of externalities and information asymmetries. It is these features that make health care different from other goods and services, and thus there is greater possibility of market failures in the case of the health sector in contrast to other types of services. Externalities in public health expenditure imply that the expenditure on one group may also benefit the others for whom the expenditure was not originally meant. Negative externality in contrast means that expenditure on certain items has adverse effect on the others, such as pollution. Here the role of the state assumes importance because it means that public expenditure has to be stepped up in those sectors of health which have the largest extent of positive externalities so that the overall public welfare may rise and health status is not adversely affected. In a similar manner, public expenditure has to be curtailed in those sectors where negative externalities are the highest.

Public health expenditure can therefore be of two categories, which will be highly relevant for the purpose of our analysis. Public health expenditure can be on general health-care services, termed as ‘public health’, like doctors, nurses and other health personnel, hospitals and other health infrastructures, the health impact of which is of long-term nature and indirect. The other category of public health expenditure has more direct and immediate impact on health outcomes. These expenditures relate more to those areas of public health which target to change the overall conditions of nutrition and sanitation that effect health outcomes. Investment on clean drinking water, immunisation or treatment for communicable diseases results in direct health benefits through reduced rates of disease. Private expenditures on all such items will not take into account the positive external effects and therefore yield less than socially optimal levels of such activities. It is asserted that public expenditure on general health care services can have positive externalities not only because of social costs of morbidity and illness but also because inequalities in health care can create other social problems. State intervention therefore becomes essential either in the form of price subsidies to encourage the consumption of health-care services or direct public expenditure for the provision of such services with the additional important goal of reducing inequalities in health between the rich who can afford expensive health care and the poor who are deprived of even the basic health-care services.

Another reason for market failure in the health-care sector is due to asymmetric information between two parties, i.e. patient and the health service provider, where one of the parties has access to some information which is not known to the other party. Situations of this nature arise when the interests of the two parties do not coincide. State intervention in the form of licensing of health-care providers and insistence on some professional norms prohibiting low-quality, regulated advertisements becomes imperative in an attempt to ensure and raise welfare by improving quality of health-care and health delivery services.

The case for health expenditure by the government thus becomes extremely important for the purpose of striking the right balance between efficiency and equity, unlike as in the case of other goods and commodities.

4.6 Health Expenditure Policies

In most developing nations and poor countries, as discussed, there is a perennial problem of scarcity of financial resources to be allocated to the health sector. However, what is a matter of even greater concern is the misallocation and inefficient use of the limited resources allocated to the health sector. While the former relates to the principals of economics, the latter deals with management techniques. Allocation of financial resources in favour of the rich and urban population and inaccessibility of the poor and the rural population to health-care services have been a plaguing issue characterising the developing countries for many years. This poses a serious challenge to the health system for seeking ways and means of striking the right balance between equity and efficiency in the health sector so that no section of the population is deprived of the benefits of public health expenditure. Such problems assume a greater degree of seriousness in the health sector in comparison with other economic sectors particularly because investment in the latest and expensive technology in the health sector, particularly to benefit the poor, can be incurred only by the public health system.

The concerns relating to equity and efficiency require that the sources of health financing is understood because these sources in turn determines the services to be provided in the sector. The nature and type of services provided in turn again determine the health status in a society. There are certain types of funding which encourages capital spending on the health sector while others encourage current expenditure on health. Some sources of finance favours expenditure on preventive measures and others on curative measures of health. The type of health personnel employed is often influenced by the sources of finance. For instance, paramedical personnel get greater attention by public health expenditure, whereas expenditure on health professionals is favoured by the private health providers.

Health expenditure can also influence consumers' behaviour by either encouraging or restraining the uses of certain types of health services. The effects of such policies on consumers' behaviour however depend on the determinants of the consumers' response. The determinants are the ability and the willingness of the health consumers to pay, which in turn depends on the socioeconomic factors like the level of education, age, gender and the status of health and economic factors like the income level, costs of medicine, etc. Universal access to health-care services particularly by the poor and the disadvantaged sections of the population of the developing countries is thereby facilitated by enhancing public expenditure in the health-care system. Studies have revealed that increased expenditure in reducing infant and maternal mortality, on immunisation and other preventative and curative health measures, better sanitation and drinking water facilities has a direct positive impact on health status of the population. Out of pocket expenditure on such health-care facilities prevents accessibility by the poor and thereby prevents the requisite extent of health care. This adversely affects the various indicators of health and health outcomes. The gap needs to be filled in by public expenditure on health services which indeed is a formidable challenge in a resource-constrained overpopulated developing economy. This results in low level of per capita health expenditure which adversely affects the status of health in a nation.

Merely concentrating on health expenditure, in the absence of any proper guidelines for the same, has often led to skewed distribution of health expenditure across space and time. This in turn prevents achieving the target of health expenditure in developing countries, resulting in low health status of the population. The gap in such expenditure is often met by private sector health investment for health infrastructure and health delivery system. The result is that health-care services is denied to the underprivileged and the socially deprived which in turn adversely affects social welfare, labour productivity and the overall growth and development of the nation. Though there may not be immediate and direct correlationship between health expenditure and health outcomes as highlighted earlier, nevertheless where health expenditure is high, people are much better off in terms of health conditions which in the long run increase longevity, reduce morbidity and diseases and reduce maternal and infant mortality. It is therefore pertinent and extremely crucial that proper policy for health investment and health expenditure be formulated. This is more pertinent for developing nations than for the already developed nations. It is therefore essential to examine not only the proportion of health expenditure to GDP of a nation, which, though, indicates the importance public authorities attach to the health sector, but more importantly also the sectoral allocation of resources in the health sector, which actually determines the status of health in a nation. Data on health expenditure by itself do not reveal the status of health in a society and what should be done to improve these indicators. However, health expenditure does focus attention to certain dimensions that are ignored by descriptions of mortality, fertility and health services. Therefore decision of a country's health policies and programmes requires the understanding of the size, structure, nature and composition of health expenditures of the country so that their effect on the health status and the factors that affect the status may receive the requisite attention by researchers and policymakers.

Expenditure on the health sector conveys the status and importance of the sector vis-a-vis the other sectors. It helps to identify the real priorities in contrast to stated or official priorities. It also focuses attention to the areas of the health sector that need to be addressed by the policymakers. For instance, it provides a different perspective from the usual descriptions of facilities and outputs such as immunisation. Policymakers may need to relook into the fact as whether raising health spending is the only solution to better health outcomes or managing the existing resources would give better results. It is no doubt that more resources are needed for many of the cost-effective public health interventions. In most developing countries, low levels of fund utilisation in public health services indicate that in the absence of any major restructuring and improving the way money is spent, merely increasing spending will surely not improve the health outcomes. Better use of the existing resources is included within the purview of health management. For instance, quality and efficiency of public health service could be improved through effective management system. Better management of both the public and private health systems to achieve the goals of health policy increases the effectiveness and also gives better health outcomes. Therefore, health economics and health managements are in reality only two sides of the same coin.

4.7 Health Status and Health Expenditure

The status of health in a nation therefore is often assessed by the extent of investment made in the health sector by the government, which in turn is determined by the health system of a nation. Consequently, health investment is an issue which dominates health policy formulations across all countries of the world. It is also a means of comparing the health status among different nations. Comparisons among nations in terms of health investment often pose problems due to the absence of consistency and comparability, because health expenditure is compiled at a national level. In the present study, such comparisons are made in the Indian context for different states of India so that the relationship between health status and health expenditure can be assessed.

The proportion of health expenditure to GDP is the most common indicator of the relative importance that is assigned to the health sector. This is a macroeconomic approach where comparisons of the proportion of national income allocated for health-care services can be made. Studies have revealed (Hopkins 2010) that health expenditure in high-income nations is not always explained by a high level of economic development, though higher quantum of health expenditure has to be inevitably supported by higher level of economic development. There is also no specific relationship between GDP per capita and the proportion of GDP for health care. This is mainly due to the fact that it is not a technical relationship but determined by variation in economic, institutional and cultural factors of the country concerned and role of private sector across nations and regions.

Where public health investment is inadequate, 'out of pocket 'expenditure which is an important component of private spending on health is higher. Out of pocket expenditure particularly in a poor nation with low health status often leads people to impoverishment, since it imposes heavy financial burden on the households. Countries with high GDP are able to maintain a sustainable health-care system, as a result of which out of pocket expenditure is low. Studies have revealed (Hopkins 2010) that out of pocket expenditure averaged 17.95 % in OECD countries and 34.9 % in non-OECD countries. Standard deviation for the former group of countries is 8.7, whereas it is 16.8 for the latter. OECD countries accounted for less than 20 % of the world population in 2000 but had spent 20 % of the world's health expenditure. In other words 80 % of the world's population had spent less than 10 % of the world's expenditure on health.

4.8 Health Expenditure in India

There is a general consensus that India spends less on health than is warranted by the needs of the nation in terms of absolute amount, though studies reveal that the proportion of health spending to GDP in India is higher than some of her neighbouring countries. However, the health outcomes such as life expectancy and infant mortality, which are normally accepted as the indicators of health status, are highly unfavourable in India in comparison to the other nations. This is a clear indication of the fact that health expenditure is not judiciously invested or spent in an effective manner. Health-care system is often not well managed and resources are not allocated where they are most needed, with the result that users prefer private health services in spite of higher prices. Questions are therefore raised regarding the present structure between curative and preventive health financing, since the high-morbidity rate and infant and maternal rates are still a matter of serious concern in

India, so many years of independence notwithstanding. Health expenditure in the public health for any country therefore necessitates adopting the appropriate models for health policies.

Ad hoc policies on health care and health services have also resulted in ad hoc policies on health financing in the Indian context. Misutilisation of financial resources takes places often due to the superimposition of new programmes on health, even before the existing health policies and programmes have been monitored or evaluated, which results in multiplicity of health schemes. Health financing has to be linked up with financing of clean drinking water, sanitation, compulsory primary education, food and nutrition, greater public awareness and participation in health. All these issues cannot be viewed in isolation but need to be integrated into well-coordinated health policies in a holistic manner for the overall development policies of a nation so that investment in the health sector can be meaningful and can be used as an effective means for economic development.

Poor health status in India notwithstanding public spending on health in India has always been miserably low. This has resulted in higher proportion of private health spending and high 'out of pocket' expenditure on health, often to the extent of impoverishment of the people. Among the low- and middle-income nations, there is very little difference between the proportions of public and private spending on health, both of which are extremely low. This is in sharp contrast to the high percentage of public spending on health among the developed nations, leading to high per capita health spending as well. Under the former category, value of public health spending to private and to a large extent the ineffectiveness of health spending are grossly inadequate even by the standard of poor nations. Almost the entire amount of private expenditure in India is constituted by out of pocket expenditure. This is highly regressive and puts a disproportionate burden for health care on poor households. Studies have revealed that (2005) households spend three fourth of their health expenditure, which in some Indian states is as high as 80 % of health spending, imposing extremely high financial burden on the poor.

An alarming experience in the Indian context in recent years is the farmer's suicides due to rising indebtedness. One of the reasons for such distress is the extremely high expenditure on health care. All these imply the adverse effect of inadequate quantity and quality of public expenditure on health. The nature and extent of health financing can have tremendous socioeconomic implications. The post-liberalisation era in India has witnessed rising trend of private health expenditure particularly in rural areas. According to the study conducted by Economic Research Foundation (2006), three broad factors can be attributed for such disturbing trend. One of the reasons according to the study could be greater importance assigned to health care, to the extent that they are ready to even incur debt for the purpose. Another reason could be worsening condition and limited accessibility to public health-care services. The reason for this could be ascribed to curtailment of expenditure on the social sector including health in the post-liberalisation period. The third reason could be higher user cost of public health system. This too could be due to resource crunch in the health sector because of which citizens are made to pay more for medicines and other medical services.

As mentioned in Sect. 4.7, the % of GDP for public health implies the relative importance assigned to health, which can thereby influence the health status of the people. India has devoted less than even 1 % of its GDP for public health as against 5 % in the developed countries and 3 % in the other Asian nations. The percentage of health expenditure in India had declined even further to 0.9 % thereafter, though recently it has increased marginally. Even out of this meagre amount, a greater proportion is spent on meeting the salaries of doctors and other medical staff, leaving very little for meeting the other important health-care needs of the poor. There is also a wide variation in public health investment across different states in India. What is a matter of concern in health investment in India is that states with poor health record have been witnessing declining trend of per capita public health spending. Another matter of equal concern is that even this paltry amount is devoted more for curative rather than preventive health care.

The implications of health expenditure are even greater for a poor country because if it is biased in favour of the poor, it can increase their capabilities and raise human development which is another area in which the record of India leaves a lot to be desired. There is indeed a clear impact of per capita public health spending on certain vital health indicators such as life expectancy, infant mortality, maternal mortality and the spread of communicable diseases. Though direct impact on health status of public health spending cannot be established, the positive impact of health expenditure on health status cannot be denied either.

It has therefore been considered pertinent to work out the correlationship between per capita health expenditure and life expectancy, infant mortality and other health indicators in the Indian context. Regression models have also been developed to examine the impact of various types of health expenditure on different health indicators. Although a good number of studies have already been conducted in this area, what the present work proposes to undertake is to get an overall idea by taking the broad scenario of all the states in India. Experience of improved health status reveals that growth of public expenditure on health has been associated with better record on immunisation and eradication of communicable diseases such as malaria and diarrhoea which is the consequence of greater expenditure on pure drinking water and sanitation. In India, on the other hand, low level of public investment in health has resulted in poor health infrastructure and also poor health delivery system particularly to the poor. Added to this has also been the mismanagement of the meagre resource and infrastructure, poor coordination, monitoring and supervision. The poor are therefore compelled to meet their own medical expenses which most of them are unable to afford. All these have resulted in very poor health status in India in spite of high growth rate of the economy. This only goes to indicate that it is not always the lack of resources but more importantly the lack of commitment towards the health sector. This has resulted in the absence of any definite, holistic and concrete health policy, as well as unequal distribution of resources for health care across different regions and states of the country.

The significance of public expenditure therefore assumes crucial importance for the health status as revealed in the work of Paxson and Schady (2005), who in their study have shown that infant mortality had gone up by 2.5 % in Peru between 1981 and 1990, which according to them was due to a decline in per capita GDP by 30 % during the corresponding period. Public health expenditure also declined by 58 % and proportion of health expenditure to GDP from 4.3 % to 3 %.

4.9 Econometric Analysis of Health Expenditure in India

In view of the immense role of health expenditure and health investment, the present work has used health investment as an independent explanatory variable and the various indicators of health status such as life expectancy and infant and child mortality as the dependent variables. Per capita public and private health expenditures have also been adopted in the models as independent explanatory variables. For this purpose data on health expenditure for all the states of India has been used in the models, which have then been regressed on the various health indicators. Consistent annual data for various aspects of health expenditure for the states are not available. Though some information for rural sectors is available from the Bulletin on Rural Health Statistics, a few data are available for the urban sectors.

Public health expenditure consists of recurrent and capital spending from government (central and state) budgets, external borrowings and grants, including donations from international agencies and nongovernmental organisations and social compulsory insurance funds. Total health expenditure is the sum of public and private health expenditures. It covers the provision of health services, prevention and curative, family planning activities, nutrition activities and emergency aid designated for health but does not include water and sanitation. On the basis of the above, the models developed are as follows:

1. The first model that is specified for our purpose is

$$\mathrm{L\,exp} = \mathrm{a} + \mathrm{b}pche_{+\mathrm{U}} \tag{4.1}$$

where Lexp represents life expectancy and is the dependent variable and *pche* represents per capita health expenditure, being the independent variable, and 'u' is the residual term.

The result of the estimated model is as follows:

$$\begin{aligned} &\mathrm{L\,exp} = 73.66 + .657pche + u \qquad \mathrm{R}^2 = .431;\ \mathrm{F} = 45.52 \\ &\mathrm{t} = (144.5)\ (6.74) \end{aligned} \tag{4.1}$$

The results of the model are theoretically and statistically sound as revealed by the signs and the significance of the coefficient of the independent variable. In fact, 65 % of the change in life expectancy is explained by 1 % change in total per capita expenditure on health consisting both of private and public expenditure. The model is also accepted as revealed by the value of R^2 which is .43 and it is also statistically significant as revealed by the value of F.

It may thus be concluded that life expectancy is determined to a significant extent by the expenditure incurred in the health sector. This is quite evident because it is an accepted fact that life expectancy is the result of overall investment in proper sanitation, clean drinking water, immunisation of children, unpolluted environment, investment in health centres, hospitals, medical equipment, laboratory, medical research facilities, medical education, nurses, paramedical workers, technicians and a host of other direct and indirect expenses that need to be incurred in the medical sector.

It is important to mention here that establishing a direct and casual relationship between higher investment in health care and higher life expectancy is difficult to establish. The mechanism of the causal relationship is unclear and therefore marginal increase in health care may not increase life expectancy in the short period. The impact works over a period of time through interactions among various variables. Care has also to be taken of the definition of health-care expenditure, which differs from country to country.

It is also a fact that as percentage of GDP increases on health care, rate of return goes on diminishing. Studies have indicated (Baal et al. 2013) that in the Netherlands between 2000 and 2010, about 0.3–50 % (1.6 years) of the increase in life expectancy is due to increase in health-care spending. Though the study has been conducted in connection with pension burden due to increase in life expectancy, nevertheless the study highlights an important fact that though the exact impact of higher health-care spending on life expectancy is difficult to ascertain, it is true that given the age profile of mortality risk, gains in life expectancy through increased health-care spending will probably be reached through decreasing mortality rates at higher ages. The study further maintains that if research allows better quantification of the strength of the effect of health-care spending on life expectancy, the role of such spending on determinant of mortality could be acknowledged, when making forecasts of life expectancy.

However, it is also a fact that reduction of various types of infectious diseases and spread of epidemics does increase life expectancy. Some of the findings of research work in the area reveal (Nolte and McKee 2004; Macenbach et al. 1988) that medical care has contributed to the increase in life expectancy in western countries since the 1950s. Other studies have further revealed (Cutler et al. 2006; Cutler and McClellan 2001) that medical care plays a crucial role for life expectancy and investment in medical care was good value for money. Cutler and McClellan (Cutler et al. 2006) concluded that 'the benefits from lower infant mortality and better treatment of heart attacks have been sufficiently great that they alone are about equal to the entire cost increase for medical care over time'.

It needs to be mentioned here that due to the time lag between investment in the health sector and rise in life expectancy, the exact quantitative relationship is difficult to establish. Besides, increase in life expectancy is due to many factors including higher income, better nutritious food and improved quality of life, and health expenditure may only be an insignificant factor. The above figure clearly demonstrates the direct relationship between per capita health spending and life expectancy.

The figure below shows the important relationship between per capita health expenditure and life expectancy. It shows that the higher the per capita health expenditure, the higher the life expectancy, and the explanatory power of the regression equation is 0.52. USA is the only nation with the exception, where higher per capita health expenditure does not raise life expectancy. The reason could be as discussed above that per capita expenditure might have already reached the highest level, and therefore any further increase cannot raise life expectancy any further, and in fact it only results in diminishing returns.

However, attention also needs to be focussed to the fact that though per capita health expenditure may appear to raise life expectancy in general, there is always wide spatial variation in terms of expenditure incurred in the urban and rural area. Variation may also be evident due to differences in income level.

The relationship between health expenditure and life expectancy as per the study of the World Bank for the OECD countries is depicted in the figure below, which shows that till a certain age level, higher health expenditure results in raising life expectancy. However, beyond a certain level of age, life expectancy increases in a diminishing rate with an increase in health expenditure (Fig. 4.1).

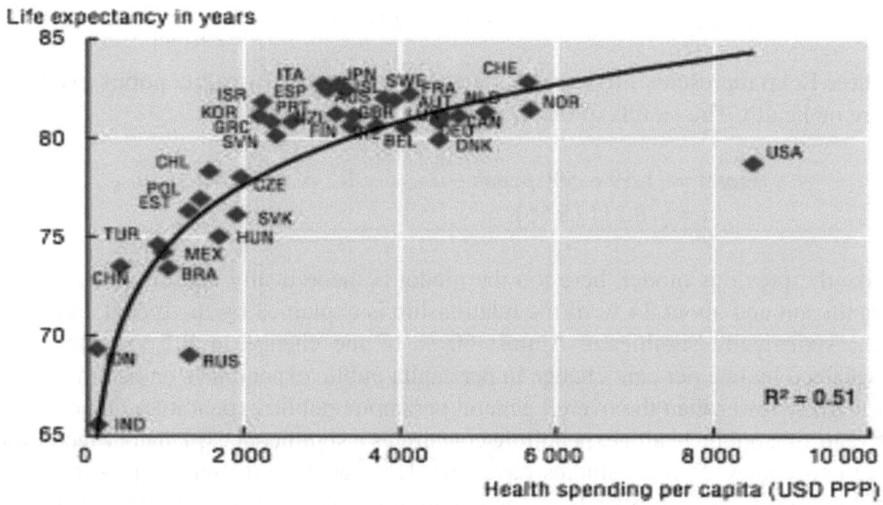

Fig. 4.1 Relationship between health expenditure and life expectancy (Source: OECD Health Statistics 2013, http://dx.doi.org/10.1787/health-data-en; World Bank for non-OECD countries Statlink http://dx.doi.org/10.1787/888932916040

4.9.1 *Relationship Between Health Expenditure and Life Expectancy*

It also needs to be highlighted that rise in health-care spending may be due to increase in price or provision of more and better health-care services. Higher spending may also be due to higher wages and salaries so that in some cases higher health expenditure may not result in raising life expectancy. The effectiveness of health-care spending on life expectancy has to be determined by examining the reason behind higher spending. The impact may be studied both by the micro-level studies as well by macro-level studies. In the former case, we confine to higher investment mainly for the purpose of controlling a particular kind of disease or a policy reform in one specific area of health sector and its impact on life expectancy. Macro studies to which the present work is confined examine the impact of the general rise in health expenditure and its impact on life expectancy.

2. As against the total health expenditure, in the next model we have examined the impact on life expectancy of per capita public health expenditure.

The model adopted for the purpose along with the estimated results is stated below:

$$\mathrm{L\,exp} = \mathrm{a} + \mathrm{b}pcpeh + u \qquad (4.2)$$

where Lexp represents life expectancy and *pcpeh* is the per capita public expenditure on health. The results of the model are as follows:

$$\begin{aligned} \mathrm{L\,exp} &= 71.59 + .590pcpeh + u \qquad \mathrm{R}^2 = .348;\ \mathrm{F} = 31.96 \\ \mathrm{t} &= (78.21)\ (5.56) \end{aligned} \qquad (4.2)$$

Like the previous model, here too the model is theoretically and also statistically significant and about 34 % of the relationship is explained by the model and R^2 is also statistically significant. Almost 60 % of the change in life expectancy is explained by one per cent change in per capita public expenditure on health, which is slightly lower than the overall general per capita public expenditure on health. It reveals that public health expenditure constitutes a significant explanatory factor for life expectancy. Similar studies have revealed that the explanatory power of the model can improve further by disaggregating expenditure into public and private expenditure and studying its impact on life expectancy (Issa and Quattara 2005).

Public health expenditure is a reflection of long-term health policy of a government. This is reflected in terms of the proportion of GDP allocated to the health sector. The intrasectoral allocation within the health sector reveals the goals of the health policy of a nation. Insufficient public health spending in most developing nations, including India, manifests itself in poor health status, since most health consumers who are in the ‘lower end of the pyramid ‘are unable to meet all the health expenses on their own. High costs of private health services mean denial of such facilities to the poor and therefore public health expenditure is associated with large positive externalities.

India records one of the lowest percentages of public health expenditure amounting to a very insignificant proportion of GDP. Elasticity of public health expenditure with respect to GDP was 0.94 for the period of 1996–1997 to 2005–2006, which is much lower than the average for low-income countries which was 1.16 for the same period (Tandon and Cashin 2010). It needs to be mentioned here that India ranked 18th among the 191 countries in terms of public expenditure on health as a percentage of GDP. Public health care in India is the responsibility shared by both the central and the state governments. State governments bear the primary responsibility for health care, accounting for almost two thirds of the total burden. Central government on the other hand bears about one third of the responsibility. Some responsibilities however overlap. Resource constraint particularly on the part of the state governments is often cited as the reason for inadequate public health expenditure in the Indian health scenario. According to a study (Stenberg and Other 2010), low-income countries need to spend at least $ 54 per capita for a basic package of health service, though the actual per capita health service is only $ 27 in these countries, with India recording $ 29 per capita health expenditure.

Regarding the importance of public health spending, there has recently been some effect at raising the health status in India through NRHM (National Rural Health Mission), introduced by the government of India in 2005 and Rashtriya Swasthya Bima Yojana (RSBY), a national health insurance scheme for people living below the poverty line. In spite of these efforts, actual public expenditure on health has neither increased nor has there been any substantial improvement in the health indicators. The result has been poor performance in terms of diseases, both preventive and curative, and poor health infrastructure, all of which have their impact on life expectancy at birth and infant and child mortality, all of which result in high incidence of deaths, which in turn lowers life expectancy. Inadequate preventive health-care services result in high incidence of deaths from communicable diseases. The WHO data for 2008 'Global Burden of Diseases' reveal that among 192 countries in the world, India accounts for almost one fourth of the deaths due to diarrhoea, more than one third due to childhood-cluster diseases, one third due to leprosy, more than 50 % due to Japanese encephalitis and almost 30 % due to prenatal conditions. The result of this is that India occupies the 132nd rank in terms of life expectancy among 193 nations according to UNDP Human Development Report, 2010, and 143rd and 124th ranks for infant and maternal mortality rates respectively.

Though public health spending should be directed mostly towards prevention and primary and secondary care, in India, however, most of it is incurred for curative and tertiary health-care services. The figure according to the National Health Accounts Data for 2004–2005 is 28 % as against the target of 10 %. Even out of this small amount, a major proportion is for wages and salaries as against drugs and other medical requirements.

Though public health expenditure in India is shockingly low, 'out of pocket' expenses are rather high as mentioned earlier. In 2007 total health expenditure, consisting of both private and public, was as high as 4.1 % of the GDP. Private spending on health during the corresponding period was almost 74 % out of the total spending on health, as against 18 % in the UK. About 90 % of this expenditure was in the form of 'out of pocket' expenditure on health by households, being the highest in Asia (Van Doorslaer and Others 2007). Consequently a large section of the poor people in India is deprived from health-care facilities, as they are not able to avail of expensive health care provided by the private sector.

It is therefore evident from our study that in view of the significant influence of public health expenditure on life expectancy in India and the small percentage of government allocation in this sector, a lot more needs to be done in raising public spending on health, which may go a long way in raising the health status in India, through higher life expectancy. In this context it is pertinent to mention that the theoretical model for studying the relationship between life expectancy and economic growth has been examined by Barro and Sala-I_Martin (1995) in the 'conditional convergence model' which focusses attention to the importance of investment in the health sector. It is postulated by the study of Levine and Renelt (1992) and Sala-I_Martin (1997a, b) that out of more than 32,000 regressions involving permutations of over 60 variables, initial life expectancy was a positive and significant predictor of economic growth during 1960–1992 in more than 92 % of the specifications (Bloom and Canning, 2005), reiterating the role of health as an important determinant of economic growth.

3. The model which we have developed for the purpose of our analysis to examine the impact of per capita health expenditure (including both private and public) on infant mortality is as follows:

$$\mathrm{imr} = \mathrm{a} + \mathrm{b}\,pche + \mathrm{u} \tag{4.3}$$

where 'imr' is the infant mortality rate, which is a dependent variable, and *pche* is the per capita health expenditure, being the independent variable.

The estimated results reveal the following:

$$\begin{aligned} \mathrm{imr} &= 12.063 - .579\,pche \qquad \mathrm{R}^2 = .336;\ \mathrm{F} = 30.31 \\ \mathrm{t} &= (13.520)\ (-5.506) \end{aligned} \tag{4.3}$$

This model too can be accepted due to the theoretical and statistical soundness of the results. If per capita health expenditure rises by 1 %, infant mortality can be reduced by 57 %. The coefficient of the independent variable too is statistically significant. However, R^2 is only .33, implying a low level of coefficient of determination and lower level of explanatory power of the model. Similar studies have revealed that rather than an aggregative level, the explanatory power of the model improves by disaggregating expenditure into public and private expenditure and studying its impact on life expectancy (Issa and Quattara 2005).

The importance of public expenditure on health assumes great significance for a nation like India where about 33 % of the people are still below the poverty line and cannot afford to pay for health expenditure since they are too poor even for meeting the expenses for the basic needs of life.

Studies have revealed (Gupta et al. 2001) from an evidence of 70 countries that public health expenditure on health is more important for the poor in low-income countries than in the high-income ones. This suggests higher return on health spending in the former group of countries than in the latter. Consequently the impact of private and public health expenditure has important policy implications for reducing infant mortality in a country dominated by people below the poverty line. However, a study by Musgrave (1996) indicates that there is no instance of expenditure on health as a share of GDP reducing child mortality, for either rich or poor countries. The share of public health expenditure to the GDP is found to have no impact separately for those who spend on child mortality, whether for all countries taken together or separately with high or low proportion of public health expenditure according to Musgrave. According to the study, per capita income or the economic status has a greater degree of explanatory power to explain child mortality. However, the study did not disaggregate health expenditure into public expenditure and private expenditure. On the other hand, it is maintained (Issa and Quattara 2005) that expenditure on health is an influential determinant of IMRs, but measuring the impact necessitates disaggregating it into private and public expenditure. Secondly, public expenditure on health is the main channel through which health of children at low stages of development is improved, but as development takes place and as a country attains a higher level of development, private expenditure on health takes the lead and becomes the primary channel that affects IMRs. The paper further concludes using data for 160 countries for the period from 1980 to 2000 using panel data techniques, supporting the findings strongly. Specifically public health expenditure was found to be highly significant among the low-income countries, where according to the study, increase in public health expenditure by 1 % reduces infant mortality by 0.16 % Rich countries did not reveal any such relationship for public health expenditure. In contrast, for private health expenditure, even among low-income countries, no relationship of the above two variables was evident, though it is significant for rich countries, where 1 % increase in private health expenditure results in 0.36 % to 85 % fall in IMRs.

4. The next model on similar lines that were estimated was developed to regress infant mortality rates on the rates of per capita public expenditure on health which is specified below:

$$\mathrm{imr} = \mathrm{a} + \mathrm{b}\,pcpeh + \mathrm{u} \tag{4.4}$$

$$\mathrm{imr_r} = \mathrm{a} + \mathrm{b}\,pcpeh + \mathrm{u} \tag{4.5}$$

$$\mathrm{imr_u} = \mathrm{a} + \mathrm{b}\,pcpeh + \mathrm{u} \tag{4.6}$$

where *pcpeh* is per capita public expenditure on health and the subscripts ‘r’ and ‘u’ refer to the rural and urban sectors respectively.

The estimated results are as follows:

$$\text{imr} = 15.70 - .571 pcpeh + u \qquad R^2 = .326;\ F = 29.014 \qquad (4.4)$$
$$t = (10.42)\ (-5.39)$$

$$\text{imr}_r = 53.803 - .406 pcpeh + u \qquad R^2 = .212;\ F = 8.869 \qquad (4.5)$$
$$t = (11.450)\ (-2.978)$$

$$\text{imr}_u = 37.83 - .550 pcpeh + u \qquad R^2 = .303;\ F = 14.26 \qquad (4.6)$$
$$t = (11.450)\ (-2.978)$$

It is therefore revealed that the results are acceptable and they corroborate the results of other studies on similar lines. In other words, the model is acceptable both on theoretical and statistical grounds. However, R^2 is only .326, implying a low level of coefficient of determination and lower level of explanatory power of the model, which may be due to the fact that the impact of per capita public health expenditure on infant mortality works out over a period of time. The models have also been examined separately for the rural and urban sectors. It is revealed that the model has better explanatory power in the urban than in the rural sector. This may imply that poor health management in the rural sector results in the health expenditure being not as effective as in the urban sector, where management may be slightly better in comparison to the rural sectors. This may also imply that mere allocation of resources is not always the only determinant factor; what may sometimes be more important is the proper management and best utilisation of the allocated resources.

5. In the next models, we have attempted to examine the impact of per capita public health expenditure on maternal mortality. The models developed for the purpose of this analysis are as follows:

$$\text{mr} = \text{a} - \text{b}\ pcpeh + u \qquad (4.7)$$

$$\text{mr}_u = \text{a} - \text{b}\ pcpeh + u \qquad (4.8)$$

$$\text{mr}_r = \text{a} - \text{b}\ pcpeh + u \qquad (4.9)$$

In the above models, 'mr ' is maternal mortality, with the subscripts 'u' and 'r' representing urban and rural sectors, respectively, and ' *pcpeh*' represents the per capita public expenditure on health and 'u' the usual error term.

The minus sign before the coefficient of the explanatory variable indicates the theoretical relationship of the model, meaning that maternal mortality rate and per capita public health expenditure are inversely related. The higher the amount of such expenditure, the lower the rate of maternal mortality. We have also attempted to examine separately the impact of public health expenditure in the rural and urban sectors since the level of poverty is higher in the rural areas in India, and therefore the dependence on public health expenditure is higher than in the urban sectors, where due to better economic condition, dependence on public health system is lower than in the rural sectors.

The results of the estimated models of maternal mortality are reported below:

$$\begin{aligned} mr &= 74.816 - .610\,pcpeh + u \qquad R^2 = .405;\ F = 10.08 \\ t &= (10.690)\ (-3.175) \end{aligned} \tag{4.7}$$

$$\begin{aligned} mr_u &= 51.449 - .670\,pcpeh + u \qquad R^2 = .469;\ F = 13.856 \\ t &= (13.662)\ (-3.722) \end{aligned} \tag{4.8}$$

$$\begin{aligned} mr_u &= 80.314 - .620\,pcpeh + u \qquad R^2 = .395;\ F = 10.688 \\ t &= (11.063)\ (3.262) \end{aligned} \tag{4.9}$$

The estimated result of the above models is quite satisfactory both in terms of the value of the independent variables and the coefficient of determination R^2, the value of which though not very high can nevertheless be accepted, in view of its statistical significance as revealed by the value of 'F', as well as the theoretical and statistical significance of the coefficient of the independent variables. Though per capita public health expenditure is extremely crucial, the fact remains that the impact on maternal mortality is determined by many more factors than only per capita health expenditure which may have long-term impact on maternal mortality, and therefore cross-sectional panel data may not always capture the full influence and role of public health expenditure as in the case of infant mortality.

It may be noted that examining the model separately for the urban and the rural areas, due to the fact that the impact of public health expenditure has a spatial significance, reveals some interesting information. The results particularly for the urban sector are more acceptable in contrast to the rural sector, as well as the overall result for the country as a whole. Though it was assumed earlier that the impact of public health expenditure in the rural areas will be more due to the greater level of poverty, the results indicate a different pattern. The model is better explained for the urban sector than for the rural sector, implying that the public health expenditure has a greater impact on maternal mortality in the urban sector than in the rural sector. The reason for this could be that public expenditure in the urban sector results in better health infrastructure, availability of trained doctors, nurses, midwives and drugs and medicines as well as equipment, all of which are grossly lacking in the rural sector. Better education, better awareness of health, cleanliness and regularity in check-ups for the mother in the urban areas may result in greater impact of public health expenditure. It may thus be that while the explanatory power of the model as revealed by the value of R^2 is .405 in the rural sector, it is almost .5 in the urban sector. The value of the explanatory variable in the estimated equation, that is, per capita public health expenditure, is also higher in the latter case, being as high as .670 as compared to the rural sector which is .620. However, both the models are theoretically as well as statistically significant, implying that maternal mortality is surely determined by public health expenditure. Therefore, what is important to realise is that, though such expenditure is crucial as a determinant of health, its impact is determined by the way health investment is made. If there are no ways of incurring the expenditure either on physical or manpower infrastructure, free drugs and medicines, the ability of public health expenditure to influence health status is surely and certainly restricted. Therefore mere expenditure by itself is not enough; the expenditure has to be judiciously spent in a planned manner. In its absence resource allocation for the sector will be meaningless and the measurement of health outcome cannot be compared with the health cost per unit. Due to this the effectiveness of health expenditure may be lost and inefficiency will be the ultimate result. This will result in wastage of the scarce resources and may also result in diversion of resources to some other channels, which in turn is likely to adversely affect future allocation of resources to the sector.

It is therefore essential for policymakers in the health sector to realise that allocation of scarce resources in the health sector should be accompanied by a judicious planning on the exact items on which the expenditure needs to be incurred. It is only then that health investment will be meaningful and can positively impact the health outcome of a nation. This highlights the fact that health policy and health management are equally important even if not more than health expenditure in determining the health status of a nation.

There is no one single factor to determine maternal mortality; a strong health system, skilled delivery attendant and women's right for maternal health are crucial. Studies (Buor and Bream 2004) have revealed that in sub-Saharan Africa, births attended by skilled health personnel and life expectancy at birth strongly correlate with maternal mortality. Gross national product (GNP) and per capita health expenditure also have strong correlation with maternal mortality. Per capita health expenditure is therefore only one of the factors affecting maternal mortality and not the only factor according to the study. The other determinant factors accepted in the study were availability of skilled delivery personnel, life expectancy and national economic wealth. It is therefore not surprising that health expenditure taken alone, as an explanatory variable, did not emerge as a highly significant factor in our analysis. In another study of a similar nature, relating to data for 141 countries, it is revealed that proportion of deliveries assisted by skilled birth attendants and health expenditure per capita emerge as important determinants. Another study for sub-Saharan Africa reveals (Alvarez and Other 2009) that maternal mortality rates were high and vary among countries. Some correlation between maternal mortality ratio and some educational, economic and sanitary factors was observed in the study. The study revealed that there exists an inverse and significant correlation of maternal mortality ratio with prenatal care coverage, birth assisted by skilled personnel, access to improved water, adult literacy rate, primary female enrolment ratio, educational index, GNP per capita and per capita government expenditure on health.

It is therefore evident from the findings of the studies above that health expenditure is an important determinant of maternal mortality, but there are also many other important factors along with health expenditure that determine maternal mortality. However, since the present work confines itself only to expenditure as a determinant of health status, we have not incorporated the other factors for the purpose of the present study.

The model has also been tested with some other health indicators such as death rates, crude death rates, underweight children and also children with stunted growth. However, since the results are not satisfactory in terms of either the explanatory power of the model or the independent coefficient or the theoretical or statistical significance of the results, we have not reported the results here, though in no way do they diminish the significance of health investment for these health outcomes. In other words, we have concluded that though health expenditure is an important determinant for all the indicators of health status, they do not influence these indicators directly, and therefore to improve these indicators, instead of emphasising on the expenditure alone, which is no doubt extremely crucial, we may need to explore the other determinants of these health outcomes as well.

6. In the final analysis, to capture the essence of the various components of health expenditure separately, in the next model, all the explanatory variables are taken separately as independent variables to develop a multiple regression model.

   The model thus adopted is as follows:

$$\mathrm{L\,exp} = \mathrm{a} + \mathrm{b}pche + \mathrm{c}\,pvhe + \mathrm{d}pcphe + u \tag{4.10}$$

where

$pche$ = per capita health expenditure,
$pvhe$ = per capita private health expenditure,
$pcphe$ = per capita public health expenditure and
u = error term.

The model has been examined with respect to all the other indicators of health status mentioned earlier. However, the estimated equation that is most acceptable theoretically as well as statistically is reported below.

The estimated results are as follows:

$$\begin{aligned} \mathrm{L\,exp} &= 70.35 + .440pche + .381pvhe + .073pcphe + u \\ \mathrm{t} &= (73.55)\ (4.182)\qquad (3.63)\qquad (1.788) \\ &\qquad\qquad\qquad\qquad \mathrm{R}^2 = .503;\ \mathrm{F} = 19.598 \end{aligned} \tag{4.10}$$

The explanatory power of the model is as high as 50 % as is evident from the value of R^2, which is also statistically significant as indicated by the value of 'F'. The independent variables too are all statistically significant with appropriate 't' values, and they also have the requisite positive signs, implying that life expectancy can certainly improve when health expenditure, be it private or public, increases. Therefore a certain way to improve life expectancy is to increase health expenditure as is also evident from the health expenditure and its impact on life expectancy in all other nations of the world, particularly those nations which have not yet reached totally maturity as far as health status is concerned.

Taking an overall view of the entire analysis of the impact of health expenditure on the various parameters of health status, the study reveals that the impact of health expenditure on all the other parameters does not appear to be very significant.

However, this in no way suggests that the importance of health expenditure can be ignored. It may imply that the effect is spread over a long time period or the effects work out through other variables in an indirect manner. The important parameters of health status on which health expenditure can have a direct impact are represented in a diagrammatic form (Diagram 4.1):

Here it needs to be mentioned that the impact of private health expenditure on health indicators is higher than that of public expenditure and is immediate and is experienced in the short run. This is in contrast to the often indirect as well as long-term permanent impact of public health expenditure. The reasons for the difference are not far to seek. Private health expenditure is incurred to tackle the immediate health problems of the individuals, such as illness and diseases. The costs are in the nature of medicines and drugs, cost of hospitalisation, fee for the doctors and nurses, laboratory tests, etc. Public health expenditure is mostly in the nature of investment in health infrastructure both physical and manpower, including their salaries and wages, medical equipment and tools and machineries; expenditure on such items mostly have long-term impact. Public health expenditure is incurred on immunisation, safe drinking water, sanitation-related problems, investment in health infrastructure and also medical education. The impact of such investment is often spread over the years to be experienced. Moreover it is also a matter of policy decision whether public expenditure on health is to be incurred simultaneously on the entire sector or in terms of certain priorities. In case priorities are not right, the desired impact on health status will also be delayed. The health management issues in the

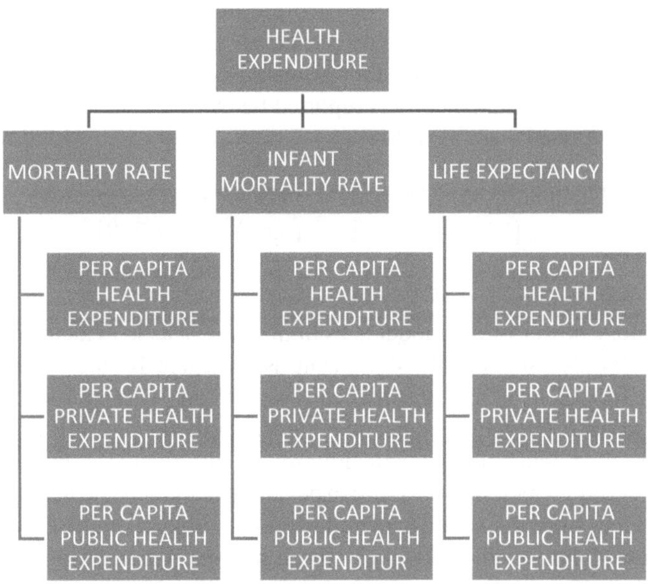

Diagram 4.1 Health indicators affected by health expenditure

public health sector often leave a lot to be desired in contract to the private sector where health service delivery is undertaken in a much more professional manner. Consequently health service delivery mechanism is less ineffective in spite of substantial financial investment in public health. That perhaps could be the reason why the explanatory power of the coefficient of the public health expenditure is lower than that of the private health expenditure. That is also the reason for the average of health expenditure per capita falling in between the two types of expenditure, private and public.

Though a good number of studies have been conducted on health expenditure for high-income countries, the same is not true for the low-income countries. Most nations incur health expenditure, which varies between 3 % and 12 % of their GDP. The extent of public health expenditure in India is shockingly low, as is evident from the very low proportion of GDP allocated for the purpose, which is lower than the minimum of 3 % by the global average. Public health expenditure in India is not only low but is also highly uneven across different states of the country. According to a study (Rao and Govinda 2008), the reason for this is the unequal distribution of resources for health across different states. The result of this is that the states which are unable to generate enough resources through revenue generation are also unable to allocate a greater proportion of budgetary resources for health care. This has also resulted in lower per capita expenditure on health, in spite of higher proportion of GDSP allocation for health purposes by the low-income states. According to the study, the reason for this is the fact that the specific purpose transfer under the Centrally Sponsored Health Schemes has weaker equalisation impact than the shares of taxes and grants as per the Finance Commission recommendations. Though equalisation of health expenditure does not ensure equalisation of health status, it is certainly an important step towards equalisation of opportunities.

The importance of health expenditure as a factor determining health status was all too evident when government initiated the NRHM as the centrally sponsored schemes incorporating all aspects of health and family welfare. The purpose was to ensure countrywide minimum expenditure on health so that due to inadequacy of funds, small and low-income states should not be adversely affected.

It is a matter of concern in India that the cost of health care has in recent years increased much more than the increase in the general price level. This has imposed a greater burden in terms of health finance particularly for those low-income and low-revenue generating states like Madhya Pradesh, Orissa, Bihar, Uttar Pradesh and Rajasthan. Health policy in the country is therefore to be reviewed and restructured periodically. This will improve the national health status which otherwise is abysmally poor, due to poor performance of these few states and due to inadequate health resources and investment.

4.10 Conclusion and Main Findings

The conclusion that is drawn from the analysis is that health expenditure in general and public health expenditure in particular can determine the extent to which health status in a country can be determined by health investment. This in turn can reveal the extent of influence that health expenditure can have on some of the indicators of health status such as life expectancy, infant mortality and maternal mortality. For policy purpose this has a crucial significance, because policymakers will be able to understand where only expenditure plays an important role; more expenditure may need to be invested in that area. Indicators of health status which is not influenced in any significant manner by expenditure may indicate that investing more in that sector of health will not give the requisite result. In such cases the remedy lies perhaps in better ways of utilising the existing resources or perhaps better health management. The findings have also been segregated into rural and urban sectors. This kind of findings can help the policymakers delving further into the analysis in deciding whether health expenditure on a certain indicator of health is equally relevant in both the urban and the rural sectors or whether different types of policies need to be adopted for the urban as well as the rural sectors. It is often the case that uniform policies for health sector is adopted for a vast country like India without taking into consideration that different factors are at play in different places depending upon the amount of allocation of financial resources to the health sector. It is true that such micro policy analysis is extremely difficult. However, for an important sector like the health which is still in a deplorable state, there is no alternative to such efforts even at the cost of being a little cumbersome for the clients of the health-care delivery system. The result is the same set of policies which are successful in one place and unsuccessful in another place, and there is still a wide disparity in health condition among different strata of the society in different parts of the country and regions as well as between rural and urban areas. Universal access and universal coverage of health-care delivery system are therefore still a far cry, all this in spite of allocating huge resources in the health sector.

The study reveals that the relationship of health expenditure with infant mortality and maternal mortality is inverse and the relationship between life expectancy and health expenditure is direct. This only goes to mean that when health expenditure is increased, both infant mortality and maternal mortality go down and life expectancy increases. The impact of health expenditure on these various indicators of health status is however not direct and involves long-term process for the full effect to be evident. This could be the reason for the low impact of health expenditure on maternal mortality, because the effect to be evident on maternal mortality involves a longer process than the effect on infant mortality, the impact of which involves a shorter period. It is also interesting to note that the effect of health expenditure is again different in rural and urban areas, and the explanatory power of the independent variable is higher in the urban sectors. This could also be due to the poor management of health delivery system in the rural areas.

However, in spite of the importance of health expenditure, particularly in developing countries, there are very few studies on this aspect. In view of poor health status in most of these countries, it is extremely crucial that greater in-depth study needs to be undertaken to examine the impact of health expenditure in such countries and health policies formulated accordingly. It is a fact that low-income countries record as low as $30 per capita on health expenditure in contrast to high-income countries which spend as high as $ 300 per capita on health. Even the proportion of GDP spent on health as revealed varies from as low as 3 % to 12 % between low-income and high-income countries. Studies relating to OECD (Wagstaff and Others 2009) revealed that health expenditure per capita was higher in countries where social health insurance mechanism exists. It is revealed that per capita public health expenditure was higher in countries that relied solely on general taxes. Health expenditure is also determined by technological progress and variation in medical practice and health system characteristics. For instance, technological progress determines the variation in medical practices, which in turn determines health indicators like life expectancy and infant mortality (Dreger and Remers 2005). However, such studies have not been conducted for low-income countries but confined mostly to the OECD nations.

The age structure of the population is an important determinant of public health services; public health expenditure in places where the population structure is dominated by the aged will rise. In case health expenditure is not elastic in response to change in age structure, health status is bound to go down. The prevalence of diseases and the nature and type of the same also impact health expenditure. For instance, as highlighted earlier, India is confronted with the diseases of a low-income nation like malaria, diarrhoea, TB and leprosy and also with the aliments of a developed country like cancer, diabetes, heart diseases, etc. The nature and pattern of such diseases demand a higher proportion of spending on the health sector. However, the irony is that the health expenditure in India is appallingly low and much lower than the global average or the lower margin of health expenditure by global standard.

It may thus be concluded that health expenditure is undoubtedly an important determinant of health status, due to which it is imperative that nations characterised by low health status should increase health expenditure. However, increase in health expenditure is determined by higher GDP. A low-income nation is constrained to raise health expenditure and there are numerous alternative demands on its meagre resources. On the other hand, high GDP is also determined by better health status of the population as is revealed from the discussion on this aspect in the first chapter. Therefore higher health expenditure and GDP have a causal relation with a time lag. It is very different to say as to which is the cause and which is the effect. When public health expenditure does not increase, OOP (out of pocket) expenditure increases and reaches the catastrophic level, meaning that health expenditure reduces the consumption of necessities below the required levels as is the case in India. It is revealed that (Pal 2010) OOP is higher among the poor and among those households with children and elderly people. Therefore health policies should emphasise more on spending for such category of the population, particularly in the rural areas among the poorer classes.

The low priority assigned to the health sector in India is thus evident from the very low percentage of GDP for public health expenditure. As per the data for the

National Health Accounts (2008–2009), out of the total health expenditure in our country, as high as 71.6 % was private expenditure and only 26.7 % was public expenditure, and external assistance was only 1.7 %. The Steering Committee on Health constituted by the Planning Commission has also admitted that the health-care system in the country suffers from inadequate funding, existence of structural problems, lack of integration between disease control and other programmes in the social sector, suboptimal use of traditional systems of medicines, weak regulatory systems for drugs as well as for medical practice and poor capacity in public health management. A sound health system requires participation and awareness by the community, the importance of which is discussed in the subsequent sections. The committee has also further recommended making the health system responsive to the needs of the citizens and attaining financial protection for the health care of the households.

References

Al Varez JL, Gil R, Hernandez V, Gil A (2009) Factors associated with maternal mortality in Sub Saharan Africa: an empirical study. https://creativeconomics.org/licenses/by/2.0

Anand S, Ravallion M (1993) Human development in poor countries: on the role of private income and public services. J Econ Perspect 7:133–150

Baal P, Obulquasim P, Brouwer P, Nusselder W, Mackenbach W (2013) The influence of health care spending on life expectancy. J Health Spend Life Expect, Panel Paper 35

Baroo RJ, Sala-I-Martin X (1995) Economic growth. McGraw-Hill, New York

Betron AP, Wojdyla D, Posner SF, Gulmezoghu AM (2005) National estimates for maternal mortality: an analysis based on WHO systematic review of maternal mortality and morbidity. http://www.biomedcentral.com/1471-2458/5/131

Bhalotra S. Spending to save? State health expenditure and infant mortality in India

Bloom DE, Canning D (2005) Health and economic growth: reconciling the micro and macro evidence. Working Paper No. 42, Centre on Democracy, Development and the Rule of Law, Stanford Institute of International Studies, pp 2, 3

Buor D, Bream K (2004) An analysis of the determinants of maternal in mortality Sub Saharan Africa. J Women's Health 13(8):926–938

Carrion-i-Silrestre JL (2005) Health care expenditure and GDP: are they broken stationary? J Health Econ 24(5):839–851

Cutler DM, McClellan M (2001) Is technological change in medicine worth it? Health Aff 20(5):11–29

Cutler D, Deaton A, Lieras-Muney A (2006) The determinants of mortality. J Econ Perspect 20:97–120

Dreger C, Romers HE (2005) Health care expenditure in OECD countries: a panel unit root cointegration analysis. Discussion Paper, 1469, Bonn

Economic Research Foundation (2006) Government health expenditure in India: a benchmark study. Economic Research Foundation, New Delhi

Filmer D, Pritchett L (1999) The impact of public spending on health: does money matter. Soc Sci Med 49(10):1309–1323

Fortney JA, Smith JB (1999) Measuring maternal morbidity. In: Berer M, Ravindran TKS (eds) Safe motherhood: critical issues. Blackwell Science, Oxford

Gerdtham U-G, Jonsson B (2000) International comparisons of health expenditure. In: Culyer AJ, Newhouse JP (eds) Handbook of health economics (vols 1A and 1B:Chapter I). Elsevier, Amsterdam

Govt Health Expenditure in India: A Benchmark Study (2006) Economic research Foundation, New Delhi

Grossman M (1972) On the concept of health capital and the demand for health. J Polit Econ 80:223–255

Grossman M (2000) The human capital model. In: Culyer AJ, Newhouse JP (eds) Handbook of health economics, vol 1a. Elsevier, Amsterdam

Gupta S, Verhoeven M, Tiongson E (2001) Public spending on health care and the poor, IMF weekly papers No. WP/99/21. International Monetary Fund, Washington, DC

Hansen P, King A (1996) The determinants of health care expenditure: a cointegration approach. J Health Econ 15(1):127–137

Hopkins S (2010) Health expenditure comparisons, Low, middle and high income countries. Open Health Ser Policy J 3:111–117

IIPS (2010) District Level Household and Facility Survey (DLHS-3) 2007–08: India. International Institute of Population Sciences, Mumbai

Issa H, Quattara B (2005) The effect of private and public health expenditure on infant mortality rates: does the level of development matter? Damascus University, Damascus

Levine R, Renelt D (1992) A sensitivity analysis of cross country growth regressions. Am Econ Rev 82(4):942–963

MacDonald G, Hopkins S (2002) Unit root properties of OECD health care expenditure and GDP data. Health Econ 11:371–376

Macenbach JP, Looman CWN, Kunst AE, Abbema JDF, Van Der Maas PJ (1988) Post-1950 mortality trends and medical care “gains in life expectancy due to decline in mortality from conditions amenable to medical intervention in the Netherlands”. Soc Sci Med 27:889–894

Musgrave P (1996) Public and private roles in health: theory and financing pattern, Health, nutrition and population (HNP), discussion paper. World Bank, Washington, DC

Muskin SJ (1962) Health as an investment. J Polit Econ 70:129–157

Nolte E, McKee M (2004) Does health care save lives? The Nuffield Trust, London

Pal, R (2010) Analysing catastrophic OOP health expenditure in India: Concepts, Determinantsand Policy Implications, W.P. IGIDS, Mumbai

Paxson C, Schady N (2005) Child health and economic crisis in Peru. World Bank Econ Rev 19(2):203–233

Preston SH (1976) Mortality patterns in national population. Academic, New York

Rajkumar AS, Swaroop V (2002) Public spending and outcomes: does governance matter. In: World bank policy research, working paper 2840. The World Bank, Washington, DC

Rao M, Govinda C (2008) Inter state equalisation of health expenditure in Indian Union, National Institute of Public Finance and Policy

Rao MDR, Krishna AK, Shiva M, Kumar C, Sundaraman T (2011) Human resources for health in India, The Lancet Series, India: Towards Universal Health Coverage

Riley JC (2001) Rising life expectancy: a global history. Cambridge University Press, New York

Sala-I-Martin X (1997a) I just ran four million regressions. Economic Working Paper 201, Department of Economics and Business, Universitat, Pompeu, Fabra

Sala-I-Martin X (1997b) I just ran two million regressions. Am Econ Rev 87(2):178–83

Sen A (1998) Mortality as an indicator of success and failure. Econ J 108:1–25

Stenberg KR, Elovainio D, Chisholm D, Fuhr A, Perucic M, Rekve D, Yurekli A (2010) Responding to the challenges of resource mobilisation. Mechanisms for raising additional resources in India, Background paper. WHO, Geneva

Tandon A, Cashin C (2010) Assessing public expenditure on health from a fiscal space perspective, Health nutrition and population (HNP), discussion paper. World Bank, Washington, DC

Van Doorslaer E, O’Donnel O, Rannan-Eliya RP et al (2007) Catastrophic payments for health care in Asia. Health Econ 16:1159–1184

Wagstaff A, Yip W, Lindelow M, Hsiaowilliam C (2009) China’s health system and its reform: a review of recent studies. Health Econ 18(S2):S7–S23

Chapter 5
Determinants of Health Status

5.1 Introduction

There is no single index for measuring the health status of a country or society, as it is a multidimensional concept. In the absence of such an index, we use a number of indicators to represent health status. Though the health status of an individual is diagnosed by a physician, for evaluating the health status of a society or population, aggregation of health data is the only way to assess the health status. There is, however, no comprehensive or absolute measure to assess the health status of a population. It may be mentioned here that most of the health indicators are actually negative aspects of health. These negative indicators in fact help us in estimating the status of health since a decline in these indicators implies an improvement in the health condition. Some of these indicators which have been selected for the present study are infant mortality, child mortality, maternal mortality, death rates, crude death rates, percentage of underweight children, percentage of stunted children and life expectancy as already discussed in the earlier sections. For most of these indicators, we have tried to segregate them into rural and urban sectors in an attempt to know the difference in health status between the two sectors.

For policy purposes and also for sectoral allocation of resources within the health sector, it is extremely crucial that the determinants of the health sector along with its indicators are identified. As all determinants do not affect all the indicators of health status in an identical manner, it is important to understand the differences in weightage of these determinants for different indicators. In fact, the way a certain determinant affects a certain health indicator in rural area may not be the same as it affects the same indicator in the urban area. This is more relevant for a vast country like India with so much of disparity between the urban and the rural areas in terms of their socioeconomic condition, which in turn affects the health status and their determinants. As a result, the analysis of the entire study through the use of econometric models has been done separately for the rural and the urban sectors as far as feasible. Such a methodology is expected to provide a spatial picture of the health

K. Sengupta, *Determinants of Health Status in India*,
DOI 10.1007/978-81-322-2535-5_5

status in the country, since disaggregated data reveals a clear picture for facilitating the policy makers. The determinants of these health indicators selected for the purpose of the present study are the level of literacy, particularly female literacy, immunisation, health infrastructure both physical and manpower, clean drinking water as well as sanitation facilities. Some of the determinants have direct impact on health status, while the others have an indirect impact. The impact of some of these factors is evident immediately, while for some others the effect works out over a period of time. This experience is evident from the study of health expenditure and its impact on health indicators, which we have been analysed separately in the previous chapter. Apart from these factors, many other factors combine to affect the health of the individuals and the community. Environment and circumstances, such as the living conditions, surrounding environment, income level, social status and sometimes even the working environment and occupation, can influence the health status. Access and use of health-care services also have an impact on the status of health of the people.

Depending upon the state of development of the country concerned, the social support system of the country, like the support from the health schemes of the government, community, families and friends, also determines the health status of the people. Genetic condition also influences in a very significant way the status of health. Longevity apart from all other factors is also determined by inheritance which can determine the possibility of developing certain illness which is gene determined. Personal behaviour and traits such as food habits, balanced eating, drinking and smoking habits or a disciplined and regulated lifestyle all combine to determine the status of health of the people.

In this context it is extremely important to mention the health status of women in determining the general health status of the people of a nation. Since the child is dependent on the mother right from the time of conception, many aspects of a woman's life such as her physical and psychological aspects, her nutritional status and her general health status affect the health status of the child. Poor health status of women particularly in developing countries is only too evident from all the data on health indicators of those nations. Women in all nations are worse off in comparison with men in all health indicators. This in turn is a matter of great concern as poor health of women has a wide ramification and great implications for overall health status of a nation.

5.2 Education as a Determinant Factor of Health

Education and health are very closely related which is evident from the experience of both the developed and the less developing nations and also highlighted in the literature survey in Chapter three. Common experience reveals that a person's ability and the knowledge to maintain his health are determined by his level of education. Knowledge about various types of diseases, the ways to prevent them or the curative measures is determined totally by the extent of knowledge which in turn depends on the level of education. Even the ability of a child to attend school regularly and continue his education is determined by his health condition. The attitude towards sanitation, utility of clean drinking water and hygienic condition of living depends on the degree of awareness, attitude which again depends on people's knowledge.

Experience throughout the world has also revealed that citizens with more education are also more health conscious. They understand the utility of good nutritious food, clean drinking water and sanitation. Therefore increasing the level of education and health awareness particularly among the disadvantaged groups has direct impact on health status. It is a fact that infant and maternal mortality, low life expectancy at birth and incidence of diarrhoea, malaria and tuberculosis are more among the disadvantaged sections who often possess little education. This is the experience throughout the world. Therefore assessing the status of health is incomplete and meaningless without a study of the educational level of the health service consumers, since the two social aspects cannot be studied in isolation. A well-coordinated health policy should thus incorporate literacy, education and awareness along with health programmes.

Though education does not directly affect health status, however it does create the potential mechanism through which health status can be improved. A study conducted for Swedish men born between 1945 and 1955 reveals that an additional year of schooling reduces the risk of bad health by 18.5 % (Spasojevic 2003). Another study conducted for Indonesia reveals that an increase in the average number of years of education in the household reduces child mortality by approximately 10 % points from a mean level of 22.5 % (Breierova and Dufla 2004). There are a good number of studies which have estimated the benefits of education and additional years of learning on the increased income due to better health, mortality rates, life expectancy and other health indicators. However, the effect certainly varies depending on the type of education or the stage and age of life when education was imparted. Though many studies have been conducted on the economic effect of education, similar studies on health status have not received much attention mainly due to the fact that the impact of education on health is much broader in scope effecting wider set of outcomes. Apart from general education, literacy is all about harnessing the benefits of education and learning that extend beyond the acquisition of information towards overall personal growth.

According to a Report by the National Bureau of Economic Research (2012, January), the causal effect of education on health necessitates subsidies for education if individual's investment in education is at a suboptimal level. The rationale behind this is that individuals may be unaware of the health benefits of education when they make their decisions about education. They may also be unaware of the externalities to education and health beyond the individuals affected. The Report further highlights the fact that an additional 4 years of education lowers the mortality below 5 years by 1.8 % points. It also reduces heart diseases by 2.16 % points and the risk of diabetics by 1.3 % points. The relationship between health and education has now been accepted as causal (Lieras-Muney 2005; Clark and Royer 2008), so that a way to improve the health status may be to restructure educational policies. Education can therefore be used as a means of improving health status, particularly when resources are limited for investing in the health sector. Raising the age of compulsory education from 14 to 15 years in the UK as a policy reform in the education sector in 1947 had improved adult health outcomes including mortality (Clark and Royer 2008).

In the developing countries, there is indeed a strong correlation between education and adult health outcomes. However, it has also been shown that (Clark and Royer 2008) there exists a strong correlation between education and even infant mortality. In the Indian context this works out through female literacy. When the mother is educated, she is more aware of and also concerned about the health condition of her children. This reduces the infant mortality rate by reducing the incidence of diarrhoea, malaria and tuberculosis. This is mainly due to the fact that educated mothers are more conscious about the importance of cleaning water, sanitation and general hygiene. Therefore investment in education, particularly female education, can go a long way in improving the health status of children. This was also evident from the study of Sagan (1989) in 'The Health of Nations' after examining historical data for 150 nations, from premodern to highly modern complex societies, that 'by far the most consistently powerful predictor of life expectancy was the prevalence of literacy'. The study also focusses attention to the co-relationship between literacy and mortality in all developing nations, across all cultural regions and time particularly after the Second World War.

Cutler and Muney (2007), too, confirm the relationship between literacy and health status, but conclude that it is highly complex and the mechanisms by which the causal effect works out are difficult to identify. They, however, identified income as one of the important factors working to establish the link between education and health. Better education means better income, which in turn enables the people to allocate more resources for health care. It is also true that even when income is taken as constant, the relationship between health and education still works out to be positive. Apart from income the authors also identify factors such as access to information, general cognitive skills, individual characteristics, rank in society and social networks as well as the differences in value assigned to the future, which are some of the direct consequences of education. These factors in turn have a positive impact on most health indicators.

Fonsica and Zheng (2011) too confirm the strong relationship between education and health. The mechanisms for this relationship identified by them are productive efficiency, i.e. raising efficiency in health production, and allocative efficiency, i.e. changing inputs in health production and changing time preference.

In view of the role that education plays in influencing the health status of a nation, the present work has taken literacy rate to examine the relationship between education and the various indicators of health. Data from the Indian context has been used to test the models that have been developed for the study. Secondary data from the health statistics of India for the year 2011 for the 35 states and UT in India has been used for the purpose of the study. To examine the effect of education on health, separate regression models have been used for general education and also female education, separately for the urban and the rural sectors. Separate models have been developed for the two sectors, because health status as mentioned earlier is a multidimensional aspect; as such the same factors that determine health status in a certain way in one sector may not work exactly in a similar fashion in another area. Consequently, we have examined the model separately for the rural and the urban sector of the Indian economy and the overall impact on the entire economy.

5.2.1 Education as a Determinant of Infant Mortality Rate (Urban and Rural)

The first models to examine the effect of education on health status that has been specified for the purpose are as follows:

$$\text{imr} = \text{a} - \text{b}\mathit{lit} + u \quad (5.1)$$

$$\text{imr}_\text{r} = \text{a} - \text{b}\mathit{lit} + u \quad (5.2)$$

$$\text{imr}_\text{u} = \text{a} - \text{b}\,\mathit{lit} + u \quad (5.3)$$

where 'imr' denotes infant mortality; the subscripts 'r' and 'u' denote rural and urban infant mortality rates, respectively; *lit* denotes the general literacy rate; and 'u' is the usual residual term which represents the composite impact of all other variables which are not explicitly identified in the model.

The negative sign before the independent coefficient implies the inverse relationship between literacy and infant mortality, meaning that the higher the literacy rate, the lower the infant mortality rate.

The estimated results of the above models are as follows:

$$\begin{aligned} \text{imr} &= 144.286 - .717\mathit{lit} + u \qquad \text{R}^2 = .514;\ \text{F} = 34.895 \\ \text{t} &= (8.056)\ (-5.907) \end{aligned} \quad (5.1)$$

$$\begin{aligned} \text{imr}_\text{r} &= 151.521 - .700\mathit{lit} + u \qquad \text{R}^2 = .490;\ \text{F} = 31.67 \\ \text{t} &= (7.738)\ (-5.628) \end{aligned} \quad (5.2)$$

$$\begin{aligned} \text{imr}_\text{u} &= 72.060 - .619\mathit{lit} + u \qquad \text{R}^2 = .383;\ \text{F} = 20.519 \\ \text{t} &= (7.468)\ (-4.530) \end{aligned} \quad (5.3)$$

The first model which examines the impact of education represented by literacy infant mortality rate reveals that the model explains more than 50 % of the relationship as evident from the value of R^2 which is .514. R^2 is also statistically significant as indicated by the value of 'F' which is 34.89. In fact, 70 % of infant mortality is explained by 1 % change in general literacy rate. The coefficient of the independent variable as is evident from the estimated model is also statistically significant as is revealed by the value of ‘t’. The negative sign in the model reveals the theoretical significance of the relationship, implying that as literacy rate rises, there is a decline in the infant mortality rate. It therefore implies that the model is acceptable for our purpose, and it confirms the earlier findings of other studies that education is an important determinant of one of the crucial components of health status that is infant mortality.

With an attempt at spatial confirmation of the above findings, we have examined the model separately for the urban and the rural areas. It is possible particularly in the Indian context that factors determining health status in the rural areas may be different from that in the urban areas, in view of the differences in the socioeconomic condition and also the level of literacy, which in the rural sectors is much lower than in the urban sectors. Consequently, the uniform health policy decisions for all the areas may not yield the expected results.

The estimated model of the impact of education on infant mortality in the rural sector reveals that the explanatory power of the model declines marginally, as R^2 is .490, but is statistically significant as revealed by the value of ‘F’. The negative sign of the coefficient of the independent variable signifies that theoretically the model can be accepted, and the ‘t’ value of the coefficient also signifies that the model is statistically significant. The value of the coefficient of literacy is as high as .70, all of which implies that education plays a significant role in determining infant mortality rate in the rural areas. As the level of education is lower in the rural sectors, any rise in the educational level can immediately affect favourably the infant mortality rate in such areas.

The estimated results of the model in the urban areas reveal that the coefficient of determination R^2 has come down significantly from its national figure. The value is only .383 though it is still statistically significant as is evident from ‘F’ value. The model is however theoretically and statistically acceptable since the coefficient of the independent variable has a negative sign and the ‘t’ value too is 4.530. The value of the coefficient of the explanatory variable has however declined, and in the urban areas, about 60 % of the change in infant mortality is explained by one 1 % change in the general literacy rate. The reason could be that most of the people in the urban areas already possess a certain level of literacy and therefore any further rise in the rate of literacy can affect the infant mortality rate only marginally. Education already plays an important role in such areas due to which the infant mortality rate in general is lower in the urban sectors than in the rural sectors.

The above analysis reveals that education occupies a significant role as a determinant of one of the important indicators of health status that is infant mortality. This corroborates the universal finding of the crucial relationship between education and health. In our analysis an important finding is that the role of education is more dominant in the rural areas in comparison with the urban areas. The reason as mentioned is that the level of education in the urban areas is already high and therefore any further rise in the level of education in the urban sector may not have any more positive effect on infant mortality rate. To reduce infant mortality further, it is not education but ‘other factors’ which might have to be tackled. This finding may be the focus of attention for the policy makers – that to tackle health condition, especially in the rural sectors, greater emphasis needs to be put on education because basic education creates awareness of basic health, which is still lacking in the Indian rural sector, whereas in the urban sector, more emphasis needs to be put on some other determinants, which will be revealed in the course of our study.

5.2.2 *Female Education as a Determinant of Infant Mortality (Urban and Rural)*

Education of women in particular has always been considered to be more effective in controlling infant mortality since it is the mother's awareness about the infant's health care which is more important in this respect. Therefore the next model that has been developed for the study is to examine the impact of female education on infant mortality rate. The following are the models developed for this purpose.

The second set of models to examine the effect of female education on the parameter of infant mortality of health status that has been specified for the purpose is as follows:

$$\mathrm{imr} = \mathrm{a} - \mathrm{b}lit_f + u \tag{5.4}$$

$$\mathrm{imr_r} = \mathrm{a} - \mathrm{b}lit_f + u \tag{5.5}$$

$$\mathrm{imr_u} = \mathrm{a} - \mathrm{b}lit_f + u \tag{5.6}$$

where lit_f represents female literacy; the negative sign indicates that the higher the education of women, the lower the infant mortality rate will be; 'imr' is the infant mortality rate; and 'u' is the usual residual term. The estimated results of the models are stated below:

$$\begin{aligned} \mathrm{imr} &= 112.79 - .714 litf + u \qquad \mathrm{R}^2 = .510;\ \mathrm{F} = 34.377 \\ \mathrm{t} &= (8.870)\ (-5.863) \end{aligned} \tag{5.4}$$

$$\begin{aligned} \mathrm{imr_r} &= 118.849 - .698 litf + u \qquad \mathrm{R}^2 = .488;\ \mathrm{F} = 31.418 \\ \mathrm{t} &= (8.567)\ (-5.605) \end{aligned} \tag{5.5}$$

$$\begin{aligned} \mathrm{imr_u} &= 89.204 - .608 litf + u \qquad \mathrm{R}^2 = .370;\ \mathrm{F} = 19.37 \\ \mathrm{t} &= (6.467)\ (-4.401) \end{aligned} \tag{5.6}$$

The estimated results of the role of women's education on infant mortality reveal that the coefficient of determination reveals that the model explains 50 % of the relationship. Female education explains more than 70 % of the change in infant mortality rate. In other words 1 % rise in female literacy rate can reduce infant mortality by more than 70 %. The model is also statistically significant as revealed by the value of ‘t’ which is 5.863, and it has the requisite sign implying the theoretical significance of the model.

A break-up of the role of women’s education between urban and rural areas reveals that the significance of women’s education is once again more in the rural areas than in the urban areas. The reasons here too could be similar to that for the general education, that is, since the level of education for the females in the urban sectors is already high, any more rise in female literacy does not result in any more substantial decline in infant mortality rate. In contrast, female literacy is still very low in the rural sectors, so that raising can result in a fall in infant mortality rate. This is a finding which can be very significant for the policy makers to decide in which type of education and in which subsectors to make educational investment, in an attempt to tackle infant mortality. This again confirms the findings of all other studies in this respect that women’s education plays an important role for controlling infant mortality. However in the Indian conditions, the significance of women’s education is almost similar to the general education level and the impact is more in the rural areas. In other words, it is not only general education but special attention has to be given to women’s education particularly in the rural sectors.

5.2.3 Education as a Determinant of Mortality Rate (Urban and Rural)

Another concern for declining status of health condition particularly in the developing countries has been the high mortality rates (give some statistics from UNDP Report and WHO Report).

In view of the urgency of reducing the rates of mortality, the present study has attempted to examine the extent of the role of education in this respect. The models developed for the purpose are therefore as follows:

$$\mathrm{mr} = \mathrm{a} - \mathrm{b}\ lit + u \tag{5.7}$$

$$\mathrm{mr_u} = \mathrm{a} - \mathrm{b}\ lit + u \tag{5.8}$$

$$\mathrm{mr_r} = \mathrm{a} - \mathrm{b}\, lit + u \tag{5.9}$$

where ‘mr’ represents the mortality rate; the subscripts ‘u’ and ‘r’ represent urban and rural sectors, respectively; and ‘u’ is the usual residual term.

The estimated results of the models are stated below:

$$\begin{array}{ll} \mathrm{mr} = 197.825 - .733 lit + u & \mathrm{R}^2 = .537;\ \mathrm{F} = 19.68 \\ \mathrm{t} = (6.158)\ (-4.437) & \end{array} \tag{5.7}$$

$$\begin{aligned} mr_u &= 94.604 - .732\mathit{lit} + u \qquad R^2 = .536;\ F = 19.644 \\ t &= (7.538)\ (-4.432) \end{aligned} \tag{5.8}$$

$$\begin{aligned} mr_r &= 205.93 - .718\mathit{lit} + u \qquad R^2 = .515;\ F = 18.087 \\ t &= (5.982)\ (-4.253) \end{aligned} \tag{5.9}$$

The results reveal that R^2 is .561 and is also statistically significant. About 73 % change in mortality rate is explained by 1 % change in education, meaning that education has a very dominant role in determining mortality rates. This is also supported by the negative sign for the coefficient for education and the statistical significance of the coefficient for education which is 4.657.

For spatial analysis, the results of the estimated models reveal that the explanatory power of the model for the urban sector is identical with that for the national figure, though the explanatory power declines marginally in the case of the rural area, though it is still above 50 % as in the case for the national figure. For both the models, the coefficient of the independent variable, i.e. education, continues to be above 70 % like the national figure, and the theoretical and statistical significance of the models leads us to conclude that education has a significant role in determining mortality rates of children, which is equally significant both in the urban and the rural sectors.

It can therefore be concluded that like infant mortality, mortality rate too can be controlled through education which in turn creates awareness about health care, clean water, sanitation, immunisation and general hygiene and cleanliness which are so essential for better health status.

5.2.4 *Female Education as a Determinant of Mortality Rate (Urban and Rural)*

Investment in education of women has been particularly more effective in having a direct impact on the health condition of her children and the family members. Several studies have revealed that every year increase in average education of reproductive age women results in 9.5 % decrease in child deaths. It has been further revealed that in 2009 among the children of less than 5 years, a decline of 8.5 million deaths in comparison with 1070 has been due to educated mothers. The results are more apparent in fewer developing countries. In view of the close relationship between female literacy and infant mortality as discussed above, the following model has been examined. In view of the role of women's education, the following models stated below have been specified taking mortality rate as the dependent variable and female literacy as the explanatory variable:

$$mr = a - b\ \mathit{lit}_f + u \tag{5.10}$$

$$mr_u = a - b\,lit_f + u \tag{5.11}$$

$$mr_r = a - b\,lit_f + u \tag{5.12}$$

where lit_f denotes female literacy.

The estimated results are as follows:

$$\begin{aligned} mr &= 153.98 - .749 lit_f + u \qquad R^2 = .561;\ F = 21.69 \\ t &= (97.24)\ (-4.657) \end{aligned} \tag{5.10}$$

$$\begin{aligned} mr_u &= 117.130 - .697 lit_f + u \qquad R^2 = .486;\ F = 16.098 \\ t &= (6.0300)\ (-4.012) \end{aligned} \tag{5.11}$$

$$\begin{aligned} mr_r &= 161.428 - .738 lit_f + u \qquad R^2 = .544;\ F = 20.302 \\ t &= (7.112)\ (-4.506) \end{aligned} \tag{5.12}$$

The results of the estimated models reveal that the explanatory power of the models with female literacy as the explanatory variable and mortality rate as the dependent variable is .561, .486 and .544, with significant values of 'F'. The models can therefore all be acceptable for our purpose. The models can also all be acceptable in view of the statistical and theoretical significance of the estimated equations. In fact, the explanatory power of the model and the value of the coefficient for the independent variable for women's education are slightly higher than that of the general education discussed in the earlier section. This implies that women's education plays a greater role in this respect. It is further interesting to note that women's education plays a more dominant role in the rural areas than in the urban areas as is clear from the results of the models above. This is extremely important from the point of view of the policy makers since the findings will guide them in making the requisite financial allocation between education, female education and the health sector.

The role of women's education for determining some of the parameters of health in India is thought to be slightly higher than that of general education, yet it is not as high as in most other developed countries because India is still a male-dominated society, where women's say in matters of health care is not always taken into account. In spite of this structure of societal set-up, education both general and women's in particular continues to play a significant role in determining the infant mortality and mortality rates of health status in India (Diagram 5.1).

The above diagram reveals the various indicators of health status that is determined by education, identified by our study.

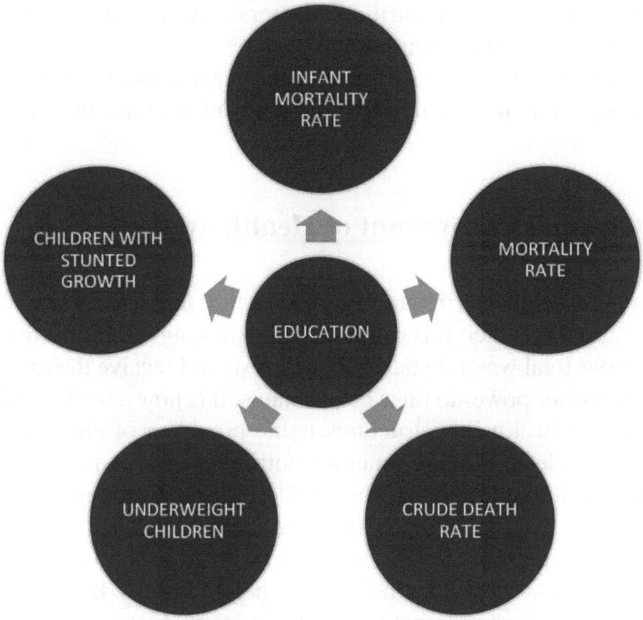

Diagram 5.1 Education and the indicators of health status

5.2.5 *Education as Determinant of Crude Death Rate, Underweight Children and Children with Stunted Growth*

We have further made an attempt to examine the role of education on the other indicators of health status such as death rate, crude death rate, children with stunted growth and also underweight children. The exercise has been undertaken separately for education in general and also women's education in particular. In all the cases the models have theoretical significance and the coefficient of the independent variable is also significant, but due to the low value of R^2 implying poor explanatory power of the models and also statistical insignificance of R^2, the models have not been accepted for our purpose. For this reason the estimated results have therefore not been stated here.

However, this does not belittle the implication of education and women's education for determining these indicators of health status. The reasons for the estimated results not being as per our expectations could be that literacy takes some time to work out and therefore a lagged model might have been more acceptable. Moreover as mentioned earlier the impact of education on health has broad ramifications and involves complex issues of interrelated phenomena and the direct and linear causal relationship may not work out. However, it also implies that for determining these parameters of health, education alone is not the only determining factor and other economic, environmental, and nutritional factors may also be equally important as, if not more important than, education.

On the whole it emerges that education in general and women's education in particular does play an important role in determination of health status of a nation.

5.3 Water as a Determinant of Health Status

One of the most crucial determinants of good health, free from disease, is the provision of clean drinking water. It is estimated that drinking water constitutes even less than 1.0 % of our total water demand, though it should receive the top most priority due to its tremendous power to raise health status. It is now a well-accepted fact that one of the pivotal health infrastructures is the provision of clean drinking water. Health benefits of clean drinking water are both short term and long term. In China, studies have shown that improving the quality of clean drinking water has directly enhanced people's health (Zheng 2010). The illness incidence of adults decreases by 50 % and their weight for height increases by 26 g/cm purely due to clean drinking water. Children's weight for height and height rise by 8 g/cm and 2.49 cm, respectively, due to improved quality of clean drinking water. According to a study conducted by WHO and UNICEF (2006), every year about 1.6 million children under the age of 5 years die due to unsafe water and lack of sanitation and 84 % of the population of the world with access to clean drinking water live in rural areas. About one sixth of the world's population, i.e. a total of 1.1 billion people, remain without access to improved drinking water. It is further revealed that 80 % of the population without access to clean drinking water are from the three regions of sub-Saharan Africa, Eastern Asia and Southern Asia. Figures also reveal that the health statistics of these regions too is the worst by world standard. It is with this purpose that WHO and UNICEF targeted 2015 as the year by which population without access to clean drinking water should be halved.

Monitoring organisations under the supervision of the Joint Monitoring Programme (JMP) define 'safe drinking water' as water from 'improved water source', which includes household connections, public standpipes, boreholes, protected dug wells, protected spring and rainwater connections (Fogdens 2009). International monitoring organisations define 'access to safe drinking water' as the availability of at least 20 l of water per person, per day, from an improved source within one kilometre of the user's dwelling.

There is thus a crucial relationship between access to safe drinking water and health status. According to World Bank Report, 88 % of diseases in the developing world are caused by unsafe drinking water. About 140 cases of cholera, 1,000,000 cases of diarrheal diseases and 114,000 cases of poliomyelitis in a year are caused by the presence of bacteria and viruses in water. Chemical pollution is also a frequent cause of disease, the health effect of which is intergenerational. It is maintained that the increased incidence of cancer in China is due to chemical pollution in waters. Five million people mostly children die every year due to diseases caused by unsafe drinking water. It is also estimated that 80 % of all diseases in the developing world are related to unsafe drinking water supply and inadequate sanitation. Due to the same reason, about 15 million children aged between 0 and 4 years die each year. Half the hospital beds in developing countries are filled with people suffering from diseases associated with poor water, sanitation and hygiene.

The weight of water that women in the less developing countries like Africa and Asia carry on their heads is about 20 kgs, the same as the average UK luggage allowance (HDR). The average person in developing world would use 10 l of water every day for drinking, washing and cooking (WSSCC), while a European uses 200 l. The consumption of water is likely to increase further with time. It is not enough to consume enough water; what is even more important is consumption of clean drinking water. Waterborne diseases such as cholera, diarrhoea, viral hepatitis A, dysentery and typhoid are transmitted through contaminated water. Skin and eye infections are spread when there is a lack of sufficient quantity of water for washing and personal hygiene, and people are unable to keep their hands, bodies and domestic environments clean and hygienic. The incidence of these problems is much higher among the poverty-stricken people. Their children are much more malnourished and therefore more likely to suffer for prolonged period from diarrhoea and other waterborne diseases resulting in weight loss, stunted growth and vitamin deficiency. This leads to greater chances of school dropouts resulting in reduced earnings and more poverty. Poor are therefore caught up in a vicious trap of poverty and poor health status.

It may also be mentioned here that a 'threshold saturation theory' is proposed by researchers on the relation between water supply, sanitation investment and health. The theory attempts to incorporate in one general theoretical framework result of numerical empirical findings. A 'two-tiered S-shaped' logistic form relationship is proposed. The theory maintains that at the lower end of the socioeconomic spectrum, there is a threshold below which investment in water supply facilities in the community may result in a little perceivable improvement in health status. At the higher end of the socioeconomic scale, since a certain level of saturation has been reached, an investment beyond a certain amount of substantial benefit, satisfactory results have been obtained on the theoretical structure by using data for 65 developing countries, though no concrete conclusion has been derived as yet.

It is therefore evident that the supply and use of clean drinking water is a crucial determinant of health status in every country. However, in developing and poverty-stricken nations, the supply of clean drinking water is difficult because of inadequate finance and investment for providing the infrastructure for the same. On the other hand, due to lack of education, literacy and awareness, the users too are not conscious of the necessity and importance of clean drinking water for their health. This once again focusses on the importance of education for good health. Therefore better health status necessitates adequate finance and allocation of the right quantum of resources for investment for the provision of clean drinking water. It is maintained by Cutler and Miller that clean water technologies, filtration and chlorination, were responsible for nearly half of the mortality reduction in major cities between 1900 and 1936 with greater impact on infant and child mortality. These technologies resulted in eradication of typhoid fever and other waterborne diseases. The authors therefore maintain that water infrastructure and the benefits of reduced mortality are highly cost-effective. In other words, the benefits of improved public health are much more than the cost of such water investments. According to them, the estimated benefit of $23.00 is against $ 1.00 investment; the ratio works out to be as much as 23:1. If the ancillary benefits of clean drinking water and the overall reduced illness and gains in productivity were estimated, the economic benefits would certainly be much more. It is therefore suggested by them that developing nations should adopt inexpensive water disinfection technologies to attain their goal of improved health status.

Cutler and Miller also estimated the cost of a water system serving 100,000 persons to be $30 million per year in 2003 dollar terms. The normal annual death with the provision of........ clean drinking water technologies was 1484, and the number of persons saved yearly was 57,922 and the financial benefits were to the extent of $679.

It is therefore clear that the application of the tools of analysis of health economics will enable the researchers as well as the policy makers in the health sector to understand the relative importance of water as a determinant of health sector. The application of the knowledge of health economics will also enable them to decide whether the objective is to achieve better health status, whether the better option is to invest financial resources directly in an attempt to tackle the problems of child mortality or whether investment is to be made in water infrastructure. It will also help them to measure the cost and benefits of various types of expenditure in the health sector. They may also weigh the short-term benefit against long-term benefits of various types of investment. The tools of cost-benefit analysis will be useful in this aspect.

In India, waterborne diseases have always been the single most important factor leading to deaths and morbidity. In most developing countries, including India, 21 diseases out of a total of 37 diseases are waterborne. Since independence, water has been considered as an important factor for low health status. Though provision of clean drinking water in the Constitution of India is the duty of the State (Article 47), the Central Government too has launched many schemes for drinking water since the states are often starved of finances and are unable to make the adequate investments for the provision of clean drinking water. Some of the significant schemes launched by the Central Government are ARWSS; Swajaldhara Schemes (2007); Bharat Nirman Programme (2005) for rural infrastructure, including water infrastructure; RWNGWM (2004); and National Water Policy (2002). In spite of all the efforts and the various schemes, about 30 % of the households still lack access to clean drinking water. It is noted that India faces a major challenge in this respect not only due to the enormity of the size of the population but also due to the non-uniformity in the level of socioeconomic development, education, poverty, practices and rituals.

Another challenging task is the quality of drinking water provided. In addition to the problem of water quality being caused by pollution and overexploitation, sewage discharge and discharge from industries and runoff from agricultural fields and urban areas are the other causes of drinking water pollution in India. Added to these problems is also the quality of water being affected due to chemical 'contamination' and persistent organic pollutants (POP). All these affect the health status directly.

For instance, the presence of 'fluoride' causes digestive disorders, skin diseases, dental fluorosis, crippling and skeletal fluorosis. The presence of 'arsenic' causes severe poisoning with oesophageal and abdominal pain and blood diarrhoea, and long-term exposure to arsenic causes skin, lung and kidney cancer. The presence of 'iron' in water is another problem in many parts of India which leads to digestive disorders and skin diseases and can also affect the blood tissues of children. 'Nitrate' causes blue baby diseases due to decreased efficiency of haemoglobin to combine with oxygen and also increases risk of cancer. Persistent organic pollutants lead to HBP hormonal dysfunction and growth retardation. Pesticide on water due to runoff from agricultural fields leads to general weakness and immunity problems and tumours.

The result of such chemical contamination on health status in India is highly alarming. It is estimated that 66 million Indians are exposed to the risk due to excess fluoride and 10 million due to arsenic in groundwater. About 195,813 habitations are still affected by poor water quality (Khanna, Sen). Apart from this, as many as 1.5 million children in India, an alarming figure, die due to diarrhoea, and 73 million working days are lost due to waterborne diseases each year. The economic burden of all these diseases is estimated to be $ 600 million per year (Khanna, Sen). The study further focusses attention on the findings of 'Down to Earth' which concluded that in India rural people spend at least Rs. 1000 each year for the treatment of water-/sanitation-related diseases. According to the government of India, this amounts to Rs 6700 crores annually, which is just Rs .52 crores less than the annual budget of the Union Health Ministry and more than the allocation for education.

5.3.1 Water as a Determinant of Infant Mortality

The reason for selecting safe drinking water as a determinant of health status is due to the important co-relationship between safe drinking water and health status and economic growth, which is evident throughout the world. The economic costs of unsafe drinking water are immense in terms of health and education of the population. This in turn may adversely affect economic growth. At the same time, higher economic growth can result in better accessibility to safe drinking water, since governments with higher growth can also afford to invest more in water infrastructure.

In view of the pivotal role of safe drinking water as a determinant of health status, particularly its impact on the health of the child, the following are the models that have been adopted for the purpose of the work:

$$\mathrm{imr} = \mathrm{a} - \mathrm{b}drw + u \tag{5.13}$$

$$\mathrm{imr_r} = \mathrm{a} - \mathrm{b}drw + u \tag{5.14}$$

$$\mathrm{imr_u} = \mathrm{a} - \mathrm{b}drw + u \tag{5.15}$$

where drw = percentage of population having access to safe drinking water.

The results of the estimated models are not statistically significant, and therefore they have not been accepted for the purpose of the study. The results are indeed very surprising, but the conclusion may be that the mortality rates among infants may be dominated more by other factors rather than waterborne diseases, which may indeed be only one of the factors.

However, to ensure that no other significant determinant is excluded from the models, we have included literacy rate along with clean drinking water to examine whether the two independent variables taken together improve the explanatory power of the model and specified the models stated below:

$$\mathrm{imr} = \mathrm{a} - \mathrm{b}drw - \mathrm{c}\,lit + u \tag{5.16}$$

$$\mathrm{imr_r} = \mathrm{a} - \mathrm{b}drw - \mathrm{c}\,lit + u \tag{5.17}$$

$$\mathrm{imr_u} = \mathrm{a} - \mathrm{b}drw - \mathrm{c}\,lit + u \tag{5.18}$$

The estimated results are as follows:

$$\begin{aligned} \mathrm{imr} &= 112.077 - .009drw - .713lit + u \qquad \mathrm{R}^2 = .510;\ \mathrm{F} = 16.67 \\ \mathrm{t} &= (6.894) \quad (.073) \quad (-5.739) \end{aligned} \tag{5.16}$$

$$\begin{aligned} \mathrm{imr_r} &= 119.414 - .007drw - .699lit + u \qquad \mathrm{R}^2 = .488;\ \mathrm{F} = 15.23 \\ \mathrm{t} &= (6.733) \quad (-.052) \quad (-5.498) \end{aligned} \tag{5.17}$$

$$\begin{aligned} \mathrm{imr_u} &= 71.87 + .003\mathrm{drw} - .619lit + u \qquad \mathrm{R}^2 = .383;\ \mathrm{F} = 9.948 \\ \mathrm{t} &= (5.827) \quad (.025) \quad (-4.437) \end{aligned} \tag{5.18}$$

With the inclusion of education, the explanatory power of all the models has improved and the coefficient of literacy rate for all the three models is also statistically significant and has the desired negative sign. However, the explanatory power of the coefficient for safe drinking water has not gone up significantly. The reason could be that water is more a factor for determining morbidity rather than direct infant mortality. However, the fact is established that literacy has a greater role in inducing the use of safe drinking water which therefore emerges as an important determinant of health status in terms of infant mortality. The reason could be that it is education which enables the users of water to understand the importance of clean drinking water.

5.3.2 Water as a Determinant of Mortality Rates (Below 5 Years)

Studies have also revealed (Woldemicael 2000) that the survival rates of children go up along with the rise in accessibility to piped water and toilet facilities. The study for Eritrea reveals that the unadjusted effect of household environment like water supply and toilet facilities is large and statistically significant during postneonatal and childhood periods. However, it is relatively small and statistically insignificant during neonatal period. According to Woldemicael the effects of household environment remain substantial during neonatal period when socioeconomic factors are controlled.

Due to the important role which safe drinking water can play in determining mortality rates of children, the following are the models that have been adopted for the purpose of the study:

$$\mathrm{mr} = \mathrm{a} - \mathrm{b}drw + u \tag{5.19}$$

$$\mathrm{mr_r} = \mathrm{a} - \mathrm{b}drw + u \tag{5.20}$$

$$\mathrm{mr_u} = \mathrm{a} - \mathrm{b}drw + u \tag{5.21}$$

The results of the estimated equations however are not accepted due to statistical insignificance, though theoretically the model is sound.

In view of the insignificance of the results which are indeed a little surprising, we have included literacy rate along with safe drinking water to examine whether the explanatory power of the models improves. The next models developed therefore are as follows:

$$\mathrm{mr} = \mathrm{a} - \mathrm{b}drw + clit + u \tag{5.22}$$

$$\mathrm{mr_r} = \mathrm{a} - \mathrm{b}drw + \mathrm{c}\,lit + u \tag{5.23}$$

$$\mathrm{mr_u} = \mathrm{a} - \mathrm{b}drw + \mathrm{c}\,lit + u \tag{5.24}$$

The estimated results are as follows:

$$\begin{aligned} \mathrm{mr} &= 144.204 - .005drw - .750lit + u \qquad \mathrm{R}^2 = .514;\ \mathrm{F} = 16.922 \\ \mathrm{t} &= (7.904) \quad (-.030) \quad (-5.817) \end{aligned} \tag{5.22}$$

$$\begin{aligned} \mathrm{mr_r} &= 161.012 - .017drw - .733lit + u \qquad \mathrm{R}^2 = .545;\ \mathrm{F} = 9.56 \\ \mathrm{t} &= (6.722) \quad (-.097) \quad (-4.1560) \end{aligned} \tag{5.23}$$

$$\begin{aligned} \mathrm{mr_u} &= 91.711 - .318drw - .669lit + u \qquad \mathrm{R}^2 = .580;\ \mathrm{F} = 11.028 \\ \mathrm{t} &= (7.325) \quad (-2.287) \quad (-3.948) \end{aligned} \tag{5.24}$$

Inclusion of literacy rate as an explanatory variable along with accessibility to safe drinking water has increased the explanatory power of all the variables, as well as their statistical significance. However the statistical significance of the coefficient for drinking water is significant only in case of mortality rate in the urban sector, and the explanatory power of the model too is the highest in case of the urban mortality rate. Therefore out of the three models, only the model for the urban sector is accepted. The results therefore imply that education is more effective in the urban sectors for creating awareness among the population about the health benefits of safe and clean drinking water.

5.4 Sanitation as a Determinant of Health Status

Sanitation is another determinant of health status which is closely associated with clean drinking water. Sanitation which is defined as safe disposal of human excreta is fundamental to good health as adequate and proper sanitation can lead to reduced mortality and morbidity rates. World Health Organisation (WHO) states, 'Sanitation refers to the provision of facilities and services for the safe disposal of human urine and faeces. Inadequate sanitation is a major cause of diseases throughout the world and improving sanitation is known to have a significant beneficial impact on health both in households and across communities. The word sanitation also refers to the "maintenance of hygienic conditions through services such as garbage collection and waste water disposal"'. Studies have revealed that (Fink et al. 2011) access to sanitation is associated with lower risk of child diarrhoea and lower risk of mild or severe stunting.

Sanitation is another determinant of health status which is closely associated with high infant and child morbidity and mortality and accounts for 10 % of the burden of diseases in the world. This has been the experience of the poor countries of Africa, Asia and Latin America. Diarrhoeal deaths account for 1.6–2.5 million deaths annually for less than 5 years in developing countries. Studies have revealed that rates of diseases of diarrhoea can be reduced by 32–37 % with improved sanitation facilities.

Proper sanitation has both social and economic benefits as it can reduce various sanitation-related diseases which may result in improved health and higher productivity. It is estimated that (MDG, Report) by averting 190 million diarrhoea cases per year, 180 thousand lives per year could be saved and in terms of economic benefit, $552 per year could be saved, while non-medical costs in terms of monetary value amounted to $ 57. The value of lost working days avoided due to proper sanitation was $ 1056 and the value of convenience time savings was 31,320. It is estimated that one extra dollar spent on sanitation can generate almost $ 10 worth of economic benefit mainly by productive work time gained from not being ill. It has also been revealed through studies that $7 billion per year in health system can be saved through proper sanitation and clean water, because half the hospital beds in developing countries are occupied by patients of diarrhoea.

India too witnesses an alarming record of sanitation inadequacy. More than half the people of 1.2 billion populations who need proper sanitation live in India. According to WHO and UNICEF with the current alarming affairs of sanitation worldwide, by 2015, there will be 2.4 million people with sanitation facilities. In India, progress of sanitation has been slow, because only a few relatively well-off people have benefitted from the schemes who normally know and understand the benefits of improved sanitation and therefore can take advantage of subsidy. Moreover, toilets for the needy and the poor have been constructed in a way which is neither technically sound nor culturally suited for the users. There is also absence of any concrete policy on sanitation. The common constraints to sanitation, particularly in developing countries, are fast-growing rate of population, illiteracy and high density of population in urban areas and migration to urban areas, without proper infrastructure and rising poverty.

The impact of this on public health can very well be visualised. As discussed in connection with the analysis of water for public health, major diseases such as cholera, diarrhoea and trachoma are caused through contamination of water resources, soil and food through the transfer of bacteria, viruses and parasites found in human excreta. The solution to these problems worldwide is the creation of adequate sanitation facilities. Realising the crucial role of sanitation for good health, the year 2008 has been declared as the International Year of Sanitation as a means to raise the profile of sanitation issues. This was done in an attempt to meet the MDG of reducing the proportion of people in the world without sanitation by half by the year 2015 from 1990. It needs to be mentioned here that though sanitation is such an important determinant of health status, yet it is also one of the most complex and most neglected and receives attention much less than what it deserves. Concrete sanitation policy with its focus on people-centric demand creation coupled with support to service providers to meet that demand is considered as a means for the successful provision of sanitation facilities.

5.4.1 Infant Mortality and Sanitation

We have attempted to examine the relationship between sanitation and infant mortality in view of the crucial role of adequate sanitation facilities on the health, particularly that of the children.

The models adopted are as follows:

$$\mathrm{imr} = \mathrm{a} - \mathrm{b}san + u \tag{5.25}$$

$$\mathrm{imr_u} = \mathrm{a} - \mathrm{b}san + u \tag{5.26}$$

$$\mathrm{imr_r} = \mathrm{a} - \mathrm{b}\,san + u \tag{5.27}$$

The estimated results are as follows:

$$\begin{array}{ll} \mathrm{imr} = 68.927 - .714san + u & \mathrm{R}^2 = .510;\ \mathrm{F} = 34.502 \\ \mathrm{t} = (12.706)\ (-5.857) & \end{array} \tag{5.25}$$

$$\text{imr}_u = 47.945 - .675san + u \qquad R^2 = .456;\ F = 27.67 \qquad (5.26)$$
$$t = (12.406)\ (-5.260)$$

$$\text{imr}_r = 73.151 - .699san + u \qquad R^2 = .489;\ F = 31.563 \qquad (5.27)$$
$$t = (12.381)\ (-5.618)$$

All the models relating to the relationship between sanitation and infant mortality rates are accepted as they are satisfactory both on theoretical and also on statistical grounds. Almost 70 % of the changes in infant mortality are explained by 1 % change in sanitation accessibility, and the coefficients also possess the negative signs and are statistically significant. Explanatory power of the models as is evident from the value of R^2 is quite high and also significant.

It is also interesting to note that the model for the rural arcas has greater acceptability. It reveals that the condition in the rural areas of India is quite bad and therefore any improvement in sanitation can have greater positive impact on infant mortality in comparison with urban areas where sanitation and health facilities are relatively better and therefore any improvement in sanitation does not have as much impact on infant mortality as much as it is experienced in the rural areas where sanitation facilities are in a deplorable condition.

5.4.2 *Infant Mortality and Open Latrines*

In India and other developing nations with huge burden of population and inadequate investment in the health sector, lack of sanitation which is a very common phenomenon leads to open defecation. This results in not only polluting the groundwater and spreading diseases such as diarrhoea and cholera, but it also contaminates agricultural produce. All these have tremendous adverse impact on health. Studies have revealed that one gram of faeces contain one million viruses and 40 million bacteria. In view of the fact that India is still one of the countries with one of the highest percentages of open defecation, the adverse effect of it on health status is only too obvious. Therefore the present study makes an attempt to examine the exact quantitative relationship between open defecation and health status, particularly infant mortality. The following models have therefore been specified to study the impact of open defecation on health status:

$$\text{imr} = a + b\,oplt + u \qquad (5.28)$$

$$\text{imr}_u = a + b\,oplt + u \qquad (5.29)$$

$$\text{imr}_r = a + b\,oplt + u \qquad (5.30)$$

where *oplt* = open latrines.

The estimated results are stated below:

$$\begin{aligned} \text{imr} &= 24.791 + .670 oplt + u \qquad R^2 = .449;\ F = 26.890 \\ t &= (7.396)\ (5.186) \end{aligned} \tag{5.28}$$

$$\begin{aligned} \text{imr}_u &= 19.682 + .636 oplt + u \qquad R^2 = .404;\ F = 22.397 \\ t &= (8.350)\ (4.733) \end{aligned} \tag{5.29}$$

$$\begin{aligned} \text{imr}_r &= 27.022 + .657 oplt + \text{u} \qquad R^2 = .432;\ F = 25.076 \\ t &= (7.442)\ (5.008) \end{aligned} \tag{5.30}$$

It is interesting to note that all the models with open defecation as an explanatory variable and infant mortality in general and urban and rural sectors separately as dependent variables are acceptable for the purpose of our study. The coefficient of determination as evident from the values of R^2 is acceptable in all the cases and they are also statistically significant. The coefficients of the independent variable, which are all statistically significant as revealed by their 't' values, have the requisite signs, meaning that the higher the percentage of open defecation, the higher also the infant mortality. It may thus be concluded that just as accessibility of sanitation has a positive effect on infant mortality, similarly open defecation has exact and identical negative effect on infant mortality. The elasticity of the adverse effect of open defecation is higher in the rural areas in comparison with urban areas. The reason is only too evident, as open defecation is more a common practice in the rural areas of the country, and therefore any reduction in open defecation has a positive impact on infant mortality. Therefore attention needs to be focussed on the fact that factors which are often overlooked such as open defecation and no policy significance normally attached to it can have greater effect on health status.

5.4.3 Sanitation as Determinant of Mortality Rate (Under 5 Years)

Various studies on sanitation reveal that child mortality (under 5 years) like infant mortality is to a large extent determined by sanitation facilities. It is estimated that infant mortality is nearly seven times higher without access to proper sanitation facilities. Researchers at the United Nations University and McMaster University found that countries ranked in the bottom 25 % in terms of adequate sanitation had 6.6 more deaths per 1000 children under 5 years old, compared to countries in the top 25 % tier. Their work further adds that maternal mortality within a year of child birth due to inadequate sanitation facility increases by 48 % from the top tier to each lower tier of countries, the corresponding odds with respect to unsafe inadequate sanitation being 48 %. It therefore implies that greater investment needs to be made in sanitation facilities, an area in which India is lagging far behind. In fact, as highlighted above there is no sanitation policy in the health sector that exists at present and the sector is still neglected in spite of its crucial importance.

The following are the models adopted to examine the impact which access to sanitation facilities can have on child mortality:

$$\mathrm{mr} = \mathrm{a} - \mathrm{b}san + u \tag{5.31}$$

$$\mathrm{mr_u} = \mathrm{a} - \mathrm{b}\,san + u \tag{5.32}$$

$$\mathrm{mr_r} = \mathrm{a} - \mathrm{b}\,san + u \tag{5.33}$$

The estimated results are reported below:

$$\begin{aligned}&\mathrm{mr} = 86.46 - .626san + u \qquad \mathrm{R}^2 = .391;\ \mathrm{F} = 10.937\\ &\mathrm{t} = (8.722)\ (-3.307)\end{aligned} \tag{5.31}$$

$$\begin{aligned}&\mathrm{imr_u} = 55.87 - .583san + u \qquad \mathrm{R}^2 = .339;\ \mathrm{F} = 8.737\\ &\mathrm{t} = (9.417)\ (-2.956)\end{aligned} \tag{5.32}$$

$$\begin{aligned}&\mathrm{mr_r} = 91.006 - .603san + u \qquad \mathrm{R}^2 = .326;\ \mathrm{F} = 9.690\\ &\mathrm{t} = (8.564)\ (-3.114)\end{aligned} \tag{5.33}$$

The models for mortality rates too are acceptable though the explanatory power of the model is much lower than that of the infant mortality rates, implying that apart from the ill effects of sanitation, malnutrition and the related diseases may also be having some impact on child mortality. Moreover, the newborn are much more susceptible to the ill effects of inadequate sanitation, whereas the slightly older children are marginally better off to withstand the adverse effects. However they too are not totally immune to the impact of poor sanitation. As a result, the coefficients of the independent variables are both statistically and theoretically significant as revealed by their negative signs. R^2 too is significant though their values are lower than that for infant mortality.

For the reasons stated above in Sect. 5.4.2, for assessing the effect on mortality rates under five, here too we have included open defecation as an explanatory variable to determine its impact on child mortality rate:

$$\mathrm{mr} = \mathrm{a} + \mathrm{b}oplt + u \tag{5.34}$$

$$\mathrm{mr_u} = \mathrm{a} + \mathrm{b}\,oplt + u \tag{5.35}$$

$$\mathrm{mr_r} = \mathrm{a} + \mathrm{b}\,oplt + u \tag{5.36}$$

The estimated results are reported below:

$$\begin{aligned} &\text{mr} = 38.146 + .509 oplt + u \qquad \text{R}^2 = .259;\ \text{F} = 5.932 \\ &\text{t} = (4.556)\ (2.435) \end{aligned} \tag{5.34}$$

$$\begin{aligned} &\text{mr}_u = 28.519 + .549 oplt + u \qquad \text{R}^2 = .301;\ \text{F} = 7.317 \\ &\text{t} = (6.1090)\ (2.705) \end{aligned} \tag{5.35}$$

$$\begin{aligned} &\text{mr}_r = 42.425 + .485 oplt + u \qquad \text{R}^2 = .235;\ \text{F} = 5.226 \\ &\text{t} = (4.760)\ (2.228) \end{aligned} \tag{5.36}$$

The coefficients of the independent variable are theoretically and statistically significant. However the explanatory power of the model as is evident from the values of the R^2 is quite low. Therefore open defecation may not be accepted as a very strong determinant of mortality rate, though it may not be altogether ruled out either. The reasons could be that children are more prone to deaths perhaps due to water-borne disease which is due to open defecation. Consequently their impact is indirect and therefore cannot be captured directly.

5.4.4 Sanitation and Education

In view of the pivotal role which education, particularly female education, plays in determining the health status, we have included general literacy rate along with the percentage of the population having access to sanitation facilities in the subsequent models. Studies have revealed (Adukia 2014) that school sanitation facilities increase the enrolment rate of girls and reduce the dropout rate, with a 3-year lag. Therefore sanitation facilities affect female education which in turn can affect the health status. It is also maintained in the same study that sanitation facilities in schools also affect attendance of female teachers. Absenteeism of teachers in general and female teachers in particular has been seen to greatly reduce school attendance of girls, though the impact on boys is much lesser (Banerjee et al. 2000). Studies have also shown that (Stephens 1984) the advantages of better sanitation facilities are severely limited when mothers are not educated. It is postulated that 1–6 years of formal education results in considerable reduction in child mortality risks, even among mothers using poor toilet facilities, and the combination of some education and adequate facilities reduces substantially the risks of death. The studies further reveal that there is a wider difference in child mortality between the best and the worst toilet types than between different water sources. The worst child mortality is exhibited by mothers whose families have no toilet facilities and must resort to open latrines. The child mortality rate is 35 % higher than the average and is well above the index for mothers who use the pit latrines. In contrast, mothers using modern flush toilets experience lowest child mortality. The use of flush toilet is associated with lower child mortality risks than with all other toilet types. Mothers with middle school or higher level of education had, in general, the lowest relative risks of child mortality, while mothers with only primary school education maintained a clear and often statistically significant advantage in child survival over others with no education, almost regardless of the quality of the sanitation facilities used. It is therefore established beyond doubt that health status particularly among child is determined largely by the level of mother's education via sanitation facilities. Therefore simultaneous improvement of sanitation and female education can have a positive impact on child mortality rates, rather than trying to solve the problem of sanitation alone.

The next models developed by us therefore incorporate female education along with sanitation facilities as determinants of child mortality:

$$\mathrm{mr} = \mathrm{a} - \mathrm{b}san - clitf + u \tag{5.37}$$

$$\mathrm{mr_u} = \mathrm{a} - \mathrm{b}\,san\_clitf + u \tag{5.38}$$

$$\mathrm{mr_r} = \mathrm{a} - \mathrm{b}\,san - clitf + u \tag{5.39}$$

where *litf* denotes female literacy.

The estimated results are reported below:

$$\begin{aligned} \mathrm{mr} &= 156.172 - .0351\mathrm{san} - .779litf + u \qquad \mathrm{R}^2 = .561;\ \mathrm{F} = 10.222 \\ \mathrm{t} &= (5.319)\quad (.112)\quad (-2.483) \end{aligned} \tag{5.37}$$

$$\begin{aligned} \mathrm{mr_u} &= 99.581 - .139san - .850litf + u \qquad \mathrm{R}^2 = .541;\ \mathrm{F} = 9.447 \\ \mathrm{t} &= (5.778)\quad (1.443)\quad (-2.655) \end{aligned} \tag{5.38}$$

$$\begin{aligned} \mathrm{mr_r} &= 166.729 - .084san - .809litf + u \qquad \mathrm{R}^2 = .546;\ \mathrm{F} = 9.630 \\ \mathrm{t} &= (5.336)\quad (2.264)\quad (-2.541) \end{aligned} \tag{5.39}$$

The addition of female education has improved the explanatory power of all the models, though the value of the coefficients of sanitation has gone down and has also changed their signs. This could be due to the presence of multi-collinearity which is only normal in view of the interrelationship between the independent variables. However, due to the higher value of R^2 in all cases and also their statistical significance, we accept all the models for our purpose.

Similarly we have also developed models for infant mortality rates taking female education as an additional variable:

$$\mathrm{imr} = \mathrm{a} - \mathrm{b}san\_clitf + u \tag{5.40}$$

$$\mathrm{imr_u} = \mathrm{a} - \mathrm{b}\,san\_clitf + u \tag{5.41}$$

$$\mathrm{imr_r} = \mathrm{a} - \mathrm{b}\,\mathrm{san}\_clitf + u \tag{5.42}$$

The estimated results are as follows:

$$\begin{aligned} \text{im}_{\text{r}} &= 95.173 - .385 san - .388 litf + u \qquad R^2 = .552;\ F = 19.686 \\ t &= (5.929)\ (1.719)\ (-2.483) \end{aligned} \tag{5.40}$$

$$\begin{aligned} \text{imr}_{\text{u}} &= 55.475 - .536 san - .164 litf + u \qquad R^2 = .464;\ F = 13.830 \\ t &= (5.778)\ (-2.188)\ (-.671) \end{aligned} \tag{5.41}$$

$$\begin{aligned} \text{mr}_{\text{r}} &= 100.0 - .381 san - .375 litf + u \qquad R^2 = .582;\ F = 17.915 \\ t &= (8.708)\ (-1.685)\ (-1.634) \end{aligned} \tag{5.42}$$

The explanatory power of the model increases marginally as revealed by the value of R^2 for all the three models, which are also statistically significant. The coefficients of both sanitation and female literacy retain their usual signs and are also statistically significant, though with inclusion of female literacy as an additional explanatory variable, the explanatory power of the coefficient of sanitation falls marginally. In view of the results, we accept the models for our purpose.

It is therefore evident that for the positive effect of sanitation on infant mortality and child mortality rates, female literacy rates play an important role, which is supported by other empirical works as well. The interrelationship between female education, the use of sanitation facilities and infant and child mortality is shown in the chart diagram below (Diagram 5.2).

This implies that policy measures to improve health status should aim at investing simultaneously in female education and sanitation, so that greater degree of awareness can be created among the members of the family for the use of sanitation facilities. This in turn can improve the parameters of health status in India.

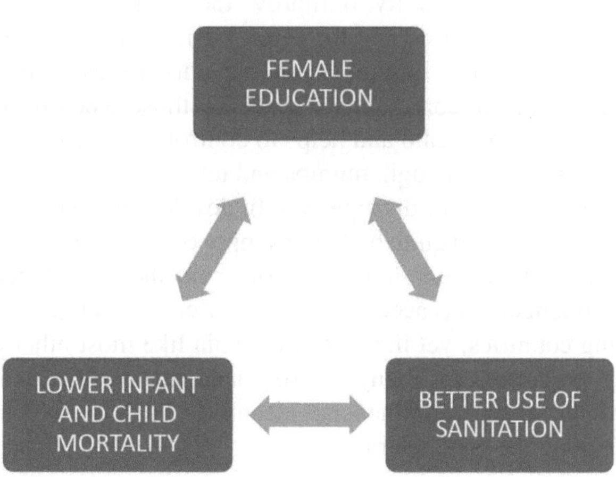

Diagram 5.2 Relationship between female education, sanitation and infant and child mortality

5.5 Immunisation as a Determinant of Health Status

Immunisation is another crucial determinant of health status, the impact of which is much wider in poor and developing nations than in the already developed countries with better health status. The major goal of immunisation is the reduction of infant and child mortality which can have both short-term and long-term health benefits, which in turn also affects the labour productivity and economic development of a nation. Immunisation is considered as one of the most cost-effective health interventions to prevent a series of major illness, more so in poor nations where children are undernourished and may die from preventable diseases (World Bank 1993). Immunisation also has great social externalities.

It is estimated (Bonu et al. 2003) that about three million people die every year due to vaccine preventable diseases, with a majority of them belonging to developing countries. About 98 % of the children not immunised are from developing countries. The Global Immunization Vision and Strategy (GIVS) was developed by WHO and UNICEF to strengthen the national immunisation programme and protect as many people as possible against diseases and epidemics through immunisation, including new vaccines. Vaccines have major contributions to public health, such as eradication of small pox, measles and polio. The result has been quite encouraging as mortality related to measles has been reduced from 750,000 in 2000 to 197,000 in 2007. It is revealed that the factors that led to the success of immunisation have been national multiyear planning, district level planning and monitoring, reestablishment of outreach services and enhancement of national budget for immunisation.

In spite of a lot of efforts by WHO and UNICEF, much remains to be done if the full potential of immunisation is to be exploited. About 1.1 million deaths of children under the age of 5 could be prevented through immunisation with new vaccines. The full potential of immunisation is not attained mostly due to unequal coverage, both in terms of gender and rural urban bias. Nations with poor health systems face these challenges in a much greater proportion. The development of an appropriate framework for maximising the benefits of immunisation provides a tremendous opportunity to improve the health status of those nations, particularly the poor, marginalised and the rural communities, who always have to bear the burden of poor health. Immunisation prevents diseases and thereby helps to protect the health of the community, especially those who are not immunised. Immunisation also prevents death and helps to control many diseases like polio, measles, diphtheria, whooping cough, mumps and tetanus which were at one time very common but have now almost disappeared. In developing countries where the incidence of such diseases is still quite high, the supply of free immunisation and incentives to improve the demand for immunisation can thereby increase the immunisation rate. Immunisation is accepted as another crucial determinant of health status in developing countries, yet the record of India like most other developing nations is equally poor in spite of many efforts made in this regard. Experience has revealed that financial and nonfinancial incentives are effective in encouraging immunisation among the beneficiaries.

In view of the crucial role of immunisation as determinant of health status especially with respect to infant mortality, mortality below 5 years, underweight children, children with stunted growth and also life expectancy at birth both for males and females separately, we have developed a number of models in this respect with immunisation as explanatory determinant factor for these health parameters.

5.5.1 Immunisation as a Determinant of Infant Mortality

The first models in this respect developed by us are mentioned below:

$$\text{imr} = \text{a} - \text{b}\,imz + \text{u} \tag{5.43}$$

$$\text{imr}_\text{u} = a - b\ imz + u \tag{5.44}$$

$$\text{imr}_\text{r} = \text{a} - \text{b}\ imz + \text{u} \tag{5.45}$$

where

imz = percentage of immunised children
u = the residual term

The estimated results are stated below:

$$\begin{array}{ll} \text{imr} = 74.358 - .614\text{imz} + u & R^2 = .377; F = 19.353 \\ \quad t = (9.045)\ (-4.399) & \end{array} \tag{5.43}$$

$$\begin{array}{ll} \text{imr}_\text{u} = 80.091 - .623imz + \text{u} & R^2 = .388; F = 20.247 \\ \quad t = (9.228)\ (-4.500) & \end{array} \tag{5.44}$$

$$\begin{array}{ll} \text{imr}_\text{r} = 44.427 - .399\ imz + \text{u} & R^2 = .159; F = 6.045 \\ \quad t = (6.834)\ (-2.459) & \end{array} \tag{5.45}$$

Taking total infant mortality rate and also the rural and the urban rates separately as dependent variable with total immunisation as independent variable, it is interesting to note that the models are theoretically acceptable. This is evident from the negative signs of the coefficient of the independent variable, implying that the higher the percentage of children with immunisation, the lower the infant mortality rates, which is only natural. The coefficients of the independent variables too are statistically significant. The value of R^2 however is not very high implying that the coefficient of determination of the model is not very high. It is due to this that the models have been rejected for the present work.

5.5.2 Immunisation and Literacy as Determinants of Mortality Rate

However, in view of the literacy rate particularly the female literacy rates in determining these factors of health statistics, we have included the percentage of literacy along with immunisation as the other explanatory variables in the next models specified below:

$$\mathrm{mr} = \mathrm{a} - \mathrm{b}\,lit - \mathrm{c}\ imz + \mathrm{u} \tag{5.46}$$

$$\mathrm{mr_u} = a - b\ lit - c\ imz + u \tag{5.47}$$

$$\mathrm{mr_r} = \mathrm{a} - \mathrm{b}\ lit - \mathrm{c}\ imz + \mathrm{u} \tag{5.48}$$

where

lit = literacy rate
imz = percentage of immunised children
u = the residual term

We report below the results of the estimated models:

$$\begin{aligned} \mathrm{mr} &= 166.552 - .260lit - 654imz + \mathrm{u} \qquad R^2 = .783; F = 28.803 \\ \mathrm{t} &= (6.986)\ (-2.1991)\ \ (-4.256) \end{aligned} \tag{5.46}$$

$$\begin{aligned} \mathrm{mr_u} &= 98.725 - .260lit - .670imz + \mathrm{u} \qquad R^2 = .745; F = 22.336 \\ \mathrm{t} &= (66.53)\ \ (-2.807)\ \ (-4.102) \end{aligned} \tag{5.47}$$

$$\begin{aligned} \mathrm{mr_r} &= 173.007 - .290lit - .657imz + \mathrm{u} \qquad R^2 = .750; F = 25.887 \\ \mathrm{t} &= (6.64)\ (-2.809)\ \ (-4.102) \end{aligned} \tag{5.48}$$

It is evident from the estimated results that the coefficient of determination is .783, .745 and .750, for the total infant mortality, urban and rural rates, respectively, implying that all the models have high explanatory power. It is also to be noted that the explanatory power of immunisation as an independent variable has increased in comparison with the models where we had taken immunisation singly as an explanatory variable. The negative signs of all the coefficients have been retained implying negative relationships of the variables, as suggested by the theoretical underpinnings of the models. It is interesting to note that for all the cases the value of R^2 has gone up significantly and the models are also theoretically and statistically acceptable. It therefore implies that immunisation by itself may not be too effective to improve the health indicators. However, immunisation works only in those cases where there is some extent of literate parents who ultimately have to decide whether their children need to be immunised.

5.5.3 Immunisation and Female Literacy as Determinants of Infant Mortality

In view of the crucial role of literacy as is evident from the results of the models above, we have also developed some more models with female literacy and immunisation as the explanatory variables, since it is the literacy rates of the mother which can actually influence the health of the child:

$$\text{imr} = 173.007 - .542\,litf - .143\,imz + \text{u} \qquad \text{R}^2 = .483; \text{F} = 15.803$$
$$\text{t} = (6.980)\;(-2.991)\;(-1.256) \qquad (5.49)$$

$$\text{imr}_\text{u} = 112.87 - .537\,lit\text{f} - .325\,imz + \text{u} \qquad \text{R}^2 = .582; \text{F} = 21.59$$
$$\text{t} = (6.653)\quad(-2.564)\quad(-4.024) \qquad (5.50)$$

$$\text{imr}_\text{r} = 71.991 - .565\,litf - .095\,imz + \text{u} \qquad \text{R}^2 = .386; \text{F} = 9.739$$
$$\text{t} = (7.266)\quad(-3.385)\quad(-.567) \qquad (5.51)$$

However, the explanatory power of the models as revealed by the value of R^2 has gone down significantly though they are still statistically significant. The coefficients of the female literacy rate are low, though they are still theoretically and statistically still significant. The findings of the estimated equations, incorporating female education, are a little surprising because in all other cases of infant mortality rate, female education plays a major role as a determinant factor. The reasons could perhaps be that in those cases the role of the mother relating to taking decisions for her child is reflected in her own behavioural aspects which are confined within her home. However, decision regarding whether the child needs to go for immunisation is a decision which extends beyond the boundary of her home. Such decisions in India, more so in the rural areas, are taken not so much by the womenfolk of the family but by the male members as in normally the case in a male-dominated patriarchal society where womenfolk have hardly any say about decisions about their children outside the four boundaries of her home. It is therefore that general education rather than only female education has a greater impact on infant mortality in this respect. Consequently, the models with immunisation and female literacy are not accepted for the study.

5.5.4 Immunisation as a Determinant of Mortality Rate (Below 5 Years)

Mortality rates under five (mr) which are also determined very importantly by immunisation are taken in the next models as dependent variables, separately both for the urban and rural areas. The models developed are as follows:

$$\text{mr} = a - b\,\text{imz} + \text{u} \qquad (5.52)$$

$$mr_u = a - b \text{ imz} + u \tag{5.53}$$

$$mr_r = a - b \text{ imz} + u \tag{5.54}$$

The estimated results are as follows:

$$\begin{aligned} mr &= 122.943 - .854\text{imz} + u \qquad R^2 = .729; F = 45.673 \\ t &= (12.050)\ (-6.758) \end{aligned} \tag{5.52}$$

$$\begin{aligned} mr_u &= 77.409 - .840\mathit{imz} + u \qquad R^2 = .706;\ F = 40.76 \\ t &= (12.68)\ (-6.385) \end{aligned} \tag{5.53}$$

$$\begin{aligned} mr_r &= 129.770 - .846\mathit{imz} + u \qquad R^2 = .716; F = 42.78 \\ t &= (11.855)\ (-6.541) \end{aligned} \tag{5.54}$$

In contrast to the models where immunisation is taken as a single explanatory variable for determining infant mortality rate, which was not very satisfactory, immunisation emerges as a highly satisfactory explanatory factor for mortality rates below 5 years. The results reveal that the explanatory power of the models as indicated by the value of R^2 is .729, .702 and .716 for mortality, urban mortality and rural mortality rates, respectively. The value of R^2 in each case is also statistically significant. The negative signs before the coefficients imply that the model is theoretically acceptable, because it implies that the higher the immunisation, the lower the mortality rate which is only too obvious. The values of the coefficient of immunisation which are also all statistically significant as implied by their ‘t’ values also reveal that over 85 % of the changes in mortality rate are explained by 1 % change in immunisation rate. All these imply how crucial immunisation is for determining health status especially for children.

5.5.5 *Immunisation and Education as Determinants of Mortality Rate*

In the next analysis along with the percentage of immunisation, we have also taken literacy rate as the independent variable to examine whether the explanatory power of the models has increased. The models are as mentioned below:

$$mr = a - b\ \mathit{lit} - c\mathit{imz} + u \tag{5.55}$$

$$mr_u = a - b\ \mathit{lit} - c\mathit{imz} + u \tag{5.56}$$

$$mr_r = a - b\ \mathit{lit} - c\mathit{imz} + u \tag{5.57}$$

The estimated results are reported below:

$$\text{mr} = 166.552 - .306\,lit - .654\,imz + \text{u} \qquad \text{R}^2 = .783;\ \text{F} = 28.803 \qquad (5.55)$$
$$\text{t} = (6.980)\ (-2.991)\ (-4.256)$$

$$\text{mr}_\text{u} = 98.725 - .260\,lit - .670\,imz + \text{u} \qquad \text{R}^2 = .745;\ \text{F} = 23.336 \qquad (5.56)$$
$$\text{t} = (6.653)\ (-2.564)\ (-4.024)$$

$$\text{mr}_\text{r} = 173.007 - .290\,lit - .657\,imz + \text{u} \qquad \text{R}^2 = .764;\ \text{F} = 25.871 \qquad (5.57)$$
$$\text{t} = (6.644)\ (-2.807)\ (-4.102)$$

Examination of the estimated results reveals that the value of R^2 is .783, .745 and .764 for total, urban and rural mortality rates, respectively. The value of coefficient of determination has improved with the inclusion of literacy rate as an additional independent variable along with only immunisation. All the values of R^2 are also significant as is evident from the 'F' values. The independent coefficient of literacy and immunisation too has negative signs implying that the lower the literacy and immunisation rates, the higher the mortality rate of infants below 5 years. The coefficients are also statistically significant as is evident from their 't' values. In all cases however, immunisation has a higher explanatory power, which is only too obvious as mortality rate of children is determined directly by various types of immunisation such as HBV, DTaP, DTP, OPV, rotavirus, Hib vaccines, pneumococcal vaccines, MMR vaccines, VZV vaccines, hepatitis A vaccines, etc., and literacy rate has only an indirect and long-term impact due to which the explanatory power of the variable is much lower. The better explanatory power of the models with education as an additional explanatory variable means that parents of newborn babies without any education may have difficulty in availing the benefits of immunisation as due to inadequate education, the awareness level of the benefits of education is absent. Therefore any rise in their level of education also results in a rise of the benefits of immunisation. This in turn has direct impact on infant mortality rates.

5.5.6 Immunisation and Female Literacy as Determinants of Infant Mortality

In view of the strong impact of female literacy rate as a determinant of health status, in the next models, female literacy instead of the general literacy rate has been taken as explanatory variable. The estimated results are accepted both on theoretical and statistical grounds. The coefficient of determination is also satisfactory both in terms of their value and in terms of statistical significance. However, there is only marginal decrease in the value of the coefficients of the explanatory variables as well as in the values of R^2 as revealed by the estimated results stated below:

$$\text{mr} = 146.576 - .307\,litf - .643\,imz + \text{u} \qquad \text{R}^2 = .779;\ \text{F} = 28.122 \qquad (5.58)$$
$$\text{t} = (9.351)\ (-1.896)\ (-3.968)$$

$$\begin{aligned} imr_u &= 90.383 - .293\mathit{litf} - .638\mathit{imz} + u \qquad R^2 = .751; F = 24.147 \\ t &= (9.471) \;\; (-1.709) \;\; (-3.718) \end{aligned} \tag{5.59}$$

$$\begin{aligned} imr_r &= 153.671 - .296\mathit{litf} - .642\mathit{imz} + u \qquad R^2 = .762; F = 25.610 \\ t &= (9.024) \;\; (-1.765) \;\; (-.3.826) \end{aligned} \tag{5.60}$$

Immunisation as a determinant factor for mortality rates for children below 5 years emerges as a better explanatory factor in comparison with infant mortality rates. The reason could perhaps be that immunisation of the infants is still viewed with fear and scepticism in comparison with immunisation for slightly grown up children. As a result immunisation is more effective in case of mortality for children within 5 years rather than infants. This is more so in the rural areas. Education like in the previous case acts as boosting factor. However like in the case of infant mortality also, female education does not play a significant role, the reasons for which could be similar to that of infant mortality.

It is therefore concluded that immunisation along with general literacy rate is a major determinant of mortality rate as far as health status is concerned.

5.5.7 Immunisation as a Determinant of Life Expectancy

In view of the important impact of immunisation on the children which in turn can have long-term effect on the longevity of the population in general, we have also developed another model to test the impact of immunisation and literacy on the life expectancy of females and males.

The estimated results of the models developed in the same lines as above with '*lexpf*' and '*lexpm*' representing female and male life expectancy, respectively, are stated below:

$$\begin{aligned} \mathit{lexpf} &= -28.62 + 1.001\mathit{lit} + .035\mathit{imz} + u \qquad R^2 = .963;\; F = 47.817 \\ t &= (-7.999) \; (23.89) \; (.826) \end{aligned} \tag{5.61}$$

$$\begin{aligned} \mathit{lexpm} &= 60.300 + .399\mathit{lit} + .175\mathit{imz} + u \qquad R^2 = .282;\; F = 3.528 \\ t &= (13.783) \; (1.507) \quad (.659) \end{aligned} \tag{5.62}$$

The results reveal that R^2 explains the model satisfactorily and they are statistically significant in both the cases and are much higher than when immunisation is taken as a single explanatory factor. Though the explanatory power of the independent coefficient of immunisation goes down slightly, however the requisite signs are maintained. The explanatory power of education is much higher implying that education plays an important role here too like the earlier models in increasing the effectiveness of immunisation. It is only natural that not only mortality and infant mortality rates increase, but the higher values in turn also impact the over-longevity of the population.

It is therefore concluded that immunisation along with education has short-term health benefits, but the beneficial impact spreads over a much longer span of the life of the population, particularly when it comes to controlling the death rates through illness and diseases which traditionally characterise the developing countries.

5.5.8 Immunisation as a Determinant of Underweight Children and Children with Stunted Growth

Immunisation is not only a precaution against infant mortality but can provide a wide range of health benefits. Numerous studies have revealed the effect of immunisation on stunting and wasting in children, till the age of 5. In the Indian context, the Report on 'Children in India' published by the Ministry of Statistics and Programme Implementation revealed that 48 % children under the age of 5 have stunted growth, which means that half of the country's children are chronically malnourished. It also states that malnourishment is higher among children whose mothers are uneducated.

Malnutrition is one of the major causes of child and infant mortality throughout the world. Bloom et al. (2005) have estimated the use of vaccinations on mortality rates combined with the estimates of life expectancy on productivity. This was done to estimate that the full immunisation with six standard vaccinations has a rate of return around 18 % (about the same rate as primary education) as an investment in human capital, despite long delays between childhood vaccinations and entering work. Children who are malnourished are nine times more likely to die from infectious diseases such as pneumonia, diarrhoea, malaria and measles. Such children are the ones who become the victims of malnutrition. Immunisation can prevent some of the chronic consequences of undernourishment. Studies in India (Anekwe and Kuner 2012) have revealed that children in India with up-to-date vaccines against tuberculosis, diphtheria, tetanus, measles, polio and pertussis were less likely to show signs of stunting. Therefore immunisation is considered as the first point of contact within national health system forming an integral part of primary healthcare platform, which has the ability to reach children multiple times in their first years of life.

In view of the importance of immunisation for preventing stunted growth and underweight children, the present study has made an attempt to assess the exact quantitative impact of immunisation on these health status indicators. The following models have therefore been adopted and estimated:

$$\mathrm{uwc} = a - b\,\mathrm{imz} + \mathrm{u} \tag{5.63}$$

$$\mathrm{csg} = a - b\,\mathrm{imz} + \mathrm{u} \tag{5.64}$$

$$\text{uwc} = 58.686 - .566\text{imz} + \text{u} \qquad R^2 = .320; F = 12.258 \tag{5.63}$$
$$t = (8.984)\ (-3.501)$$

$$\text{csg} = 62.265 - .645\text{imz} + \text{u} \qquad R^2 = .416; F = 18.5 \tag{5.64}$$
$$t = (13.303)\ (-4.303)$$

The estimated results have the required signs for the coefficients of the independent variables, meaning that the higher the rate of immunisation, the lower also the percentage of underweight children and children with stunted growth. The explanatory power of the model is reasonably satisfactory, all of which imply that immunisation is an important determinant of children with stunted growth and underweight children.

5.5.9 *Immunisation and General Education and Female Education as Determinants of Underweight Children and Children with Stunted Growth*

However, in view of the important role of female literacy in this respect, in the next model, it has been included along with immunisation to examine whether the explanatory powers of the variables have increased.

We have firstly attempted to examine the models by incorporating only general education along with immunisation to assess whether the explanatory power of the models have improved in any way. The models examined are as follows:

$$\text{unw} = a - b\ \text{imz} - c\ lit + \text{u} \tag{5.65}$$

$$\text{csg} = a - b\ \text{imz} - c\ lit + \text{u} \tag{5.66}$$

The estimated results are stated below:

$$\text{unw} = 90.888 - .391 imz - .376 lit + \text{u} \qquad R^2 = .432; F = 9.488 \tag{5.65}$$
$$t = (7.485)\ (-.2.298)\ \ (-2.210)$$

$$\text{csg} = 89.742 - .452 imz - .416 lit + \text{u} \qquad R^2 = .551; F = 15.360 \tag{5.66}$$
$$t = (8.278)(-2.988)(-2.747)$$

Inclusion of education improves the explanatory power of both the models as revealed by the value of R^2 which is .432 and .551 for underweight children and children with stunted growth, respectively. The R^2 are also statistically significant. The coefficients of the model are also theoretically and statistically significant. Consequently, it may be concluded that like all the other models for immunisation,

Diagram 5.3 Diagrammatic representation of the relationship between education, immunisation, infant and child mortality and life expectancy

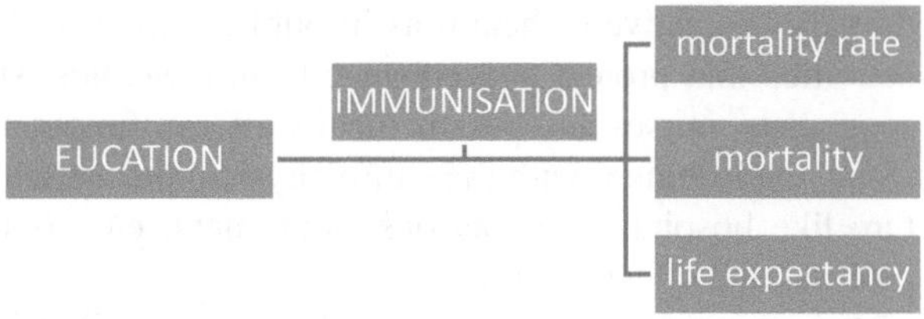

in this case also education reinforces the impact of immunisation on underweight children and children with stunted growth (Diagram 5.3).

In the next models we have used female literacy, that is, the literacy of the mothers as another variable in the following manner:

$$\text{unw} = a - b\text{imz} - c\,lit_f + \text{u} \tag{5.67}$$

$$\text{csg} = a - b\text{imz} - c\,lit_f + \text{u} \tag{5.68}$$

The estimated results are as follows:

$$\begin{aligned}\text{unw} &= 80.954 - .392\text{imz} - .405\,litf + \text{u} \qquad R^2 = .454;\ F = 10.381 \\ t &= (7.485)(-.2.390)(-2.470)\end{aligned} \tag{5.67}$$

$$\begin{aligned}\text{csg} &= 79.541 - .470\text{imz} \quad .406\,litf + \text{u} \qquad R^2 = 550;\ F = 15.291 \\ t &= (10.488)(-3.160)(-2.732)\end{aligned} \tag{5.68}$$

With the inclusion of female literacy as the other explanatory variable along with immunisation, it is seen that the explanatory power of the models increases in both the cases, as the value of R^2 increases for both the models. The coefficients of both the independent variables too retain their negative signs and are also statistically significant as is evident from their 't' values. It may therefore be concluded that immunisation and female literacy are two important determinants of the health status of children in India as far as underweight children and children with stunted growth are concerned. The impact of the mother's education here is therefore slightly better in comparison to the other parameters of health status. However, on the whole it can be mentioned that immunisation along with education has greater impact on the status of health than immunisation taken alone as a determinant factor of health status.

5.6 Health Infrastructure as a Determinant of Health Status

The formal and enduring structures that support public health are termed as the health infrastructure. They are both tangible and intangible, existing inside as well as outside the government sector. According to WHO health infrastructure may be directly protective of health as in public sanitation systems or may support other activities that protect and enhance health. Medical staff such as doctors, medical specialists, nurses and paramedical staff can function effectively only in a professional environment with the entire physical infrastructure. Such tangible infrastructure like hospitals, laboratories, equipment, etc., is the important determinant of professional effectiveness.

It is therefore clear that tangible and intangible infrastructure cannot function without each other, and existence of one without another is incomplete and meaningless as far as rendering services in the medical sector is concerned. The health service to the public which is another crucial determinant of health status is determined by three important components:

- Availability of capable and qualified workforce
- Availability of centres for delivering public health services
- Availability of physical health infrastructure

The public health infrastructure therefore provides the requisite structure for addressing the other determinants of health, discussed earlier. In fact, in the absence of public health infrastructure, most of the goals of health status would remain unattained. Therefore attaining the goals of better health status has to proceed simultaneously with the goals set for health infrastructure, both tangible and intangible. If the two sets of goals which merge with each other to attain the common goal of improved health status are not targeted simultaneously, bottlenecks will arise, as the absence of one will hamper the achievement of the other goal.

Before examining the status of the various public health infrastructures, it is essential to understand the meaning of the public health system of a country. Public health system is the outcome of a collaborative effort of a complex network of people, system and organisation, constituted through public health investments, for delivering health services to the entire population, preventing the spread of diseases and ensuring quality and accessibility of health services. It is imperative that the public health system is supported by a strong political and financial system. Therefore, as discussed earlier, the health expenditure is one of the important determinants of the strength of the public health system and the requisite health infrastructure. In other words, public health system provides the formal and enduring structures which is the backbone of the health status of the population. The activities of the public health system may directly protect health or may support other activities that enhance the health status. The health concerns that are directly controlled by such infrastructure are the spread of communicable diseases and protection of the newly born child and mother. It is interesting to note that the capacity to absorb latest technology and knowledge is a very powerful predictor of infant mortality. Thus only a nation with strong public health infrastructure will have the capacity to tackle the threats posed to the health sector of a nation. In fact, health investment is mostly for the purpose of maintaining both physical and manpower infrastructures in the health sector.

One of the most pivotal roles in the public health system is played by the health workers without whom, health services cannot be delivered to the recipients. The most important components of the health workers are the physicians, surgeons, nurses, paramedical workers, health educators, outreach workers and also health managers who are often one of the most important but often neglected components of health workers. Apart from these most essential manpower in the health sector, health workers also include social workers, nutritionists, anthropologists, psychologists, economists, political scientists and information technology scientists. However, for the purpose of the present study, we will keep this category of health workers outside the purview of the analysis.

To enable the health workers to deliver their services in an effective and meaningful manner, they have to be trained, due to which the quality of vocational and research training in public health determines the effectiveness of the health workers. Consequently, funds should be allocated on a priority basis for medical educational and training programmes, the expenditure towards which also forms an important part of health expenditure. It is the quantum of investment in this area and the quality of training imparted which in turn determines the quality of the health-care delivery models, importance of primary health care and creation of awareness of the benefits of immunisation. The quality of all these services rendered by the health workers will in turn determine the health status of a population.

Consequently funds should be allocated on a priority basis for medical education and training programmes so as to enable the health personnel to enable them to successfully deliver health services to the needy. Through their education they can educate the public on new health-care delivery models, the importance of primary health care and awareness about the benefits of immunisation, all of which will have a positive impact on the health indicators discussed above.

From our discussion above, it is evident that inadequate immunisation of a child is a major problem in developing countries affecting the health status adversely. The other problem as highlighted in the earlier sections is unsafe drinking water leading to the highest incidence of waterborne diseases and diarrhoeal morbidity and deaths. Inadequate sanitation facilities resulting in unsafe disposal of human waste and garbage are other acute causes of diseases and epidemics. All this preventive health care is therefore considered as an important broad-based category of activities, which directly affects the health status of the population. It is here that the PHEs can have a great role to play particularly in developing countries. It is only a nation with strong public health infrastructure who will have the capacity to tackle the threats to the health sector of a nation. In fact, the health investment is mostly for the purpose of maintaining the health infrastructure both physical and manpower.

It is in this context that the present study has made an attempt to examine the relative weightage of health infrastructure on the health status in India. We have taken the physical health infrastructure such as public health centres, subcentres, central health centres and also the availability of hospital beds and their relative weight in determining the health status. We have also taken the various types of constraints in health infrastructure such as non-availability of doctors, non-availability of laboratory technicians and non-availability of paramedical workers as the determinants of health status. Accessibility of health facilities often becomes the crucial determinant of health status, especially in remote and far off places and rural areas where connectivity to health centres is often a constraint for the delivery of health services. We have therefore taken some of the crucial indicators of accessibility of health facilities such as the distance of the subcentres and public health centres, existence of health and sanitation committees, awareness of the pradhan/panchayat members related to the united funds and some other determinants of health status.

Taking all the above factors both positive and negative will give us a holistic picture of the determinants of health status. The quantitative analysis will also enable us to assess the relative importance of the determinant factor separately for the urban and the rural sectors.

5.6.1 Physical Health Infrastructure and Health Status

Infrastructure in economics has a pivotal link with development in general. The same is relevant for the social sector development which also includes health sector. In the earlier section, discussion has been made relating to the importance of water and sanitation for enhancing health status. However, lack of physical infrastructure for providing clean drinking water and proper sanitation results in high infant and child mortality and many other related health problems. Similar is the case with accessibility to health facilities, which is often impaired due to long distance which in turn affects the health sector. This again can be overcome through adequate investment both in constructing roads and other means of communication and transport and also building more health infrastructure such as health centres and subcentres so as to enable greater and easy accessibility of the health service users.

Primary health-care (PHC) system forms an integral part of a country's health system. The facilities are made universally accessible to individuals and family in the community at a cost which the community can afford. It forms the first level of contact for the individuals, the family and the community with the national health system. They also reflect the economic condition and social values of a country and are the result of a country's health service research and experience. PHC addresses the main health problems in the community and provides promotive, preventive, curative and rehabilitative services to the community. They are assigned with the responsibilities of creating health awareness in the community and providing adequate supply of safe water and sanitation and maternal and child care, including family planning, immunisation against major infectious diseases, prevention and control of locally endemic diseases, education concerning prevailing health problems and the methods of preventing and controlling them and the provision of basic essential medicines.

Ideally speaking all primary health-care services should have a mutually supportive referral system. PHC centres also provide the health-care platform for utilising the services of different types of health workers mentioned earlier such as the physicians, nurses, paramedical workers and others. In fact, PHC system should be oriented in such a way that everyone in the community will be able to access health-care facilities whenever needed. In some countries, especially the developing ones, PHC steps in where the more sophisticated health-care system fails to take care of the major sections of the community. In fact, hospitals play a crucial role to support and develop PHCs, which has now been accepted as the most important means of meeting the health needs of the community. For implementing this scheme of health management, support has to come from the organised health-care sector. Hospitals with all their facilities therefore have to assume the leadership role in the health delivery system. Just as PHCs are the centres for preventive health care, hospitals are the centres for curative health care. It is only a nation with strong public health-care infrastructure which will have the ability to tackle the threats to the health sector of a nation. In fact the health investment is mostly for the purpose of maintaining the health infrastructure, both physical and manpower for the health sector.

The study therefore attempted to examine the role of health infrastructure such as health subcentres, public health care, central health-care centres, hospital beds per one lakh population, rural and urban government hospitals and also the total number of hospital beds in order to capture the role of physical infrastructure of health on health status. It is true that such infrastructure does not directly determine the health status, but they nevertheless facilitate delivery of health services. In other words absence of such facilities will directly impact health status in an adverse manner. Therefore physical health infrastructure plays an indirect and pivotal role in determining health status.

Therefore the first model, which is a multiple regression model that has been developed to assess the impact of physical health infrastructure on various indicators of health status, is stated below:

$$\mathrm{dr} = \mathrm{a} - \mathrm{b}\ subc - \mathrm{c}phc - \mathrm{d}che - \mathrm{e}hbd - \mathrm{f}dphc - \mathrm{g}hp - \mathrm{h}bd + \mathrm{u} \tag{5.70}$$

where

dr = death rate
subc = subcentres
phc = public health centres
chc = central health centres
hbd = hospital beds per 100,000 population
dphe = doctors per PHC
hp = total (rural and urban) govt hospitals
bd = total number of beds in hospitals

The availability of physical infrastructure mentioned above has been used as independent variable in the multiple regression models with urban and rural death rates, mortality rates, urban and rural mortality rates, expectancy of life for both males and females, infant mortality rates in general and also urban and rural, crude death rate, underweight children and children with stunted growth. The negative sign in the model indicates the inverse relationship between the negative health indicators and the physical infrastructure. In other words, the better the availability of the infrastructure, the better the health status.

The coefficient of determination indicating the explanatory power of the model is acceptable in case of mortality rate in general and urban mortality rates and infant mortality and rural infant mortality rates. Though theoretically the coefficients of the independent variables should all have negative signs implying that the better the physical infrastructure, the lower the negative health indicators mentioned above, some of the coefficients have positive signs. However this is not very surprising because of autocorrelation among the independent variables, due to their interrelationships, yet we do not accept the models for our purpose. The models for mortality rates have the requisite negative signs, implying that the better the physical infrastructure facility, the lower the mortality rate. Some of the estimated results which emerge as significant in our case are reported below:

$$\begin{aligned} \mathrm{mr} &= 65.489 + .219 subc - .526 phc + .036 chc - .268 dphc - .020 hp - .766 bd + u \\ \mathrm{t} &= (4.491)\ (.319)\ (-1.942)\ (.074)\ (-2.829)\ (.068)\ (-1.527) \\ & \mathrm{R}^2 = .505;\ \mathrm{F} = 12.307 \end{aligned} \tag{5.69}$$

$$\begin{aligned} \mathrm{mr_r} &= 68.784 + 232 subc - .495 phc + .080 chc - .260 dphc + .016 hp - .754 + u \\ \mathrm{t} &= (4.481)\ (1.337)\ (-2.883)\ (.166)\ (-1.801)\ (.055)\ (-1.505) \\ & \mathrm{R}^2 = .500;\ \mathrm{F} = 12.007 \end{aligned} \tag{5.70}$$

$$\begin{aligned} \mathrm{imr} &= 44.734 + .232 subc - .200 phc - .278 chc - .450 dphc + .140 hp - .620 hb + u \\ \mathrm{t} &= (7.813)(-1.429)\ (-1.432)\ (-2.687)\ (.2.55)\ (.767)\ (-2.216) \\ & \mathrm{R}^2 = 500;\ \mathrm{F} = 14.501 \end{aligned} \tag{5.71}$$

$$\begin{aligned} \mathrm{imr_r} &= 47.229 + .194 subc - .226 phc - .255 chc - .432 dphc + .126 hp - .542 bd + u \\ \mathrm{t} &= (7.543)\ (.350)\ (-1.447)\ (-1.615)\ (-2.393)\ (.673)\ (-1.885) \\ & \mathrm{R}^2 = .474;\ \mathrm{F} = 14.059 \end{aligned} \tag{5.72}$$

Among the various physical infrastructures that have been used in our present study, the estimated results reveal that for mortality rate, hospital beds emerge as the most crucial determinant both for general and rural mortality rates followed by the public health centres and the doctors per public health centres. It is interesting to note that a number of hospitals or the central health centres do not appear to be much significant in the determination of mortality rates. For the infant mortality rates in general and rural infant mortality rates in particular, a number of hospital beds emerge as the most important determinants, followed by the number of doctors per health centre and also by the number of public health centres and central health centres. It is also interesting to know that the subcentres which should ideally have been more effective determinant of health status in the rural areas do not have much impact in this matter. The reason could perhaps lie in their poor management and operation and the quality of services rendered by these subcentres, rather than their existence which as per the goals of health policies should cater to the basic health needs of the rural population. This therefore is an aspect that needs to be looked into by the policy makers, while working on the cost-benefit analysis of investment in the health sector.

The above findings can have serious implication for policy matters. Policy makers while allotting funds for the different tiers of the health system may need to have an idea about the outcome of the invested funds so that resources can be used more judiciously for the establishment of new health centres keeping the health outcome in mind.

The reasons for the estimated results working out to be different from our hypothesis could be that physical infrastructure may facilitate delivery of health services, which in turn can have favourable impact on health status, but may not contribute directly to determine health status in the immediate short run, but has its impact on the long-term health status through indirect impact. However, the indirect influence of physical infrastructure on health status in no way diminishes the importance of health infrastructure for health status. In fact, inadequate and poor physical infrastructure can impair the delivery of health services, adequate and good human infrastructure notwithstanding. It is here as discussed in Sect. 4.4 that the role of the state assumes importance because it means that public expenditure has to be stepped up in those sectors of health which has the largest extent of positive externalities so that the overall public welfare may rise. In a similar manner public expenditure has to be curtailed in those sectors where negative externalities are the highest.

Again as highlighted in the same section, public health expenditure, which is of two categories, is highly relevant. Public expenditure can be on general health-care services, termed as 'public health' like doctors, nurses and other health personnel, hospitals and other health infrastructures, the impact of which on the health status is indirect. The other category of public health expenditure has more direct impact on health outcomes. These expenditures relate more to those areas of public health which target to change the overall conditions of nutrition and sanitation that affect health outcomes. Investment on clean drinking water, immunisation or treatment for communicable diseases results in direct health benefits through reduced rates of disease, which is discussed in the sections on water and sanitation. Private expenditures on all such items will not take into account the positive external effects and therefore yield less than socially optimal levels of such activities. It is asserted that public expenditure on general health care services has positive externalities, not only by reducing social costs of morbidity and illness,but also by reducing inequalities in health care, which can otherwise create other social problems. State intervention therefore becomes essential either in the form of price subsidies to encourage the consumption of health-care services or direct public expenditure for the provision of such services.

Studies have revealed that inadequate public health expenditure has also resulted in a poor state of health infrastructure in India. A number of health-care personnel are grossly inadequate. The number of allopathic doctors, nurses and midwives is less than a fourth of the WHO benchmark. The ratio of nurses to doctors is extremely unfavourable compared to some better performing countries. The ratio is as low as 0.6:1, being less than one nurse per doctor (Rao and others 2011). In the developed countries, on the other hand, the ratio is 3 nurses per doctor.

The low component of non-salary expenditure has resulted in inadequate essential drug in the health subcentres, primary health centres and community health centres in rural areas, leading to further fall in the health status. Studies have revealed (IIPS 2007–2008) that about 35 % of the subcentres and 30 % of the public health centres have less than 60 % of essential drugs required for primary care. About one third of the public health centres has less than 60 % of the basic refrigeration facilities for primary care (IIPS 2010).

5.6.2 Non-availability of Health Manpower Infrastructure as a Determinant of Health Status

Since the above model did not reveal the expected results, we have also tried to examine the impact on health status of health manpower infrastructure, since their impact on health parameters is more immediate and has short-run implications. The model however has been specified in terms of the non-availability of health manpower and its impact rather than the availability of the same.

The model used for the purpose is as follows:

$$\mathrm{mr} = a + \mathrm{b}nd + \mathrm{c}nlt + \mathrm{d}np + u \tag{5.73}$$

where '*nd*' is the non-availability of doctors, '*nlt*' is the non-availability of laboratory technicians and 'np' is the non-availability of physicians.

The model has been tried for the different indicators of health status with positive sign for the coefficients, meaning that the greater the non-availability of health manpower facilities, the higher also the negative indicator of health status such as infant and child mortality, underweight children and children with stunted growth. Only in case of life expectancy the relationship will be negative, since the higher the non-availability of health manpower, the lower the life expectancy will be.

The model is thought to be not acceptable in the case of most indicators of health status either due to theoretical or statistical significance, but is acceptable for mortality rate in general and rural mortality in particular. It is also applicable to the case of underweight children and also for children with stunted growth. The estimated results of the model for mortality rate are reported below:

$$\begin{aligned} \mathrm{mr} &= 52.251 + .268nd + .556nlt + .615np + U \qquad \mathrm{R}^2 = .412;\ \mathrm{F} = 25.67 \\ \mathrm{t} &= (6.284)\quad (5.85)\quad (2.79)\quad (2.73) \end{aligned} \tag{5.73}$$

$$\begin{aligned} \mathrm{mr_r} &= 56.728 + 2.49nd + 6.08nlt + .682np + U \qquad \mathrm{R}^2 = .466;\ \mathrm{F} = 32.06 \\ \mathrm{t} &= (6.799)\quad (5.46)\quad (2.059)\quad (2.022) \end{aligned} \tag{5.74}$$

The statistical and theoretical significance of the above two models and thereby the acceptability of the same are not surprising because the lack of health manpower infrastructure is often responsible for a high rate of mortality particularly in the rural areas. The maintenance or functioning of inadequate health facilities, even if they are in existence, leaves a lot to be desired. The result is when the children fall ill, they are not given adequate treatment due to the lack of doctors or specialists or laboratory technicians which are so important for the diagnosis of different types of illnesses and diseases. The absence of all these facilities results in high death rate of children. This is more true in the case of non-availability of physicians as is evident from the estimated results, meaning that due to the lack of proper diagnosis of ailments because of lack of physicians, children are either not given proper treatment or in many cases not given any treatments at all, particularly in the rural areas. The results reveal that 1 % fall in the availability of physicians raises mortality rates by over 60 % in general and almost by 70 % in the rural sectors. Mortality rates can therefore be reduced to a large extent just by increasing the number of physicians, more so in the rural sectors, which only reiterates the already accepted fact of the existence of appalling state of rural health in India. In other words health status in general can be improved to a large extent just by improving the manpower infrastructural facilities in the rural areas. This is another crucial area in which the policy makers need to pay attention to. The rural health sector needs to be an independent area of planning since the approach and tackling health issues of the sector cannot be clubbed with that of the urban sector, because the problems and issues of the two sectors are quite different from one another, necessitating an altogether different approach to the two sectors.

The results of the model for underweight children and children with stunted growth are stated below:

$$\begin{aligned} \text{unw} &= 29.233 + .411nd - .086nlt + .519np + U \qquad R^2 = .505;\ F = 7.080 \\ t &= (14.256)(2.427)\quad (-.453)\quad (2.746) \end{aligned} \tag{5.75}$$

$$\begin{aligned} \text{csg} &= 38.837 + .154nd - .159nlt + .505np + U \qquad R^2 = .401;\ F = 32.06 \\ t &= (18.045)\quad (.733)\quad (-.674)\quad (2.115) \end{aligned} \tag{5.76}$$

where 'unw' and 'csg' represent underweight children and children with stunted growth, respectively.

The above two models are acceptable for our purpose in view of the satisfactory explanatory power of the model. R^2 is .505 and .401 for underweight children and children with stunted growth, respectively, which are also statistically significant. The coefficient for the explanatory variables relating to the non-availability of adequate number of doctors and physicians is significant both statistically and theoretically having the requisite signs before the coefficient. In fact, the higher non-availability of physicians by 1 % results in a rise of such children by almost 50 %. This implies that the lack of doctors and physicians to a large extent is responsible for the great number of underweight children and children with stunted growth. This implies that the lack of proper diagnosis during childhood is one of the important determinants of a growing number of such children. It is also a fact that poverty and lack of proper nutrition are the other contributory factors. However since the present study has not included these variables, we will not discuss it and leave it for the residual factor which is captured by 'U'. However, the non-availability of laboratory technicians however does not emerge as a factor determining the existence of underweight children and children with stunted growth, which is understood.

5.6.3 Accessibility of Health Centres and Health Awareness and Health Status

Pivotal role can be played in the health sector and in raising the health status through the creation of health awareness and identifying the potential risks to health. Ways of reaching out to the community particularly in the rural areas can create a positive impact on health status through awareness about the challenges and solution relating to good health. As discussed in Sect. 4.5, asymmetric information between the patient and the health service provider often results in market failure in health-care sector. This is a typical case of awareness relating to health-care service provided by the government and availing of the same. It is often experienced that one of the parties has some information which is not known to the others, so that even if adequate facilities in terms of physical or human infrastructure or other health delivery facilities are in existence, the ability to avail such facilities is non-existent or insufficient. The result is a drastic drop in health status merely due to unawareness and inadequate information.

Health status can be adversely affected when patients have to cover long distances to avail of health-care facilities. This often happens in large-sized countries, where a number of population served by physical and human infrastructure may be too high, particularly in highly populated countries like India. The use of health services can be considerably reduced due to long distance to health centres. The lack of universal accessibility to health care due to distance may thus bring down health status. Travel time often discourages particularly the poor to resort to quacks or even forgo treatment leading to high mortality rate. Studies have revealed (Schoeps et al. 2011) that in rural Burkina Faso, low health facility density and the resultant high travel time led to high mortality among infants and children. According to the study, the average walking time from each village to the closest health facility was obtained for both the dry and rainy seasons and its effect on infant and child mortality was analysed. The study also revealed that walking distance was significantly related to both infant mortality and child mortality.

The modes of transportation and distances to health subcentres become more significant in the rural areas, and studies have revealed (Mattson 2010) that distance decay effect states that the interaction between two locales decreases as the distance between them increases, which according to the study is found to occur in consumer travel behaviour, since a smaller proportion of the population travels to certain locations as the distance to those locations increases. Good number of studies (Goodman et al. 1977; Arcury et al. 2005; Winter et al. 2006) highlights that distance had a significant impact on health services and the related costs affected their health-care decisions and the time spent for travelling affected them physically and was a cause of stress. Nemet and Bailey (2000), for instance, revealed that people who had to travel more than 10 miles to go to the physicians tend to go less frequently to the physician than the ones who had to travel shorter distance. This is evident from the relationship between distance and utilisation of health care by a group of elderly residents in rural Verment, a country on the Canadian border where 82 % of the residents live in rural areas.

It is a fact in every country that there is a lower level of health-care utilisation in rural areas, where there are always fewer doctors and specialists per capita. Studies have revealed (Fordyce et al. 2007), even in the American context, that there are not only fewer specialists per capita in rural areas, but there are fewer generalists per capita. The study revealed that in rural areas with 19 % of the population in the USA, there are only 11 % of the physicians available. Therefore many rural countries do not have sufficient number of patients to have full service hospitals. The rural health model therefore emphasises on providing primary care and emergency care locally, and regional hospitals and health centres are referred to for specialised treatments.

We have therefore adopted the next set of models to examine the impact of health awareness and accessibility to health facilities with secondary data in the Indian context. In India every panchayat is allotted certain funds for rural health. However the utilisation of the funds by the patients in the rural sector depends on the awareness of the availability of such funds. This awareness in turn among the rural patients has to be developed by the panchayat/pradhan (head). It has been observed that in many cases, the pradhans themselves are not aware about the availability of such funds. The result is that the patients in the rural areas are able to avail of such facilities given by the governments only due to the lack of awareness. This has often been experienced to be an important factor that brings down the health status in the rural areas.

In certain rural areas, the function of the pradhans (village head) from Health and Sanitation Committees is to raise awareness about the positive effect on health of the proper system of sanitation to the villagers, and all other necessary assistance in this connection is given to the villagers by the panchayat. Such committees however are formed only when there is sufficient consciousness and awareness among the village head or the residents about the beneficial effect of adequate sanitation.

The travel distance as discussed is a very important determinant of health status in the rural sectors which is often overlooked by the policy makers. In the model we have taken the presence of health subcentres within a range of 3 km and public health centres within a range of 10 km and attempted to examine their impact on the health status.

The multiple regression model conceptualised by including the factors of awareness and accessibility to assess the health status is stated below:

$$\mathrm{dr} = \mathrm{a} - \mathrm{b}hsc - \mathrm{c}paf - \mathrm{d}skm_3 + \mathrm{e}pkm_{10} + \mathrm{U} \tag{5.77}$$

where

hsc = health and sanitation committees
paf = pradhan/panchayat member aware of united funds for health
skm_3 = health subcentres within a range of 3 km
pkm_{10} = public health centres within a range of 10 km

The negative sign for the coefficients on awareness implies that the lower the awareness, the higher the negative indicator of health status. Since 3 km is a reasonable distance to avail of health facilities, positive sign has been used for the coefficient, meaning that the lesser the presence of health subcentres within a range of 3 km, the better the health indicator. For exactly the opposite reasons, 10 km is a long travel distance to avail of health facilities, and therefore the more the number of public health centres located at a faraway distance, the higher also the negative health indicator.

The model has been tested for all the indicators of health status mentioned above. However in view of the statistical and theoretical significance of the models, only those models for child mortality and life expectancy both for males and females reported below are accepted for the purpose of the present study:

$$\begin{aligned} \text{mr} &= 122.95 - .512hsc - .004paf + .119skm3 + .545pkm_{10} + U \\ \text{t} &= (5.189)\ (-2.789)(-.015)\quad (.1.55)\quad (2.157) \\ & \text{R}^2 = .601;\ \text{F} = 5.27 \end{aligned} \tag{5.78}$$

$$\begin{aligned} \text{mr}_{\text{u}} &= 74.225 - .626hsc + .164paf + .201skm_3 - .196pkm_{10} + U \\ \text{t} &= (94.681)(-1.87)\quad (.491)\quad (.796)\quad (.778) \\ & \text{R}^2 = .458;\ \text{F} = 2.958 \end{aligned} \tag{5.79}$$

$$\begin{aligned} \text{mr}_{\text{r}} &= 137.038 - .507hsc + .041paf + .510skm_3 + .546pkm_{10} + U \\ \text{t} &= (5.492)(-1.764)\quad (.141)\quad (2.267)\quad (2.510) \\ & \text{R}^2 = .597;\ \text{F} = 5.181 \end{aligned} \tag{5.80}$$

The estimated models mentioned are all acceptable since the coefficient of determination as revealed by the value of R^2 in each case is .601, .458 and .597, implying satisfactory explanatory power of the model which is also statistically significant as revealed by the value of F.

As far as the first model is concerned, the results reveal that the signs of the coefficients are acceptable for all the independent variables and they are all statistically significant. It is revealed that the greater the distance of the health centres from the actual users of the health services, the higher also the mortality rate, and the closer the health centres, the lower also the mortality rates. This is in conformity with the conclusions of the other studies conducted on similar lines. What therefore transpires is that a distance of 10 km of the health centre is extremely difficult for the patient to traverse along with their sick children. As a result they are either left without any treatment or resort to quacks and home treatment even in case of acute illness. The result is a rise in the mortality rates. The same however is totally reversed when the distance of the health centres is reduced to only 3 km. It is therefore only too evident that more health centres within close range need to be set up, implying more investment and allocation of resources in increasing the number of health centres.

Among all the variables relating to awareness of health and sanitation facilities, the findings reveal that health and sanitation committees are the most significant determinants of mortality rate. This once again implies setting up more of such committees. This of course does not require more of financial investment but only requires providing incentives and encouragement to set up such awareness committees, which is therefore much easier to establish. It is also revealed that the existence of pradhan and panchayat members with knowledge of the funds of health does not have much impact on mortality rates. The reason could be that such information for the benefit of the health consumers are not disseminated. What therefore transpires from the above is that awareness about health and sanitation and distance of health centres are important determinants of child mortality in India.

Analysing the impact of awareness and distance spatially for urban and rural sectors, the study reveals that the explanatory power of the model is much higher in the case of the rural sector. Besides this, the signs of the coefficient for the urban sector are not per theoretical expectations. The reason could be that distance in the urban sector is not an impediment to accessibility to health facilities and the panchayats and sanitation committees are non-existent in the urban areas. For exactly the opposite reasons, the model is more relevant in the case of the rural sector. Not only is the explanatory power of the model better, R^2 is also statistically significant. The coefficient explaining the effect of the Health and Sanitation Committees on mortality rate is also acceptable with the requisite sign and statistical significance. The awareness of the panchayat/pradhan regarding the availability of funds for health is not relevant, perhaps due to reasons which need a thorough and separate investigation, or as highlighted above the information is not disseminated. The impact of travel distance on child mortality is also quite clear as evident from the signs of the coefficient. For the coefficient of subcentres within a range of 3 km, the more the presence of such subcentres, the lower the child mortality. In contrast, the more the number of public health subcentres within a range of 10 km, making accessibility more difficult, the higher the mortality rate. The coefficients are also statistically significant, due to which the model is accepted for our purpose. It may therefore be concluded that in the rural areas, awareness about health programmes and facilities and the travel distance of availing health facilities directly affects child mortality and might also be affecting the other indicators of health status in an indirect way.

The results of the model of impact of distance and awareness on life expectancy are reported below:

$$\begin{aligned} \mathrm{lexp}f &= 63.662 + .337hsc - .060paf - .312skm_3 - .723pkm_{10} + U \\ \mathrm{t} &= (16.018)(1.243)\ (-.224)(-1.662) \qquad (-3.957) \\ & \mathrm{R}^2 = .529; \mathrm{F} = 4.490 \end{aligned} \tag{5.81}$$

$$\begin{aligned} \text{lexpm} &= 64.104 + .509 hsc - .173 paf - .359 skm_3 - .696 pkm_{10} + U \\ t &= (23.509)(1.918)\ (-.655)\quad (-1.955)\quad (-3.890) \\ & \qquad\qquad\qquad\qquad\qquad R^2 = .548;\ F = 4.857 \end{aligned} \tag{5.82}$$

where '*lexp*' represents life expectancy and the subscripts 'f' and 'm' signify female and male life expectancy.

The models are accepted for explaining both female and male life expectancies as indicated by the value of R^2 which are statistically significant in both the cases. The results reveal that the longer the distance of the health subcentres, the lower the life expectancy, be it that of females or the males, but the value of the coefficient of longer distance is higher for the females. This only implies that it is more difficult for females to travel a longer distance to avail health services and they therefore do not receive medical attention which becomes a common feature throughout their life, which adversely affects their life expectancy, be it in the rural or the urban sector. However the reverse is the case when the distance of the health centres is reduced, which then has a direct impact on their life expectancy in the case of both males and females more or less in a similar manner. It therefore transpires that even in the case of life expectancy, the closer the health centres, the better the impact on both male and female life expectancies.

As in the case of mortality rates for life expectancy too, it is revealed that committees on health and sanitation have a favourable impact on life expectancy. This may work with better impact through awareness on sanitation, clean drinking water and general hygiene, the impact of which has already been discussed in the earlier sections. The information of the panchayats and pradhan about the existence of funds for health does not have any impact even in the case of life expectancy; the reasons could perhaps be the same as highlighted earlier.

As a whole therefore, what transpires from the finding of this section is that the distance of health centres and the health and sanitation committees can determine health status in a significant way so that strengthening these determinants of health status is a matter for policy considerations, which can ultimately determine the status of health in a nation.

5.6.4 Status of Health in India

In a vast country like India, health care either in terms of policies or budgetary allocation or even medical education has never received its due importance. The National Health Policy of the country was adopted for the first time in Parliament in 1982–1983. One of the glaring instances of the relatively low level of importance assigned to the health sector is evident from the extremely low proportion of GDP allocated for the health sector. Till 2007–2008, it was only 0.9 % of the GDP, increasing to only 1.6 % in 2011–2012. This is the scenario of the importance assigned to the health sector through policy consideration when India is a case of a nation burdened both with the illness of a poor nation like tuberculosis, malaria and diarrhoea and the illness of rich nations like heart diseases and diabetics. In other words, even before the nation is able to fully eliminate deaths and illness due to poverty, the nation is burdened with illnesses due to lifestyle.

Unprecedented disparity in health condition in India between rural and urban sectors has always been a matter of great concern. In fact, the seriousness of the issue is increasing along with higher growth rate and rapid economic development and unplanned urbanisation. Even within the urban sector, there is gross inequality in health status of the population. Rapid unplanned urbanisation on one hand is leading to pollution, slum and unhygienic condition of living and environmental degradation resulting in growing health problems. Added to all this is the lack of civic amenities. Rising population on the other hand, particularly among the lower middle class, is leading to deprivation in terms of food and nutrition, adequate housing facilities, unclean drinking water and inadequate sanitation facilities. The result of all this as stated earlier is that the population becomes the victims of all types of diseases and illnesses. The biggest challenge of the health sector in India comes from the rural sector in India which constitutes over 70 % of the total population. It is in the rural sector that there is almost total absence of any health infrastructure, absence of qualified health personnel and non-availability of basic medicines. All these make the quality of health delivery system almost deplorable. The result is that in the rural areas, health consumers have to resort to illiterate, untrained doctors and village quacks, which in most cases aggravates health problems even further. In the urban sectors, almost 92 % of the health-care visits are to private health service providers, out of which 70 % are for urban population. The result is that 'out of pocket' expenditure for health has become a menace in India. Such expenses are also unaffordable to the poor and the population of rural India. It is due to this reason that health statistics in India is still shocking, high growth rates of the economy notwithstanding.

Studies relating to the health condition in India have revealed (Perianayagam and Goli 2013) that though in India, public health-care system is the main channel for the delivery of health care to the people in vulnerable socioeconomic conditions, the system suffers mainly due to the lack of management and poor quality of services and inadequate finances. In spite of recent expansion and modernisation in public health-care system, health delivery system has not improved in India. The gap in the system is being fulfilled by private health delivery services, which is more expensive. It is the dominance of private health services in view of the inefficacy of the public health services that health consumers often have to borrow or sell assets and utilise their savings for the purpose of meeting hospitalisation expenses (Gumber 2001; Gumber and Kulkarni 2000). According to the World Bank Report (2002), a quarter of the Indians are pushed into poverty for meeting hospitalisation expenses and almost 80 % of the households incur 'out of pocket' expenses on health spending on drugs and medicines. It is further revealed that due to health-care services becoming more expensive, many sick people are forced to forgo medical treatment. The study has also revealed that financial reasons account for a quarter of untreated ailments in rural areas and over 20 % of untreated ailments in urban areas, a rise from 15 % to 10 %, respectively.

The result of all this is that health records in India are quite shocking in spite of the high growth rate of the economy in recent decades. Infant mortality according to figures available for 2012 was still 42 per 1000 and mortality under 5 years was 63 for the corresponding period. The number of underweight children for the 2006–2010 period was 42.5 %. Figure for maternal mortality was 212 per 100,000 population during 2007–2009. According to 2009 figures, adult mortality rates among females were 169 per 1000 and 250 for males. In spite of so many decades of planned development, malaria deaths constitute 1.9 % and death due to cholera is 6 %. Life expectancy has improved since independence, yet it was only 67.3 years for males and 69.6 years for females for the 2011–2015 period. Children under 5 years still die due to diarrhoea, mostly due to the reasons discussed in the preceding sections. The figure for such deaths was as high as 13 % in 2008, due to measles about 4 % and 20 % deaths due to pneumonia.

In view of the above, the determinants of the various indicators of health status as examined and highlighted in the present chapter assume crucial significance for the policy makers in the health sector.

References

Adams SJ (2002) Educational attainments and health: evidence from a sample of older adults. Educ Econ 10(1):97–109

Adukia A (2014) Sanitation and education, Working paper, Harvard University, Harvard, Cambridge

American College of Physicians (2012) Internal medicine, doctors for adults, summary of position. Paper approved by the ACP Board of Regents

Anan A (1993) Gender preference for children, Demographic and health surveys, comparative studies, no-23. Macro International, Calverton

Anekwe TD, Kuner S (2012) The effects of vaccination programmes on child anthropometry: evidence from India's universal immunisation programme. J Public Health 34(4):489–497

Arcury TA, Wilbert M, Gesler JS. Preisser JS, Spencer J, Perin J (2005) The effects of geography and spatial behaviour on health care utilisation among the residents of a rural region. Health Ser Rec 40(1):135–155, US

Arend JN (2001) Education effects of health: causal or from unobserved components: a panel data analysis with endogenous education. Institute of Economics, University of Copenhagen, Copenhagen

Arendt JN (2005) Does education cause better health? A panel data analysis. Using school reforms for identification. Econ Educ Rev 24:149–160

ARWSS, Swajaldhara Schemes (2007) Swajaldhara rural drinking water scheme. Govt of India, India

Asafu-Adjaye J (2004) Income inequality and health: a multi- country analysis. Int J Soc Econ 31:194–207

Banerjee A, Jacob S, Kremer M, Lanjouw J, Lanjouw P (2000) Promoting school participation in rural Rajasthan: results from some prospective trials. MIT, Cambridge, MA, mimeo

Bharat Nirman Programme (2005) Statewise target and achievement of national rural drinking water programme (NRDWP) under BNP in India

Blane D, White I, Morris J (1996) Education, social circumstances and mortality. In: Blane D, Brunner E, Wilkinson RG (eds) Health and social organisation. Routledge, London

Blomm DE, et al (2005) Health and economic growth: reconciling the micro and macro evidence. Working Paper No. 42. Centre on Democracy, Development and the Rule of Law. Stanford Institute of International Studies, pp 2, 3

Bonu S, Rani M, Baker TD (2003) The impact of national polio immunisation campaign on levels and equity in immunisation coverage: evidence from rural north India. Soc Sci Med 57(10):1807–1819

Breierova L, Duflo E (2004) The impact of education on fertility and child mortality: Do fathers really matter less than mothers. National Bureau of Economic Research, Cambridge, MA

Case A, Fetig A, Paxson C (2005) The lasting impact of childhood health and circumstances. J Health Econ 24:365–389

Clark D, Royer H (2008) Effects of education on adult mortality and health: evidence from UK, Working paper. University of Florida, Gainesville

Coutoyannis P, Jones AM (2004) Socioeconomic status, health and life style. Health Econ 23:965–995

Corman H, Grossman M (1985) Determinants of neonatal mortality rates in the US. J Health Econ 4:213–236

Cutler D, Miller G (2005) The role of public health improvements in health advances the twentieth century United States. Demography 42(1):1–22

Cutler D, Muney M (2007) Education and health, Policy brief. National Poverty Centre, Ann Arbor/Cambridge, MA

Cutler D, Deaton A, Lleras-Muney A (2006) The determinants of mortality. J Econ Perspect 20:97–120

Das Gupta M (1987) Selective discrimination against female children in rural Punjab, India. Popul Dev Rev 13(1):77–100

Deaton A, Paxson C (2001) Mortality, education, income inequality among american cohorts. In: Wise PA (ed) Themes in the economics of aging. University of Chicago Press, Chicago, Cambridge, MA

Erbsland MW, Volker U (1995) Health, health care and the environment, econometric evidence from German micro data. Econ Health Econ 4:169–182

Farrell P, Fuchs V (1982) Schooling and health. J Health Econ 1:217–230

Feinstein L, Hammond C (2004) The contribution of adult learning to health and social capital. Oxf Rev Educ 30(21):199–221

Feinstein L, et al (2006) Measuring the effects of education on health and civic engagement. In: Proceedings of the Copenhagen symposium, OECD, Paris

Fink G, Gunther I, Hill K (2011) The effect of water and sanitation on child health: evidence from demographic and health surveys. Int J Epidem 40(5):1196–1204

Fonsica R, Zheng Y (2011) Effects of education on health: cross country evidence. Working paper, rand, labour and population. Santa Monica: RAND.

Fordyce MA, Chen FM, Doeschen MP, Gary Hart L (2007) Physician supply and distribution in rural areas of the United States. Rural Health Research Center, University of Washington, Seattle

Fuchs VR (2004) Reflections on the socioeconomic correlates of health. J Health Econ 23:653–661

Glewwe P (1999) Why does mother's schooling raise child health in developing countries? J Hum Res 34(1):124–159

Goli S, Arokiasamy P (2013) Trends in health and health inequalities among major states in India: assessing progress through convergence models. Health Econ Policy Law 9(2):143–168. doi 10.1017/S17441331130000042

Goodman DC, Fisher E, Stukel TA, Chang CH (1977) The distance to community medical care and the likelihood of hospitalisation: is closer always better? Am J Public Health 87

Grossman M (1972) On the concept of health capital and the demand for health. J Polit Econ 80:223–255

Grossman M (2000) The human capital model. In: Culyer AJ, Newhouse JP (eds) Handbook of health economics, vol 1a. Elsevier, Amsterdam

Grossman M, Kaestner R (1997) Effects of education on health. In: Behrmeen JR, Stacey N (eds) The social benefits of education. University of Michigan Press, Ann Arbor
Gumber A (2001) Economic reforms and the health sector: toward health equity in India: National seminar on economic reforms and employment in the Indian economy. Institute of Applied Manpower Research and Planning Commission, New Delhi
Gumber A, Kulkarni V (2000) Health insurance for the informal sector: a case study of Gujarat, Economic and Political Weekly, September
Gwntkein DR (2000) Health inequalities and the health of the poor. Bull World Health Org 78(1):55–65
IIPS (2007–2008) IIPS and macro international (2007) National Family Health Survey (NFHS-3) 2005–06, India, vol 1, Mumbai
IIPS (2010) District level household and facility survey (DLHS-3) 2007–08, India. International Institute of population Sciences, Mumbai
Jalan J, Ravillion M (2003) Does piped water reduce diarrhoea for children in rural India. J Econ 112(1):153–173
Kawachi I, Kennedy BP, Lochner K, Prothrow-Stith P (1979) Social capital income inequality and mortality. Am J Public Health 87(9):1491–1498
Lieras-Muney A (2005) The relationship between education and adult mortality in US. Rev Econ Stud 72:189–221
Macagba RL (1985) Hospitals and primary health care. Sponsored: International Health Care, London
Mattson J (2010) Transportation, distance and health care utilisation for older adults in rural and small urban areas. Research sponsored by Federal Transit Administration, United States, Department of Transportation
McMichael T, Biaglehole R (2003) The global content for public health. In: Beaglehole R (ed) Global public health: a new era. Oxford University Press, Oxford
Meara E (2001) Why is health related to socioeconomic status? The case of pregnancy and low birth weight. National Bureau of Economic Research (NBER), Cambridge, MA
Mellor JM, Milyo J (2002) Income inequality and health status in the United States: evidence from current population survey. J Hum Res 37(3):510–539
Muller A (2002) Education, income inequality and mortality: a multiple regression analysis. BMJ 324:23–25
National Bureau of Economic Research (2012) Education, health and mortality: evidence from a social experiment. NBER Working Paper No. 17932
National Water Policy (2002) Ministry of Water Resources, Govt of India
Nemet GE, Bailey AJ (2000) Distances and health care utilisation among rural elderly. Soc Sci Med 50:1197–1208
Or Z, Wang J, Jamison D (2005) International differences in the impact of doctors on health: a multilevel analysis of OECD countries. J Health Econ 24:531–560
Pande P, Yazbeck AS. Beyond national averages for immunisation in India: income, gender, regional inequalities, Health, Nutrition and population (HNP) Series. Washington, DC, Washington
Perianayagam A, Goli S (2013) Pathways of economic inequalities in maternal and child health in urban India: a decomposition analysis
Peterson A, Lupton D (1996) The new public health. Sage Publications, St. Leonard
Pruss-Ustun A, Bos R, Gore F, Barstram J (2008) Safe water, better health: costs, benefits and sustainability on interventions to protect and promote health. WHO, Geneva
Rao M, Rao MD, Shiva Kumar AK, Chatterjee M, Sundararaman T (2011) India towards universal health coverage. Lancet 377:586–598
Reading R, Surridge H, Adamson R (2004) Infant immunisation and family size. J Public Health Oxf J 26:369–371
Sagan LA (1989) The health of nations: true causes of sickness and well-being. Basic Books, New York

Schoeps A Gabrysch S, Niamba L, Sie A, Becker H (2011) The effect of distance to health care facilities on childhood mortality in rural Burkina Faso, Multicentre Study, Research Support non US Govt

Sharma S (2007) Immunisation coverage in India, Working paper series. No E/283/2007. Institute of Economic Growth, Delhi

Spasojevic J (2003) Effects of education on adult health in Sweden: results from a national experiment. PhD dissertation, City University of New York Graduate Center

Status Report (2001) Public Health Infrastructure: Centre for Disease Control and Prevention, Department of Health and Human Services, USA

Stephens PW (1984) The relationship between the level of household sanitation and child mortality: an examination of Ghanian data. African Demography working paper. University of Pennsylvania, Population Studies Center

Thomas D, Strauss J, Henriques MH (1991) How does mother's education affect child's height? J Hum Res 26(2):183–211

Wildman J (2003) Modelling health, income and income inequality on health and health inequality. J Health Econ 22:521–538

Water Aid: European Commission. Abandoning open defecation: comparison and adaptation of social change dynamics

WHO and UNICEF (2006) Meeting the MDG drinking water and sanitation target: the urban and rural challenges of the decades. New York, USA

Winters CA, Cudney SA, Sullivan T, Thresen A (2006) The rural context and women's self-management of chronic health conditions. Chronic Ill 2:273–289

Woldemicael G (2000) The effects of water supply and sanitation on child mortality in urban Eritrea. University of Asmara, Eritrea

World Bank (1993) Investing in health. World development report. Oxford University Press, New York

World Bank Report (2002) Health. World development indicators. World Bank, New York

Zheng J (2010) The impact of water quality on health: evidence form drinking water infrastructure program in rural China, University of Maryland, College Park (Job market paper)

Chapter 6
Health Management for the Health Sector

6.1 Relevance of Health Management for Health Status

6.1.1 Introduction

The discussions and analysis of the preceding sections reveal the need for management skills in the health sector for the delivery of health-care services to the right people at the right time and even more importantly at affordable prices. Health economics focusses attention to the ways and means of utilising the scarce resources in the health sector in an optimum manner. Management skills in the health sector, on the other hand, ensure that the health-care system has a strong medical, operational and financial foundation so that the health needs of the consumers can be undertaken and delivered in a professional manner with optimum use of the resources allocated to the health sector. Professional management of the health system can also ensure minimum wastage, avoiding underutilisation of capacity in the health system. In a society dominated by health-care service consumers, it is necessary that the important communication relating to health issues are conveyed to the members of the society and their leaders, for which management can also play a crucial role.

The role of the state in providing health services particularly during the period when market forces have assumed a growing role has been a matter of intense debate. It is maintained by some thinkers that the role of the state in health sector has resulted in wastage of precious resources particularly in poor nations in maintaining a huge administrative set-up. Such a set-up has resulted in corruption rather than in providing the necessary health services to the needy. While this view cannot be totally ruled out, at the same time, there are certain areas of health-care system which if left outside the purview of the state will only result in growing misery among the poor. One of the most important reasons for the controversy over the role of the state in providing health care is the inadequate understanding about the role of the state in either changing the economic scenario or the health scenario. Added

K. Sengupta, *Determinants of Health Status in India*,
DOI 10.1007/978-81-322-2535-5_6

to this kind of uncertainty is the problem of inadequate resources for the health sector. Over and above this is also the rising problem of inadequate monitoring system and the absence of accountability. Consequently, what should be one of the most important social investments has lost its relevance and appears to be wastage of resources. The other associated problem has been a lack of priority regarding allocation of resources in the sector. The result has been gross misallocation of resources. Lack of prioritisation has also resulted in 'financial and human resources being spread too thinly for impact'. Studies have revealed that states in India which have experienced equity in terms of service coverage and in delivery of basic preventive services to the poor and disadvantaged groups have consistently recorded better health outcomes. In such instances adequate attention is also paid to management issues of the health sector. This shows the importance of equitable access to health services by poor and disadvantaged groups which can be ensured only by the state (IIHR 2005). Apart from these functions in the areas of health education and public awareness, planning, management and monitoring of services sensitivity to local community needs can best be ensured by the state machinery.

There is thus an integral connection between health economics, health outcomes and health management. The limited resources available for the health sector for their optimum use and maximum health benefits to the users can be given proper direction and channelised into desired objectives only through the right management techniques. The optimum use of limited resources in the health sector can thus be attained only through various management tools. Health management uses various managerial tools and techniques in an attempt to undertake the challenges of limited resources, inadequate health infrastructure both physical and human as well as spatial problems of health delivery and other critical issues of delivering health services to the needy as has been examined in detail earlier. Decision about such managerial tools and techniques is determined by the type of health problems confronting the people and the nation. It is also decided by the national income of the country, the per capita income of the people and their health expenditure, the population composition of the nation as well as the literacy of the population, all of which come under the purview of health economics. Identification of these factors and their relative weightage on health status needs to be examined before deciding upon the managerial techniques to achieve the health objectives. It is thus evident that a holistic study of health economics is incomplete without a study of the issues, tools and techniques of health management. The use of management tools can therefore be considered as the channel through which delivery of health-care services can be made to the final users. Therefore, if the route through which health services are delivered is inefficient and inadequate, health status of the place too will meet a similar fate.

It also needs to be noted that the choice of health management tools is determined by the challenges posed by the type of diseases, mortality and morbidity rates and infant and maternal mortality rates. The priority given in solving each of these problems and the formulation of health goals and objectives, which come under the purview of health policies, are in reality addressed by health management. Development of programs, cost estimation, alternative and cheaper programs and strategies for attaining the health objectives can all be achieved with the help of knowledge of health management. Study to evaluate the effectiveness of different health programmes and their modifications, expansion or even replacement or innovation is undertaken only with the help of management tools. The primary role of management is the same everywhere, be it in the service sector, production and manufacturing sector or sale of goods and commodities. Basic objectives are the same with a difference of only the complexities of the respective enterprises of the health sector. The complexities of the health sector have been only increasing in recent times with growing challenges of the sector, thereby increasing the role of health management.

As an organisation tries to handle these complex issues, managerial competence from top to bottom faces greater and greater challenges. Managerial experience therefore of not only the health officials but even the health providers therefore assumes crucial significance. Successful and professional functioning of the health sector requires managers who are able to control and make the health sector function effectively so that the health delivery system can successfully meet its goal and objectives.

With the expanding health sector, investment in the sector, too, has been rising at an increasing rate, demanding greater degree of professional management of the huge investment and finance. Efficient management of financial resources necessitates knowledge of financial management, which will not only reduce wastage but will also ensure optimum utilisation of scare resources, which is one of the goals of the study of microeconomics. It is also essential that proper health administration demands efficient personnel management and human resource management. Teamwork effort in the health sector and other types of soft skills are the key to the success of the health sector. All these efforts both at the organisational level and at the national level require a vision and a mission which can be effectively devised and handled only by managerial techniques.

Health management therefore deals extensively with the evaluation of health programmes and cost accounting, cost-benefit and cost-effectiveness of health expenditure, all of which are the economic tools of analysis. As a result, health economics play a pivotal role in the study of hospitals, demand and supply for health care, provision of health infrastructure, both physical and manpower and medical curricula with the purpose of making health management standardised and effective. Hence, the study and integration of health economics and health management is of crucial importance which neither any economist nor any health manager can afford to ignore.

Therefore, managers dealing with the health sector need to possess all the managerial skills of leadership, communication, strategic planning, budgeting and finance through which support and coordination of the services of the health sector organisation can be ensured, in addition to the knowledge of health economics.

6.2 The Concept of Health Management

Health management has always been a difficult area to understand and comprehend. Health consumers' research focusses attention mostly to health-care or health service management. It deals mostly with the various ways in which health services are organised and determined (Hunter and Brown 2007). The knowledge gained in the study of health sector is often experienced to be far from the application to real-life situation. It is here that health management can play an important and effective role.

One of the crucial areas of concern is the failure to convey and utilise the knowledge gained from research in health sector to the managers in the health sector. The reason for this is that, as is evident from our study above, the health sector is extremely wide, encompassing many areas from economics to social sectors, due to which management of the health sector tends to become unwieldy. Management in the health sector therefore takes into account all these issues of coordination and supervision so that health delivery to each and every member of the society is ensured. Health management is therefore defined as 'the activities around the development and implementation of policy and the organisation of services aimed at improving health. The focus is on delivering and effecting change in organisation concerned with improving population health' (Hunter and Brown 2007). The study of health status in our present work supports the definition of health management because it was clearly evident that the status of health is determined from financial investment for physical infrastructure such as hospital equipment to health education, both for consumers and the health personnel who delivers health services. It also extends to clean drinking water and sanitation facilities, immunisation, drugs and medicines. It also stresses to the political commitments and governance, which ultimately determines the success of the health-care system. Health management incorporates all these activities in a holistic manner so that health delivery is done in an efficient and effective manner.

The responsibility of raising health status thus is determined to a large extent by the personnel responsible for health management. As such, it is essential that health-care personnel develop professionalism and understand the complexities of the leadership skills and have an in-depth understanding of management skills relating to basic accounting, financial principles, medical practice and managerial software within health-care organisations. It is therefore essential that effective decision-making and planning skills for health-care management and all-round education in health-care practices need to be developed by health practitioners. Apart from mainstream management skills, health management also extends to management of chronic diseases. However, the fact remains that studies relating to health management, particularly in the Indian context, are scanty. Findings of the above study for policy considerations can be strengthened if supported by adequate research work on health management, since most of the gaps relating to health-care status can be overcome with the skills of health management. In fact, health management issues have always been a neglected area, though most of the problems of health inequalities, chronic diseases and inaccessibility to health-care services can be overcome if effectiveness of health management issues is addressed and assigned its due priorities by policy makers.

There is thus an integral connection between health economics and health management. Health economics enables knowing and identifying the problems of the health sector using economic tools of analysis. Overcoming and solving the problems thus identified is the domain of health management, which it attempts to attain with the help of management tools and techniques. The two aspects of health study therefore cannot be viewed in isolation. The ultimate goal of raising the health status can be achieved only when the two areas of study are synchronised in the best possible manner, because one aspect of the study is incomplete without the other. Making health policies effective requires the knowledge of both health economics and health management. It is therefore of utmost priority that more research needs to be undertaken in different areas of health management, so that research gap in the sphere of health management can be overcome and the health sector of the country can be strengthened.

The importance and the impact of the management tools and techniques is evident from the study (McKinsey and Company) where management practices such as operations management, talent, people management and performance management were studied in 1194 hospitals across the USA, UK, Canada, Sweden, Germany, France and Italy. The study recognising the rising challenges of the health sector, in terms of rising health expenditure and rising demand, can be tackled by addressing the management issues in the health sector.

The study clearly established the relationship between management practices and health outcomes. It is revealed that hospitals with better management practices have lower mortality rates, higher levels of patient's satisfaction and better financial performance. The study asserts that management does matter for patient's well-being. The study also concludes from data of hospitals in the UK that the more the number of managers with clinical degree, the better is also the management of the hospitals. Better performing hospitals give managers higher level of autonomy in comparison to lower performing hospitals.

An interesting finding of the study is that there is a strong relationship between management practices, performance of hospitals and policy-related variables, such as perceived levels of competition and percentage of health managers who have some professional training. Competition even in the health sector encourages better management. Poorly managed hospitals are therefore likely to close down or to be taken over since they are unable to withstand the stiff competition. Health care is a skill-based service and therefore quality of human skills is crucial for the success of the health sector. It was also revealed that management practices are better in larger sized hospitals than in smaller sized ones and large hospitals are therefore also more successful, which reveals the advantages of economies of scale which the larger sized hospitals are able to reap advantageously. Autonomy of managers also plays an important role in bringing about better management practices according to the study.

6.3 Public Health Management and Health Status

Public health management is defined as 'the use of the resources of the society and its health services towards the improvement of health experience of the population' (Alderslade and Hunter 1994). It is, broadly speaking, managing the health of the population or to managing for health (Hunter 1999). One of the major problems as is well known in the health sector in all nations, more specifically in the developing ones, is the implementation of health policies. This often occurs due to inadequate knowledge and experience regarding the ways of implementing the policies in a complex and a dynamic sector, like the health sector. Strengthening the management system helps in delivering the policy objectives through appropriate actions with the help of management skills. In the twenty-first century, along with the other determinants of health sector, management training in the health sector for developing various management skills is therefore of utmost importance. The ultimate success of the health sector thus depends on the combined efforts of the health practitioners and the health managers with the requisite management skills. Health management skills are the means of attaining the targets of the best health status of a nation. Lack of coordination between the two sectors particularly in the public health-care system has been responsible not only for the failure for ensuring the best use of scarce resources in the health sector but has also resulted in the duplication of efforts, time and energy in the health sector resulting in huge wastage of precious resources. In fact, it has in many cases resulted in a total failure and collapse of the public health system in a good number of less developed nations, India not been an exception. The result has been higher negative figures of health status than what is warranted by the policies and investment in the sector. Better coordinated efforts therefore demand greater leadership qualities, in the entire health sector, but more so in the public health sector, which is often the neglected one. Though consideration of equity dominates efficiency in the public health sector, in no way public health sector can justify inefficient system of management, the need for which is imperative for better health status in every nation.

Realisation has now dawned among the planners of the public health sector, in the twenty-first century, that higher level of investment and mere accessibility may not always ensure better health services, unless and until the sector is supported by a strong health management system. Good and ambitious health policies even in the developed countries have often failed merely because they were framed within the traditional public health models in which leadership and management skills of planning, coordination and organisation were not considered relevant for the health sector. Health managers therefore need to possess both management skills and knowledge of the public health sector. It is only too clear from the deplorable condition of health status of most countries that the role of health leadership in the public health system is more important today than ever before.

In order to appreciate management roles in the public health system, it is essential to know the broad features of public health management which are as follows:

1. It is multi-sectoral and professional.
2. Combines knowledge and action.

3. Has epidemiology at its core.
4. Is influential across all health determinants.
5. Involves public health reporting, leading to health strategy development.
6. Communicates with politicians, professional and the public
7. Is influential organisationally and financially.
8. Lies at the heart of the civic society.

It is therefore maintained by many (Hunter 2001) that public health management is all about leadership and managing change, which therefore brings us to the roles of public health management. These roles are advocacy and management roles, knowledge and action, managerial capacity, infrastructure and networking. These roles can create partnerships across organisations and disciplines, broad involvement and people and skills. This can be an outcome-based focus of national agenda for health and health service research.

Ineffective system of health management in most public health sector has resulted in status of health much below than what is warranted by planning and investment in the sector concerned. This has been the experience of those nations who are yet to realise the role of health management in the public health sector. Underutilisation of capacity in the health sector, underfinancing and mutualisation of existing capacity which are evident in the health sector is due to inadequate role assigned to health management. Managing collectively and effectively the issues of scientific and technical practices as well as knowledge and skills of the health sector has become more complex today than ever before. Public health management therefore implies 'managing for health' (Hunter 2001) in which attention is focussed to public health management and the various ways in which it might serve as an unifying concept, linking policy makers' interest in public health with the ability of public health practitioners to achieve the stated goals of the health sector.

The significance of health management for public health assumes greater importance, particularly in those nations characterised by wide diversity between those sections of the population who can afford the best and the most expensive health services and those who have to incur huge 'out of pocket' expenses and have to even incur huge debts to meet health service expenses. Such gaps in the health service users focus attention to the concept of equity often at the sacrifice of efficient management. The gap in health status is increasing in most nations, India not been an exception, in spite of higher and higher investment in the health sector and greater realisation of the role of public health for raising health status. It is towards this goal, reiterated with greater emphasis in the twenty-first century, that WHO has advocated strong public health action among its member nations, many with different health systems. The main objective of this was to bring results showing substantive health gains for the population which can indeed be achieved with new approaches to health promotion and disease prevention and more effective management of health care (WHO 2000).

In the Indian context too, it is evident from our study that health status as is clear from the performance of the public health system requires a lot to be desired, impressive economic growth of the country and higher investment in the health sector notwithstanding. The present work has identified the relative importance of the various determinants of the different parameters of health status and made a detailed analysis of the problem of the sector. However, changes for the better can be brought about through appropriate actions, which requires knowledge of management skills relating to the health sector and its implementation by the public health-care system. Some of the factors considered as universal truth about the public health system anywhere in the world, which act as serious obstacles for the success of health policy (Lewis 2000), are mentioned below:

1. Health-care system is an expanding sector – they are by nature expansionist.
2. Higher health spending does not necessarily lead to higher health status. Some less spending countries such as Japan has better health status than higher spending countries like the USA.
3. Universal access to health care does not lead to universally good health – the wealthier groups in society often continue to remain healthier than those who are poor.
4. Public awareness of risks to health has improved, even if much of this is media driven, with both consequences associated with such a development.
5. Health care almost always wins out in the competition for resources – even when government proclaims their commitment to health and prevention, they often fail to back it up by shifting resources.
6. Changing the distribution of health status through upstream strategies is extraordinarily difficult with interventions intended to benefit the disadvantaged, often benefitting the already advantaged, thereby widening disparities and the health gap.

6.4 Role of Health-Care Manager

One of the fastest growing sectors in the world, particularly in the developing countries, reveals that the health sector requires a lot more attention than it receives at present and the goals in the health sector have not yet been achieved, in spite of sound and positive policies and investment in the sector. To achieve the goals of the health sector, whose challenges and complexities are only increasing with time, the twenty-first century requires health-care managers, with not only the knowledge of the health-care sector, but more importantly their emphasis is more on the managerial aspects of the health-care sector. It is only with their expertise that satisfactory delivery of health care can reach the required users and objectives of the health sector can be achieved.

The crucial function of these health-care managers is to provide leadership and direction to those health units and departments which are assigned the responsibilities of delivering personal health-care services. Proper supervision and coordination of the various sectors of health departments with a professional outlook is of utmost importance for the success of the health-care sector. Managers in the health sector need to ensure through their managerial skills that the function of their respective organisations is carried out in the best possible manner with the appropriate financial and human resources necessary to support the organisational goals of the respective health sector. The crucial decisions taken by the health-care managers can shape the success and goals of the health-care sector. Managers in the health-care sector have to recruit and train the staff of the health sector and take decisions regarding allocation and spending of financial resources for the sector. He/she also ensures that health consumers receive the most appropriate, timely and effective health care, so that the gap between policy and achievement can be wiped out and the desired results as per policy and investments are attained. Health-care manager therefore is the person who works through and with other people for carrying out technical and interpersonal activities in order to achieve the desired objectives of the organisations. He/she is the person in the organisation who supports and is responsible for the work performance of one or more other persons (Lombardi and Schermerhorn 2007).

The study conducted by McKinsey reiterates that management skills do make a significant difference to the health status of a nation. The study concludes that the factors which play a significant role in the corporate sector like competition, skills, scale, autonomy and ownership play an equally important role in health-care sector. This is true for all the publicly dominated health-care system across all countries. The skills that a health manager needs to develop thus are not too different from that of a manager in any other sector. One of the most important characteristics of a health manager is that he/she should have the ability to get along with people, because they have to deal not only with the team workers but also the numerous patients with conflicting demands and complexities of problems. Management is the art and the technique of understanding people and developing a good relationship with all the stakeholders in the health sector, both directly and indirectly, to attain the goals of the health sector.

The management skills that are required by the health manager to achieve the objectives of the health sector at the right time by utilising the scarce resources allocated to the sector in the best possible manner are as follows (Lussier 2008):

(A) *Technical skills*: This type of skill is the ability to use the methods and techniques to perform the task of the health-care sector. The technical skills are the basic skills of the health-care sector which enables the manager to join the sector at the entry level.
(B) *Interpersonal skills*: As mentioned above, this type of skill is one of the most crucial skills that needs to be developed in the health-care sector which demands human touch and compassion to deal with the sick and the ill people and their relatives. They are the resources that are needed to get the job done and are made available only through relationship such as the ability to understand, communicate and work effectively through individuals or groups by developing good relationship. This kind of relationship has to be developed by the health manager both inside within the organisation and outside, with the patients, suppliers, government agencies and the different types of health centres. Such skills are termed as human skills or soft skills, which has emerged as

the most effective skills in any sector of business, more so in the health sector. The various aspects of interpersonal skills which have become imperative for a health-care sector manager are stated below:

- *Team skills*: Teamwork skills are the backbone of the success of the health sector. Unless and until there is proper understanding between the different levels of works extending from the doctor and the specialist to the health attendant and the health-care delivery to the health customers, the process will not be complete and satisfactory and the broad goals of the health sector will not be attained.
- *Motivation skills*: The team workers in the health sector have to be motivated to work in the right spirit and with utmost dedication and personal care. Unless the manager through his own personal motivation skills motivates his co-workers, colleagues and subordinates, health care will be unable to reach the required persons in an effective manner.
- *Communication skills*: Health managers have to spend a significant proportion of their time communicating with the others. Unless and until they are able to communicate in an honest, clear-cut and effective manner, the system may only become weak with time.
- *Ethical skills*: This is one of the most important skills in the health sector because ethics are the standards of right and wrong that influence the behaviour of the health manager. Unethical behaviour, meaning that the health manager indulges in doing wrong things, may mean that the patients will lose trust and confidence in the health sector. This will bring down the health status of the country as patients may refrain from going to the health centres where unethical practice is rampant. Honesty, integrity and high-value system are part and parcel of the personal characteristics of the health manager. He has to be above personal interest and selfishness in his dealings with the stakeholders.
- *Diversity skills*: Developing good working relationship with all the stakeholders particularly the patients with diverse background, complexities and problems is a skill that the health manager needs to develop. They will differ in their attitude, behaviour and response often in terms of their own identities of race, ethnicity, religion, gender and ability. Expectations and value system and socioeconomic class of the patients may also pose diverse types of problems. The health manager should be prepared to meet these additional challenges of the health sector, which may not always be so evident in the other sectors. This is crucial for the overall success of the health system.
- *Conflict management skills*: The health manager should also possess or develop those traits in his personality as a leader, which will help him to resolve misunderstandings and conflicts which often arise both between the patients and the health personnel and even within the team workers themselves.

(C) *Decision-making skills*: The health manager should also possess such type of skills, which enables him/her to conceptualise a certain situation, particularly in a difficult moment and select alternatives to resolve the situation and take advantage of the opportunities. The different types of skills that constitute the decision-making skills are stated below:

- *Conceptual skills*: Health managers need to understand the abstract ideas as well as the interrelationships of the parts of the health system and their relationship to the organisation as a whole.
- *Diagnostic, analytical and critical thinking skills*: Health managers need to understand a situation and need to make the most appropriate decisions. The ultimate success or failure of the health system depends upon the right decisions taken by the health manager. He/she therefore needs to have a keen sense of judgement so that he may take the right decision at the right time.
- *Quantitative reasoning skills*: The health manager should also be able to quantify the alternative courses of action for decision-making so that he/she can decide the most appropriate course of action to maximise the use of the resources at his disposal. Knowledge of quantitative techniques is therefore essential for the health manager.
- *Time management skills*: It is extremely essential that the health manager has to set the priorities and get more done at a less time with better results. The manager therefore needs to know the techniques of time management so that he may perform the work in an efficient and effective manner.

6.5 Management Functions

With the help of the above abilities which the manager needs to develop, he has to perform then four main managerial functions (Lussier 2008):

1. Planning
2. Organising
3. Leading
4. Controlling

6.5.1 Planning

This is the starting process in any management function, which in fact decides the path of success of any organisation or system. Health manager needs to set short-term as well as long-term goals within the broad goals of his/her own organisation and plan as how to achieve the short-/long-term targets of his plan in the health sector. Planning is therefore the process of setting the objectives and determining in advance the means of achieving the objectives of the health sector.

6.5.2 *Organising*

The plans which the health manager devises have to be implemented, for which organising the tasks at hand plays a pivotal role. An important part of organising and coordinating the activities at hand is to coordinate human resources, right from the top level to the bottom level with the various jobs and tasks. The health manager therefore needs to possess the ability to make the right choices in area of health management.

6.5.3 *Leading*

The process of influencing the staff and employees towards achieving the goals of the health sector in general displays the leadership qualities of the manager. The manager has to lead employees through different types of interpersonal skills, as they perform their daily tasks. For this, the manager should have the ability to communicate the objectives to the employees and motivate them to achieve those objectives.

6.5.4 *Controlling*

The process of establishing and implementing the mechanisms to ensure that the objectives are met is called controlling, since the objectives may not be attained without a proper follow-up action. In an organisation it often happens that some staff and employees may not do the tasks assigned to them. As a result, organisational goals become difficult to achieve. The health manager therefore needs to take extra precautions to measure the progress towards achievement of the objectives and take corrective actions, whenever and wherever necessary.

The management functions are very much distinct, though highly interrelated. The health manager can perform all the above managerial functions at the same time and may not need to follow the sequence of planning, organising, leading and then controlling. However, each managerial function depends vitally on the other managerial functions. For instance, if planning is weak, in spite of good organisational, leadership and controlling skill, the objectives of the health sector will not be achieved. The status of health will continue to be poor in spite of all efforts at other fronts. Objectives will also not be achieved if the health manager possess sound organisational and planning skills, but do not possess leadership skills. The interrelationships of management skills and functions are displayed below in a diagrammatical form (Diagram 6.1).

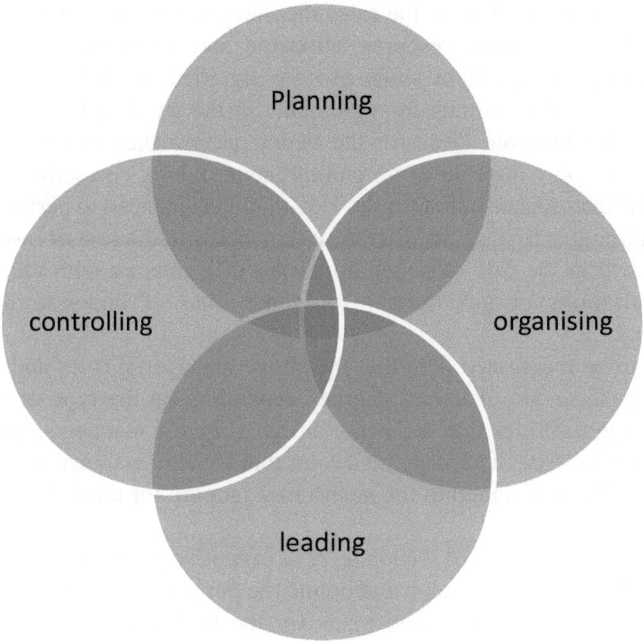

Diagram 6.1 Management functions

6.6 Management Roles

The health manager therefore needs to have a thorough idea about the roles he is to play in the health sector so that the goals are attained and the system becomes successful. Management roles are the expectations of how the health manager will behave in a given situation. Mintzberg grouped these three roles into three management role categories.

Firstly, it is the interpersonal roles which means that the health manager has to play the role of the leader, figurehead and the liaison. The use of human and communication skills as highlighted above assumes importance in this case. The figurehead role for representing the organisation in ceremonial and symbolic activities may not come into the forefront in case of the health manager. However, the leadership roles of motivating, communicating and influencing the others become highly relevant for the health manager. The liaison role too is very important for the health manager, since they have to interact with a lot of people outside their organisation to gain information and establish contacts.

Secondly, health managers also have to play informational roles which includes monitoring, dissemination and acting as a spokesperson whenever and wherever necessary. Communication and human skills are again important in this respect.

Thirdly, decisional roles are the roles that need to be performed as an entrepreneur, disturbance handler, resource allocator and negotiator. Conceptual and decision-making management skills assume significance in this respect. Health managers also need to initiate improvements in the existing health-care delivery system and also innovate ideas for the better performance of the system. When doing this, they play the role of an entrepreneur. Taking corrective actions make them play the disturbance handler role. Health managers need to perform budgeting and programming activities, and therefore they perform the role of resource allocator. They perform the role of negotiator when they interact with the members of other organisations or government for some kind of understanding and get commitments.

It needs to be mentioned here that the above managerial roles and functions of the health manager are of varied degrees depending on the type of management roles and responsibilities that are being assigned *by* the managers. This in turn is determined by the type of management roles that is being assigned *to* the managers. The responsibilities assigned to the health manager are for three different levels of management.

There may be *managers at the top level* of executive positions, who are very few in numbers. They have to develop and define the purpose of the organisation, objectives, strategies and the long-term plans for the health sector in which they are engaged. They are responsible for the management of the entire organisation or major part of it. There are then *middle-level managers* who are responsible for implementing top management's strategy by developing short-term plans of operation. The next are the *first-line managers* like the head nurse, supervisors or any other kind of team leader or office manager who are responsible for implementing middle-level managers' operational plans. They supervise employees who are responsible for the action operations. Managers at every level report to their immediate senior-level managers.

Health-care organisations are characterised by many complexities, due to which role of managers is essential at every level of health-care organisations, extending from lower-level to middle-level to upper-level managerial roles. Authority in the hierarchy is thereby delegated from the upper level where authority and responsibility is the highest to the lower level, where authority is much less. These management positions in the health sector thereby demand varied levels of skills, competencies and experience depending on whether they are senior-level managers or managers at the entry level.

The study by Mckinsey reveals the importance of health management and health managers in raising health status of a nation. The study contends that in the UK one standard deviation increase in skills, like the increase in proportion of managers having clinical qualifications by a quarter, results in 0.2 point rise in management score. An improvement in management score by 0.3 point results due to standard deviation increase in competition or size. Combined effect of skills, scale and competition can raise management score by almost 0.5 point which results in significant decline in mortality rates. It is therefore opined by the study that in the present scenario characterised by increasing demand for health-care services and constraints on government health budgets, better management practices in the health sector can definitely improve quality and efficiency.

6.7 Health Management in India

Providing efficient and effective health care to over a billion population in a vast country like India is a major challenge for health management and health managers. A matter of great concern in India is not only the large 'out of pocket' expenses, due to inadequate public spending on health, but also the quality of the services provided and the quality of human resources. Lack of accountability among the public health practitioners and inefficiency in the use of resources in the sector have resulted in poor health indicators and health status as is evident from our study. Professional management in the health sector demands improved quality of health service delivery. Quality in health management is a holistic term incorporating health-care organisations which undertakes to fulfil the needs of the customers such as the patients, the payee, doctor and also the health employer. Quality also means doing the right things for the right people at the right time. Quality also refers to the technical aspect of health care to non-technical aspect of health service delivery like the clients' waiting time, attitude of the staff and restricting the policies such as infrastructure, assessment and overall management. Quality management incorporates strategic planning of the health sector, allocation of resources and other systematic activities for quality such as planning and operations.

Primary health care is the basic structure in India which has no doubt resulted in improving the health status in India, though it is still much below the global average. A vast country like India has extensive networks of health centres, but the spatial and numerical distribution of such facilities fall much below the government guidelines. Even in these centres there is a tremendous shortage of manpower, as there is 7.8 % shortage of doctors in these centres and 50 % shortage in the subcentres. It is a fact that in spite of such extensive health centre networks, only 20 % outpatients and 45 % indoor patients avail of these services. Studies have revealed that in India (Dadwad 2013) in most of the health centres the staff is either not trained or inadequately trained and vacancies are often not filled up. It is also an experience that the health infrastructure requires many major and minor repairs and lacks amenities for clients, OTs are existing but are non-functional, citizen charter is not displayed and vehicles are not used for referrals.

It is also a matter of concern that there is almost a total absence of infection prevention practices and hospital waste is not disposed of, as per guidelines. There is not only a shortage of laboratory equipment but some essential ones are not available at all. Even the emergency drugs are not available in most public health centres. Records on these aspects are almost absent and incomplete.

There is also absence of new born baby corner and newborn protocol care is not maintained, all of which perhaps may also be one of the determinant factors for high infant mortality rates in the country. The absence of micro-planning is a characteristic feature of most of these health centres, and they also do not have any counselling for the poor. Vaccines are either unavailable or in short supply and not administered at proper age.

It is therefore not surprising that health status in India is in such a deplorable state. Better record in the health-care sector can be attained, and more efficient management of the health-care sector in India is possible to achieve. Managers of the health-care sector in India should therefore adhere to 'effectiveness' that is concentrate on the health outcomes. Another important issue that health managers need to concentrate upon in India is the degree of accessibility which should not be hampered due to geographic, economic, social, organisational and linguistic barriers.

The importance of public health management is only too clear from the experience of implementation of health policies, particularly in rural India and the consequent deplorable state of rural health in India. In spite of many ambitious policies relating to rural health in India, health condition in rural India leaves a lot to be desired, which is mainly due to the lack of implementation of the policies on health. One of the main reasons for this is the absence of any proper public health management system. There are no new practices and procedures to ensure that policies are properly implemented and health-care delivery reaches the right people at the right time even to the remotest corners of the country. There is a wide gap in the implementation of health policies in the country, which has resulted in 8 % of the public health centres having no medical doctors or medical staff. About 39 % of the health centres are without any laboratory technicians, and 18 % of these are characterised by the absence of any pharmacist. The ailments characterising the health sector in India are extremely poor quality of health care, no accountability, lack of awareness and limited accessibility, all of which can be changed if public health management was viewed as a holistic part of health-care delivery system with the sole target of raising the health status in the country.

The success of public health in India is to a large extent determined by the managerial skills of the individual health manager. Such a person needs to have interpersonal and motivational skills and competencies. He/she should be equipped with the general management skills of managing time, materials and space and have idea of all management techniques and also about all related issues of health-care management. The supervisory role of the health manager is equally important. This involves managing others in terms of effectively completing the work, by assigning the tasks to the right person, reviewing the work and monitoring the performance of the subordinates and through his/her personal management skills to ensure that health delivery is provided to the right persons at the right time and in right proportions. These managerial functions will ensure that the function of health delivery is done effectively and efficiently.

The overall efficiency and effectiveness of the health delivery system will make the health sector successful. Health managers should therefore be a part of a larger organisation of the health system to ensure the overall successful viability and success of the health system. Effective collaboration of the health manager with the health system is therefore of utmost importance. The health manager therefore has to ensure that the health system functions effectively through sharing of information, collaboration and communication. The success of many health-care organisations is determined solely by individual performances or that of the motivated employees. In many organisations this has been used as competitive advantage as against their competitors.

The role of the health manager has to be made more effective by the management, when he has all the information relating to the health policies of the nation and the extent of success of the implementation of the policies at the local, district and national level. This enables the successful health manager to gain idea about the health-care delivery, and therefore he/she can decide their own roles and functions to overcome the deficiency in the sector. The health manager therefore has to keep himself/herself updated about the knowledge of the health sector.

It is therefore evident that the scope of the public health is much wider today in the twenty-first century than ever before. Public health system does not incorporate ideas and experiences of medical knowledge only. The delivery of this knowledge to the actual users is determined by how it is coordinated and managed. The managerial aspect of health care, that is, public health management, is equally if not even more important than health sector itself. Public health management and the role of the health manager have now become a part of health services and are the only means of effective implementation of the health policies of a nation. When studying health status, it is maintained that improved access to health-care services can contribute significantly to health and an improved quality of life, but it is still a case of treating the symptoms rather than the root cause. Health policy therefore has to ensure that a balance is maintained between the two, and tackling both upstream and downstream of determinants of health as opined by experts in the field becomes extremely important.

Health sectors in many countries have not been able to optimally utilise the resources in the health sector. In fact, expenditure in the health sector reveals that there have been gross wastage and misutilisation of the scarce resources allotted to this sector. The framework of health economics and the basic fundamentals of health economics have not been followed. Most of the ailments in the sector have been due to the lack of coordinated efforts. Research findings of the health sector have never been taken seriously, and therefore there is neither any interest nor effort to formulate health policies based on research findings in most developing countries and India as well.

6.8 Health Policies and Health Management

It is maintained by experts that the health policies to be meaningful and effective needs to possess the following features:

A vision statement mentions what the health policy attempts to achieve. It defines whether the goal is to achieve a better quality of life, health status or sustainable human development. It also states whether raising health status is an end or a means. Vision also defines the role of the policy makers, health practitioners, professionals and the health managers and the interdependence of their roles. Therefore, it is imperative for the success of the health sector performance and raising the status of health that management in the health sector is improved and capacity of the health sector is raised. It is also important that innovations in the health-care provisions, management of technological innovations, should constantly undergo a change so that the best of health-care services can be provided to the consumers. A responsive, responsible and an effective system of health management can in fact result in the success of public health policies, so that the vital link between health management and health policies can be established. Accountability and responsibility can be attained through a proper organisational structure, auditing bodies and monitoring and supervisory roles, which are all in the domain of management issues.

Public health policies have an extremely significant impact on health status of a nation. It deals with the plans, actions and strategies and decisions to attain the desired health status of a nation (Brownson et al. 2009). Public health policies have to incorporate the complexities of the economy, social and political strengths of a nation in deciding on the plans and actions relating to the health policies. Since health is a complex phenomenon as is evident from our discussion above, policy implementation and the exact health outcomes can often not be determined in advance. In fact, it is a means of intervention by the government at the right time and for the right people, so that health-care services are available to each and every person of a country without any obstacles and hindrances, due to finance, general infrastructure, medical infrastructure and manpower infrastructure, with the sole goal of achieving the best health outcome. Health policies therefore ultimately boil down to administrative controls through coordinated legislations. The main consideration for public health policy is to provide health-care facilities to all based on equality, freedom and justice to one and to all.

Health policies like any other policies attempt to achieve rational outcomes. They are statement of intent relating to the health sector, which are able to incorporate a whole lot of issues from planning and management to health-care delivery systems so that the desired health outcomes can be achieved. Health policies are therefore implemented as a procedure concentrating around principles which guide actions towards those that are most likely to influence health outcomes. Health policies assume particular significance for 'health outcomes' because they focus on making important organisational decisions, including identification of different attitudes such as health programmes or spending priorities and choosing among them on the basis of the impact they have, as is very importantly revealed by the detailed study. Health policies will therefore guide actions towards those that are most likely to achieve a desired outcome by influencing health programmes and spending priorities particularly between rural and urban sectors on the basis of the impact as is revealed by our work.

Health policies can thereby avoid insignificant or negative results and seek positive health benefits. However, negative or positive, all outcomes cannot be foreseen in advance.

6.9 Role of Economics in Evaluation of Health Policies

It is here that economics play a major role in evaluating the benefits of health policies. The outcome measured in terms of benefits is measured rather than only the goals of the policies, which is often the case. The result is that the policies by themselves become important rather than the outcomes, which should in reality be the focus of attention in all studies pertaining to the health sector. For instance in the detailed analysis made above by the present study, we have highlighted the importance of different factors in determining infant mortality, mortality rates below five years and some other parameters of health status. We have further focussed attention to the factors that raise the negative parameters of health status. The relative cost of each factor may be worked out, and the effectiveness of the concerned factor may be examined. If it is revealed that more is spent on the factor concerned compared to the outcome by the use of cost-benefit analysis, then resources which are always scarce can be transferred to other sectors of health which may have better outcome. An important area of concentration of the present study is that the factors which play an important role in the urban sector are not always the ones which will play equally important role in the rural sectors. Therefore, to formulate the same health policies for the rural and the urban sectors may not give the same outcome. In other words, aiming at uniform health policies may not only provide the undesired outcomes but may entail wastage of resources. Policy makers have to be on the lookout as where and how the resources in the health sector can be used in an optimum manner. Economic evaluation can help to understand the policies which have become redundant due to cost ineffectiveness and the new policies that need to be adopted accordingly. A comparison of cost and benefit analysis will provide relevant information to the policy makers to decide if the policy should be given importance over other uses of the scarce resources.

Economic analysis of health policies further focusses attention of the government to achieve the goals of the policies in an effective way. When it comes to policy, it is not only the health status which is important but also equity is equally important. As a result, what may be clear for raising health status may not be acceptable in terms of equity, implying fairer distribution of health benefits, even if they are not always economically viable in terms of only cost-benefit analysis. Striking a balance between health status and equity is a challenge for both the policy makers and the economists. Sacrificing equity may result in widening the gap in health status between the rich and the poor, whereas equity may result in less than the optimum uses of scarce resources. For instance, in terms of our findings, it is revealed in most cases that the parameters of health status are worse off in the rural sectors in comparison to urban sectors. To improve the status of health in the rural sectors, more investment needs to be incurred, which is certainly not economically viable. However, to maintain equity and improve the health status, it is essential that the focus of health policies should be aimed at rural sectors.

It is suggested (McPake and others 2002) that total costs may be estimated by all the health services provided to the patient and multiply them by the unit cost of each service. By this method, estimate and standard deviation of costs can be provided. The cost-effectiveness can then be stated with confidence intervals. Though getting data for such a detailed work will definitely be a challenging task, particularly in a country like India, it is not impossible. Financial accounts and budgets usually used for accounting and planning may be used for the purpose, revealing the importance of health management. A single measure of unit cost is essential, which necessitates that overhead costs are accounted for in a meaningful way and the health-care services delivered to the patients are of a similar nature and the apportionments of shared costs are appropriate. These are no doubt extremely difficult especially for country like India where the system of maintaining records and getting data is indeed a herculean task. However, this is the first step for formulating a satisfactory health policy. Measuring benefits of health policies in terms of outcomes is more challenging, since in most cases it is opined that (McPake and others 2002) benefits is multidimensional which is more difficult to measure. Some benefits are spread over a longer time span, while others are immediate. If health policies are for controlling certain epidemic or diseases, for example, eradication of malaria, tuberculosis or polio, measurement may be in terms of the total eradication, though the period which is set as a goal also needs to be paid attention to. However, if benefits are in terms of reduction of infant mortality, maternal mortality and morbidity, the time span required is much longer. However, improvement in terms of raising the quality of life is more difficult to measure.

In India, till 2007 there was no organisation for laying down the guidelines for decision-making in the health sector. The ICMR, in 2007, constituted the Health Research Policy within the Health Ministry.

The means to achieve the goals according to these policies were mainly there (a) to create a National Health Research System, (b) to establish a National Health Research management forum and to (c) operationalise a 10-point action programme.

The underlying value of NHRS is health research, which is to be considered as an investment in the health sector.Such research also serves the goal of providing equity in health care services and develops and maintains ethical values in health research. Other values were that of ownership solidarity, development of research culture, intersectorality and partnerships and originality and accountability.

Health is a state subject in India, which is run with the help of the central government. The principles of health policy in India are based on participation by the community with emphasis on the grassroots level. Some of the schemes at the grassroots level are the Anganwadi Schemes of ICDS and the constitution of the village-level committees. The community action has been successfully utilised for disease control programmes such as malaria and in certain plans for drinking water and sanitation scheme and adequate supply and proper nutrition. A successful story is the total eradication of polio through pulse polio immunisation. Health policies in India are implemented through a three-tier system. They are the primary, secondary and tertiary health-care system. The principles of equitable distribution, community participation and intersectoral coordination and appropriate technology are the principles upon which policies on primary health care revolve. Contribution towards socioeconomic development of a country through primary health care is emphasised in all policy considerations. Therefore, policies in this area focus on education, concerning prevailing health problems and methods to prevent and control them; promotion of food supply and proper nutrition; adequate supply of water and basic sanitation; material and child health, including family planning, immunisation and prevention of locally endemic diseases; and provision of essential drugs.

Primary health care is provided through a network of government-owned and government-operated subcentres, primary health centres and community health centres (GOI 2011). In India, quality of health care at the first level of contact that is the primary health-care services leaves a lot to be desired. The result is that clients who first have accessibility at this level proceed to the next level that is the district hospitals. The result is overcrowding, overburden on the physical and manpower resources and poor quality of services rendered. It is here that the role of health management comes into the picture. If primary health-care centres and subcentres are professionally managed, with a certain degree of accessibility, many diseases and illness can be prevented at the elementary stage. To that extent not only the burden of disease can be reduced, but the undue pressure on the health system at the next level can also be reduced. In this way, effectiveness of the services can also be increased. This in turn will reduce the gap between the health goals and achievements.

References

Alderslade R, Hunter DJ (1994) Commissioning and public health. J Manag Med 8(6):20–31. PubMed PM ID: 10140733.9

Brownson RC, Chriqui JF, Stamakartis KA (2009) Understanding evidence based public health policy. Promot Public Health Res Pract Educ 99(9):1576–1583

Dadwad SS (2013) Quality management in healthcare. Indian J Public Health 57(3):138–143

Govt of India (2011) National health research policy, department of health research. Ministry of health and Family Welfare, New Delhi

Hunter DJ (1999) Managing for health: implementing the new health agenda. Institute for Public Policy Research, London

Hunter DJ (2001) Public health management. WHO, University of Durham, Durham

Hunter DJ, Brown J (2007) European journal of public health. Oxford J 17(Suppl.1):33–37

International Health Regulations (2005) Strengthening health security by implementing the international health regulations. WHO, Lyon

Langabeer R (2007) Healthcare operations management: a quantitative approach to business and logistics. Jones and Barlett Learning Publisher, Boston

Lewis S (2000) Reconfiguring health policy: simple truths complex solution. Sage, London

Lombardi DM, Schermerhorn JR (2007) Health care management. Wiley, Hoboken

Lussier RN (2008) Management fundamentals. USA

McKinsey and Company. Management in healthcare: why good practices really matter. Prepared by Centre for Economic performance. LSE, London

McPake B, Kumaranayake L, Normand C (2002) Health economics – an international perspective. Routledge, London/New York

WHO (2000) Regional office for Europe-1999 and innovation care for chronic condition. WHO, Geneva

Chapter 7
Policy Implications of the Main Findings of the Study

Health has been accepted as an important determinant of economic development which is evident from numerous empirical works on the subject. This is true both for the developed and the less developed countries. Good health can save scarce resources, which is particularly crucial from the point of view of development for the poor countries. Good health is also an important determinant of regular and good education, good income, higher productivity and higher national growth. Planning for good health is an integral part of overall national planning. Good health status therefore increases both the quality and the quantity in terms of both the number of workforce and the number of hours of work put in by the workers. Investment in health sector cannot be ignored either by any developed or underdeveloped nation. Development economics assigns the responsibilities of the health sector to the state, so that the minimum requisite health standard can be assured even to the deprived and poverty-stricken people of the country.

- It is thus the use of economic tools and techniques and the powerful analytical method of the subject that can provide adequate guidance to the policy makers as how best to utilise the scarce resources for obtaining the optimum health outcomes. The goal of improving the various health outcomes analysed within the purview of economic framework gives a new and a different insight of looking into the problems confronting the health sector. It is in this connection that the issues relevant for health management arise and the knowledge from the study of health economics can be utilised for the purpose of health management. Economics basically work with the idea of unlimited demands, because there is no limit to the wants of mankind. In the health sector too there are unlimited demands that require urgent attention. However, the basic problem confronting economic problems is limited resources to satisfy these unlimited claims and demands. It is here that models and tools of analysis to study health economics have evolved and the analytical tools of overcoming these problems have been used to study the health-related issues in an organised manner. The framework developed is then used to predict health-related economic behaviour. The many

K. Sengupta, *Determinants of Health Status in India*,
DOI 10.1007/978-81-322-2535-5_7

conflicting demands of the health sector can thus be attempted to be optimally satisfied by the use of these economic tools of analysis.

- From an examination of various components of health expenditure on the indicators of health status, the study comes up with some interesting findings which can have crucial significance for policy makers. The study reveals that relationship of health expenditure with infant mortality and maternal mortality is inverse and the relationship between life expectancy and health expenditure is direct. This only goes to mean that when health expenditure is increased, both infant mortality and maternal mortality go down and life expectancy increases. The impact of health expenditure on these various indicators of health status is however not direct and involves long-term process for the full effect to be evident. This could be the reason for the low impact of health expenditure on maternal mortality, because the effect to be evident on maternal mortality involves a longer process than the effect on infant mortality, the impact of which involves a shorter period. It is also interesting to note from the study that the effect of health expenditure is again different in rural and urban areas and the explanatory power of the independent variable is higher in the urban sectors than in the rural sectors. This could also be due to the poor management of health delivery system in the rural areas and also inadequate health infrastructure both physical and human, in rural sectors, so that merely rise in health expenditure always does not result in better health indicators.
- In terms of the multiple regression model, the study concludes that private health expenditure is more effective than public health expenditure. Moreover, it is also a matter of policy decision whether public expenditure on health is to be incurred simultaneously on the entire sector or in terms of certain priority sectors of health. In case, the selected priorities of the public health policies are not right, the desired impact on health status will also not be evident or the desired health outcomes may be different from what is expected. The health management issues in the public health sector often leave a lot to be desired in contract to the private sector where health service delivery is undertaken in a much more professional manner. Consequently, health service delivery mechanism is less effective in spite of substantial financial investment in the public health sector. That perhaps could be the reason for the explanatory power of the coefficient of the public health expenditure being lower than that of the private health expenditure. That is also the reason for the average health expenditure per capita, lying in between the two types of expenditure – private and public.
- The conclusion drawn from the analysis is that health expenditure in general and public health expenditure in particular can determine to a large extent the health status of a nation. This in turn can reveal at a disaggregative level the extent of influence of health expenditure on the various indicators of health status such as life expectancy, infant mortality and maternal mortality. For policy purpose such findings have a crucial significance, because policy makers will be able to identify those areas of the health sector where only expenditure plays an important role rather than exploring other determinant factor. In such areas greater degree of investment may need to be made. Indicators of health status which is not

influenced in any significant manner by incurring more expenditure may indicate that investing more in that sector of health will not give any better health outcome. In such cases, the remedy lies perhaps in better ways of utilising the existing resources or perhaps in better health management. The findings have also been segregated for rural and urban sectors. This kind of findings can help the policy makers into delving further into the analysis for deciding as to whether health expenditure on a certain indicator of health is equally relevant in both the urban and the rural sectors or whether different types of policies need to be adopted for the urban and the rural sectors. It is a fact that uniform policies for health sector are adopted for a vast country like India without taking into consideration that different determinant factors are at play in different places. It is true that such micro-policy analysis is extremely difficult. However, for an important sector like the health, which is still in a deplorable state, there is no alternative to such efforts even at the cost of being a little cumbersome. The clients of health-care delivery system in a vast country like India are characterised by different socioeconomic background, different income level and even varied superstitions and beliefs due to which homogeneity in the operation of the health delivery system cannot be expected. The result is that the same set of policies which are successful in one place is unsuccessful in another place, and there is still a wide disparity in health condition among different strata of the society in different parts of the country and regions as well as between rural and urban areas. Universal access and universal coverage of health-care delivery system is therefore still is a far cry. All this in spite of allocating huge resources to the health sector, which has been revealed from our study.

- The study has revealed a strong interrelationship between education and health status. Every aspect of health status has been examined with respect to the literacy level of the health consumers as well as the female literacy level. The study has come to the conclusion that education is indeed a strong determinant of health status. The findings reveal that education is a very important determinant of infant mortality in India, since as much as 70 % of the change in infant mortality can be explained by 1 % change in education. The model is significant in exactly the same manner in the rural areas. However, the significance of education as a determinant of infant mortality declines substantially in the urban areas though it still maintains its significance as an important determinant. The possible reason could perhaps be that in the urban areas, since the level of education is already high, any further increase in the literacy rate may not show any impact on the mortality rates. The rate which is already much lower than in the rural areas can be reduced by tackling 'other factors' and not education.
- The study also highlights the importance of female literacy on infant mortality, the elasticity of which is as high as 70 % for every 1 % increase in female literacy. This substantiates the findings of other similar studies done in India and abroad that female education increases health awareness in the mother, about child care, diseases and illnesses, hygiene and clean drinking water, all of which result in high percentage of infant mortality, interesting findings which have emerged from the present work.

- The findings also reveal the important role of education on mortality rate of children below 5 years of age. The study reveals that over 70 % of the change in the mortality rate can be explained by 1 % change in the literacy rate. The value surprisingly is similar both for the rural and urban sectors.
- The study also concludes that female education has an important impact on mortality rates of children below 5 years both in the urban and rural sectors. The models in this respect are most satisfactory with strong theoretical and statistical significance. The coefficient of the independent variables is all within a range of 0.75 %.
- Clean drinking water is well accepted as a crucial determinant of good health, the benefits of which can be short run and immediate as well as spread over a much longer term and are sometimes also indirect. This well-established conclusion has been reiterated by the present study. However, breaking up the total impact of clean drinking water on various parameters of health status separately reveals some interesting findings. Using clean drinking water as an independent variable for determining infant mortality is not acceptable in our case, according to the estimated models. However, when education is taken as an additional independent variable along with clean drinking water, the model is acceptable. This implies that accepting clean drinking water as a determinant of infant mortality education which can develop the awareness of clean drinking water plays the catalytical role. The model has higher validity in the urban than in the rural sectors, implying that any improvement in the level of education and clean drinking water in the rural sector will reduce infant mortality rates much more than in the urban sectors. The reason could perhaps be that in the rural sector the level of education is still on the lower side that any rise in the level of education has greater degree of positive elasticity on infant mortality.
- Sanitation defined as the 'safe disposal of human excreta' has universally been determined along with safe drinking water as another crucial determinant of health status. The study has therefore examined the impact of the change in the percentage of acceptability of sanitation facility on infant mortality. The findings reveal that 1 % rise in the accessibility to sanitation reduces infant mortality by over 70 % in general. In the urban sector the percentage change is 67 p.c., whereas in the rural areas it is 69 p.c. The findings come to the conclusion that the responsiveness to sanitation facilities is higher in the rural than in the urban sectors. It also means that since there are not enough sanitation facilities in the rural sectors, any marginal rise in such facilities has greater positive impact on infant mortality in the rural sectors than in the urban sectors where such facilities are much better. The study therefore concludes that sanitation facilities have a positive effect on infant mortality in general but the impact is much higher in the rural areas.
- In view of the fact that a large number of population in India do not have access to sanitation facilities, the alternative is that the percentage of the population left out of the accessibility of sanitation facilities resort to open defecation. Open defecation pollutes the water and the environment and results in various forms of diseases and illnesses. The findings of the study reveal that open defection has a

significant impact on infant mortality rates. The impact is once again higher in the rural than in the urban areas.

- The findings of the study relating to the impact of accessibility to sanitation facilities on mortality rates reveal that elasticity is significant with higher positive elasticity in the rural areas. The impact on maternal mortality is however lower in comparison to the other indicators of health status. The reason may be that maternal mortality is determined more by other factors such as the medical facilities, nutrition and other health infrastructural facilities. The findings further reveal that open defecation has negative impact on the health status. This impact is higher in the urban sectors than in the rural sectors perhaps due to higher degree of pollution, contamination, overcrowding and unhygienic living conditions in urban areas.
- The study has also established the role of female education in determining the positive effect of sanitation on health. Both the factors together have significant impact on infant and child mortality. The findings therefore imply that policy measures to improve health status should aim at investing simultaneously in sanitation and female education for the purpose of improving the health status.
- The study has also established the important role of immunisation in determining the indicators of health status such as infant and child mortality. It is already a known fact that record of immunisation in India leaves a lot to be desired. For policy consideration, it implies that much more needs to be invested in immunisation schemes. However, the study further reveals that immunisation by itself is not too effective when considered as a single independent variable, but immunisation along with education emerges as crucial determinants of health status. It is therefore concluded that parents with some level of education have a higher level of awareness and therefore understand the significance of immunisation for their newborn babies. Children of parents who are illiterate have fear and myth about immunising their newborn. The result is, even though immunisation facilities are in existence, they are not availed of merely due to ignorance of the parents. Segregating the results for the rural and the urban sectors, the findings of the work reveal that there is not much spatial difference, though the elasticity in the rural areas is marginally higher than in the urban areas. The findings also reveal that incorporating female literacy, that is, the education of the mother as an additional explanatory variable, does not improve the explanatory power of the model. This is indeed surprising since in all other aspects of infant mortality female literacy has an important role to play. However, the reason could be that unlike clean drinking water and sanitation, where the mother's role is confined to taking decisions within the walls of her household, the decision as to whether the child is to be immunised or not extends outside the home. The education of the mother therefore in the rural areas may not have much impact as far as immunisation is concerned as in most cases; such decisions are taken by the male members of the family. However, the same is not the case in the urban sector though the explanatory power of general education is still marginally higher. The conclusion is that though in the urban areas women (mother) have a greater say as far as taking their children for immunisation is concerned in comparison to the

rural areas, on the whole, men still have a greater say in taking this decision of taking their babies for immunisation even in the urban sector. The same however may not be true for women in the urban sectors who are highly educated, and hence the explanatory power of female education is higher in the urban sectors than in the rural sectors. For policy consideration in the health sector, it is apparent that for the effect of mass immunisation to be meaningful, particularly in the rural sectors, simultaneous investment in general education is equally crucial rather than more specifically female education, as is the case in other determinants of health.

- The study further concludes that though immunisation by itself is not effective in determining infant mortality, it emerges as a highly satisfactory variable in determining mortality rate of children below 5 years of age. The reason could perhaps be that the fear of getting the newborn infants immunised is much more, but this fear and uncertainty diminishes to a large extent for slightly grown-up children. Though the spatial difference is not much significant, the findings reveal slightly better elasticity with respect to the rural sectors. It is further noted that inclusion of education as assessed by the literacy rate increased the explanatory power of all the models, both for the rural and the urban sectors, with rural sectors recording marginally better values. The study therefore concludes that education is a very powerful instrument for the impact of immunisation to be effective in the case of mortality rates. Inclusion of education of the mother does not improve the impact of immunisation by any significant extent either in the rural or urban sectors. It may thus be concluded that though education of the mother is important in determining the success of immunisation for children below 5 years, general education plays a much more significant role. The fear, inhibition, myth and the mistrust associated with immunisation in India need to be broken through education after which immunisation can be used as an effective tool for improving the health status.
- The findings of the study become especially relevant for children with stunted growth and underweight children, which is a major problem in India. The study reveals that immunisation does have a positive impact on such children. The impact, however, increases with rise in general education, though, as is the experience in the previous case, inclusion of mother's education does not improve the impact significantly. The study therefore highlights the importance of education for the success of immunisation policy on the whole in India.
- Another important finding of the work is the impact of health infrastructure, both physical and manpower on the health status. This is an area of health sector which is extremely crucial but is often ignored for examining the health status in a country as vast as that of India. Findings reveal that though most of the parameters of health are not affected directly by the presence of health infrastructure such as health centres and subcentres, hospital beds and a number of hospitals, however, in rural areas, infant mortality rate and child mortality rate are determined by the presence of such health infrastructure. This is only expected because due to inadequate health-care facilities in the rural sector, a large percentage of infants and children are victims of early deaths. This is a harsh reality

which is also confirmed by our findings. However, the impact on other parameters of health status, such as death rate, life expectancy and underweight children with stunted growth, does not appear to be significant in terms of the findings of the study. The reason could perhaps be that such impacts work over a longer period of time, the exact period of which is difficult to assess. The impact is long term and spread over a much longer period due to which the effects cannot be captured by our models. Physical infrastructural facilities of health services has long term impact on healh status by raising the overall quality of health condition,though immediate short run impact of such physical infrastructure may not be evident.

- Examining the effectiveness of physical infrastructure, the findings reveal that hospital beds emerge as important determinants of health status in comparison to other physical infrastructure. This finding therefore has important significance for the policy makers when they allocate funds for different health infrastructure. The lower level of significance for the subcentres or hospitals may have to be studied separately when the cost-benefit analysis of health investment is being worked.
- The study has also revealed the role of health manpower particularly as a determinant of mortality rates, an important parameter of health status. The work examined the absence of doctors, physicians and laboratory technicians and found that the more the absence of manpower facilities, the higher the mortality rates. The findings reveal that mortality rates particularly in rural sectors are affected adversely due to the non-availability of doctors, physicians and laboratory technicians. The same direct relationship is true for children with stunted growth and underweight children. Lack of laboratory technicians however does not emerge as a significant factor in this case, the effect of which may work out over a longer period of time.
- A very important determinant of health status particularly in a country dominated by a large section of the population, who are below the poverty line and also who do not possess much education, is the awareness of the health consumers about the necessity and ways and means of maintaining good health. Education creates awareness as discussed extensively on the impact of education on health. However,the information for creating awareness among the health consumers has to be widely disseminated. In the absence of such information, though health-care service may be in existence, mere absence of awareness may also lead to the absence of availing these facilities. This can give rise to asymmetric information between the health consumers and health service providers resulting in adverse health status, an important finding which has emerged out of the study.
- Another explanatory factor, which is often ignored but has emerged as a crucial determinant of health status, particularly in rural sector, is the distance to the nearest health centre. Long-distance and inaccessible and remote areas of habitation prevent the health-care consumers to travel to the health centres for treatment, which adversely affects the health status. The study concludes that child mortality rates are affected significantly by both awareness and distance. It is

also interesting to note, as per our expectation, that the impact is much higher in rural areas than in the urban areas. The findings of the study further reveal that when health centres are within a closer range of 3 km, mortality rate declines, in contrast to when they are at a distance of 10 km, in which case, mortality rate goes up. This is more relevant in rural areas, as the distance of health centres is not so relevant in urban centres, due to better transportation facilities. As far as awareness is concerned, the more the existence of health and sanitation committees, the lower the mortality rate. However, the existence of Pradhans and Panchayats member's awareness of the existence of united funds for health does not emerge as an important determinant. The reason could be that they do not perform their functions of disseminating such relevant information among the public. The conclusion that is revealed from the study is that in the rural areas awareness of health programmes and the distance of the health centres affect the mortality rates.

- The study also concludes that life expectancy both for males and females is also affected by the distance of the health centres. This is more relevant for females than for the males. Health and sanitation committees also favourably impact life expectancy through awareness of the benefits of better sanitation and hygienic and clean drinking water. This implies that policy makers need to strengthen the determinants of health status by reorienting health plans in such a manner that there cannot be uniform focus and goal for the rural and urban health. Factors which emerge as crucial determinants of health in the rural sectors are not necessarily the same factors which are important in the urban sectors. Similarly, the challenges of the health sectors are not similar in the two sectors, so the solution to the challenges of health cannot be spatially similar. In exactly the same manner, the determinants of health for the females are different from that of the males, necessitating an altogether different approach and solution. The study also concludes that breaking up the different parameters of health status reveals that mere financial investment is not always the solution in solving all the issues of the health sector as is normally assumed. In certain areas investment in education has a greater return to the health parameters. The solutions to the challenges of health should also be broken down into short-term and long-term solutions. Inadequate understanding and a lack of in-depth knowledge relating to the challenges of the health sector may be one of the important reasons for the inability to achieve the desired health status which a nation strives to achieve.

Bibliography

Anan A (1993) India: unhealthy immunisation programme. Lancet 341:1402–1403
Arnold F (1997) Gender preference for children, Demographic and health survey. Comparative studies, no 23. Macro International Inc., Calverton
Coddington DC (1990) The crisis in health care: costs, choices and strategies. Jossey-Bass, San Francisco
Coffey RM (1983) The effect of time price on the demand for medical care services. J Hum Resour 18:407–424
Cowing TG, Holtman AG, Powers S (1983) Hospital cost analysis: a survey and evaluation of recent studies. Adv Health Econ Health Serv Res 4:257–303
Cremieux P-Y, Ouellette P, Pilon C (1999) Health care spending as determinants of health outcomes. Health Econ 8:627–639
Culyer AJ (1989) The normative economics of health care finance and provision. Oxf Rev Econ Policy 5(1):34–58
Culyer AJ, Wagstaff A (1993) Equity and equality in health and health care. J Health Econ 12:431–457
Culyer AJ, van Doorslaer E, Wagstaff A (1992) Access, utilisation and equity: a further comment. J Health Econ 11:207–210
Currie J, Reagan PB (2003) Distance to hospital and children's use of preventive care: is being closer better and for whom? Econ Enq 41:378–391
Custer WS, Willkie RJ (1991) Teaching hospital costs: the effect of medical staff characteristics. Health Serv Res 25:831–857
Davis MA (1991) On nursing home quality: a review and analysis. Med Care Rev 48:129–166
Ellis RP (1993) Hospital costs function estimation, when firms may not want to Minimise total Costs. Mimeo, Boston University, Boston
Ellis RP (1998) Creaming, skimping and dumping: provider compensation on the intensive and extensive margins. J Health Econ 17:537–555
"Esources in India" Background paper. Geneva, WHO
Feldstein MS (1970) The rising price of physicians services. Rev Econ Stat 52:121–133
Feldstein PJ (1986) The emergence of market competition in the US health care system: its causes, likely structures and implications. Health Policy 6:1–20
Feinstein JS (1993) The relationship between socio economic status and health: a review of the literature. Milbank Q 71:279–322
Folland S (1986) Health care need. Economics and social justice. Int J Soc Econ 13:98–116
Fournier GM, Mitchell JM (1992) Hospital costs and competition for services: a multi product analysis. Rev Econ Stat 74(4):627–634

K. Sengupta, *Determinants of Health Status in India*,
DOI 10.1007/978-81-322-2535-5

Fuchs VR (1982) Time preference and health: an exploratory study. In: Fuchs VR (ed) Economic aspect of health. University of Chicago Press, Chicago

Galbraith JK (1958) The affluent society. Houghton Mifflin, Boston

Garber AM, Phelps CE (1997) Economic foundation of cost effectiveness analysis. J Health Econ 16:1–31

Gerdtham UG (1992) An econometric analysis of health care expenditure: a cross section study of the OECD countries. J Health Econ 11(1):63–84

Getzen TE, Poullier JP (1992) International health spending forecasts, concepts and evaluation. Soc Sci Med 34:1057–1068

Ginsburg PB, Grossman JM (2005) When the price isn't right: how inadvertent payment incentives drive medical care. Health Aff 24:376–384

Glick P, Sahn DE (1998) Health and productivity in a heterogeneous urban labour market. Appl Econ 30:203–216

Gold MR et al (eds) (1996) Cost effectiveness in health and medicine. Oxford University Press, New York

Goldstein KP et al (1996) The effect of epidemic measles on immunisation rates. J Am Med Assoc 276:626–630

Grossman M (1972) The demand for health: a theoretical and empirical investigation. NBER, Columbia

Hansen WL (1962) Shortages and investment in health manpower. In: Economics of health and medical care, Proceedings of the conference on economics of health and medical care, University of Michigan, Ann Arbor

Harris JE (1977) The internal organisations of hospitals: some economic implications. Bell J Econ 8:467–482

Hitiris T, Posnett J (1992) The determinants and effects of health expenditure in developed countries. J Health Econ 11:173–181

Hurdley J (2000) An overview of the normative aspect of health sector. In: Culyer AJ, Newhouse JP (eds) Handbook of health economics, vol I. Elsevier, Amsterdam/New York

Makinen M (2000) Inequalities in health care use and expenditures. Bull WHO 78(1):55–65

Murray CJL, Lopez AD (1997) Regional patterns of disability- free life expectancy and disability. Adjusted life expectancy: global burden of disease study. Lancet 349:1347–1352

Peters D, Yazbeck A, Sharma R, Ramana G, Pritchett L, Wagstaff A (2002) Better health systems for India's poor. Human Development Network, The World Bank, Washington, DC

World Bank (2003) World bank report 2004: making services work for poor people. The World Bank, Washington, DC

World Bank (2004) Attaining the millennium development goals in India: role of public policy and service delivery. Human Development Unit/World Bank, South Asia Region/Washington, DC

MIX
Papier aus verantwortungsvollen Quellen
Paper from responsible sources
FSC® C105338

If you have any concerns about our products,
you can contact us on
ProductSafety@springernature.com

In case Publisher is established outside the EU,
the EU authorized representative is:
Springer Nature Customer Service Center GmbH
Europaplatz 3, 69115 Heidelberg, Germany

Printed by Libri Plureos GmbH
in Hamburg, Germany